To Vickie, Mia and Lana.
Together ye make it all worthwhile

Stallions & Power

The Scandals of the Irish National Stud

by Conor Ryan

HILLGATE PUBLISHING LTD.

AN EMERALD CLASSIC PUBLICATION

First published in 2011
by Hillgate Publishing Ltd.
The Village Pump, Batterstown,
Co. Meath, Ireland
Phone No.: 01-8241005
Email: hillgate1@eircom.net
Web: www.hillgatepublishing.ie

ISBN: 978-0-9541819-3-2

Typeset by Computertype, Dublin
Printed in Ireland by Anglo Printers Limited, Drogheda

Contents

Acknowledgements

To meet my deadlines, part of this book was written on a family holiday with my luggage allowance taken up with binders and files. Still, I was encouraged to do it. That gives some idea of the love, support and understanding I enjoy on a daily basis from Vickie, Mia and now, our newest arrival, baby Lana. They have picked up where my parents, sister and brother have never been, and will never be, able to leave off. Thank you for all your help to both pillars of my family.

My employers, the *Irish Examiner*, have never faltered even where there have been easier and safer options. It would be remiss not to mention Paul, John, Colette and Tim in particular. Through the hard work and versatility of my colleagues the paper continues to ensure that whatever wrong, small or large, it is brought to where the public can cast judgement. I am proud to be associated with it.

This book began as a trail of breaking stories uncovered by different journalists. As a result, other writers in various organisations have done sterling work on this and associated issues. Building the jigsaw would have been impossible without their efforts.

I am delighted to say I took a lot of help in my research for this book. I appreciate especially the assistance of staff at the National Library, Trinity College library and the National Archives.

Crucially, to all those who cannot be named. The bloodstock business is notoriously tightly knit. This is all tied up in commercial ties and kinship. Most people who helped me would never want to be mentioned or associated with this book. But that does not lessen their commitment to protect the legacy of aspects of the industry which they hold dear.

We made valiant attempts to contact all the photographers involved but if we missed anybody, please accept our thanks and apologies.

Thanks also to Frieda Donohue for her help in editing the text and finally, thanks to Des O'Neill and Joan O'Sullivan at Hillgate Publishing Limited – if it is true that there is a book in everybody it took Des to squeeze one out of me.

Prologue

On March 17th, 2009, Ireland's greatest ever horse, Sea the Stars, was struck by a fever. His temperature hit 103 degrees. A viral infection threatened a potentially sensational career. The bay-coloured colt was preparing for his seasonal debut. He was entered into one of the world's most glorious races, the 2,000 Guineas. But this spectacle, the first classic of the season, was less than seven weeks away. Very few horses would have been able to recover smartly enough to parade in front of the elite of English society at the revered Newmarket racecourse. But very few horses were anything like Sea the Stars.

He was just shy of his third birthday with a body sculpted for racing, and a pedigree to justify an incredibly lucrative breeding career. Born an ungainly foal, the wonderfully-bred horse had thrived throughout a tranquil upbringing inside a cherished Kildare enclave. This was his first home – the Irish National Stud. Over the course of 100 years, the Stud's 1,000-acre farm had harvested the potential of many great horses. Yet, despite those legacies still haunting the impeccably kept yard, Sea the Stars was easily the most perfect of all those bred at, raised in, or brought to, its paddocks.

For long periods, the State-owned farm had been starved of such talent. During these spells, the company had staggered through debt and depression. It was only because of chance relationships with a small number of super stallions that it held on during some terribly dark days. These had occasionally exposed the business to national ridicule. Still, the month that Sea the Stars got sick, the Stud's powerful board of directors had been confronted by its bleakest moment. It now needed a beacon, a new hope. The Irish National Stud needed Sea the Stars. If the colt raced like he promised, he would complete the coronation of the Kildare operation as one of the world's top breeding grounds. Insiders then expected his owners to crown the relationship by returning him to the paddocks in Tully to stand as an anchor multi-million euro stallion. Such a single-stallion enterprise would be worth a great deal more than the £400,000 prize fund up for grabs at Newmarket on May 2nd.

So, on St Patrick's Day 2009, the only concern for the semi-state stud farm should have been Sea the Stars' recovery. Instead, a gnawing nervousness had the Stud sweating. Its prominent directors, chaired by Lady Chryss O'Reilly, had recently learned of a scandalous mess. This had long been festering below the Stud's surface. The details were now starting to seep out through the thoroughbred industry. It could not have been worse.

It involved two key people who the directors hoped would help fashion a long and profitable stud career for Sea the Stars. They were mired in a darkly destructive dispute. The highly successful, 59-year-old chief executive, John Clarke, and his 30-year-old stallion nominations manager, Julie Lynch, had had a one-year love affair. When it ended, she bore the brunt of victimisation and belittling treatment. Rumours circulated. The Stud's precious reputation was under threat.

The Board had brought in the former chairman of the Labour Court, Finbarr Flood, to find a way for the colleagues to work together. By the time that Sea the Stars got sick, this effort had faltered. The Stud ratcheted up its response. Mr Flood was charged with investigating the entire affair, its fractious fall-out and the devastating allegations made by Ms Lynch. Yet, the company did not even have the luxury of giving the scramble for a workable resolution its full attention. Financially, it was flailing just to stay afloat.

The company had been dragged under in the downing of the Irish banks. The speed and the timing of their demise torpedoed any prospect of the Stud riding out a torturous 2008. It prayed that Sea the Stars would soon arrive as its economic lifeboat.

The torment was getting worse every day. An emergency budget from Finance Minister Brian Lenihan was imminent. All hoped this would restore calm to the increasingly chaotic market. Mr Lenihan's efforts proved insufficient. Then, two days after the Minister commended his budget to the Dáil, Julie Lynch decided the company's attempts to protect her had failed as well.

At her home, within the lush and expansive grounds of the controversial and captivating Stud, she took out a pen. Three years earlier, she had arrived at Tully brimming with optimism. Now, she wrote her last will and testament.

CHAPTER
1

It Was Seen in the Stars

It stands as the legacy of a star-gazer and a world at war. A history coursing with controversy and conflict, superstition and success. This has been the home, and the nursery, of some of the greatest thoroughbreds ever to take to the track. It is the Irish National Stud.

The gentle hills and stables at Tully, Co Kildare took 43 years to make their way into the hands of the Irish people. The land was bought and developed in 1900 by William Hill Walker, the difficult and eccentric heir to the Scottish brewing family.

The millionaire stood thin and tall, with short wispy hair. His was a pinched face, dominated by a full moustache. Distilled through the British upper-class traditions of fencing, hunting hounds and polo, Colonel Hill Walker rose, in an utterly undistinguished fashion, through the ranks of the Royal Artillery Militia. By the time he took the honorary title of colonel in 1897, his horse, The Soarer, had won the Aintree Grand National.

While serving in India, he had acquired an obsessive interest in eastern philosophies and Buddhism. His business strategies were interwoven with astrology. On a boggy patch of his developing stud at Tully, he invested more than £34,000 and four years, building the idyllic Japanese Gardens, to represent the life of man. He was a troublesome visionary.

Trainers came and went as their advice on horses was relegated behind the messages gleaned from star charts. He claimed the zodiac predicted a horse's fate and off-loaded foals immediately if the horoscopes he crafted at their birth were ominous. These stars predicted that Minoru, named after the son of his Japanese Garden's designer, would win the Epsom Derby. Col. Hill Walker was so convinced by the astrological reading that he insisted the horse be leased to King Edward VII, to improve the morale of the monarchy. Duly, in 1909, when the two best horses in the race mysteriously tripped over each other, Minoru tipped his nose in front to win it at the post.

The same man was elected a Conservative Party MP to the House of Commons. Later, he enticed the spiritual leader of the Shia Isma'ili Muslims, the Aga Khan III, to make his fateful entry into the horse world.

In December 1915, when Col. Hill Walker was serving in World War I, he felt he could do more for the war effort. He sold his studs in Kildare and Berkley, in England, to the British Government for a cut-price £66,125. He donated his entire stock of 78 horses and 300 cattle to the people of England, to help improve the standard of cavalry charges. The National Stud was born.

Britain loved the gift it had been given. So, when Ireland won its independence five years later, the 1,000 acres alongside Kildare town remained a British enclave. The Free State Government did not like the arrangement. But Britain got stubborn. Any hope of a polite handover was killed off before Christmas 1923 when Col. Hill Walker, then elevated to become the first Baron Wavertree, made it clear who his gift was intended for.

"The National Stud is the property of the people of England and, like any other property in Ireland, owned by private individuals," Lord Wavertree said in a telegram to the *Irish Times*.

Negotiations continued behind the scenes and there were rumours of a deal. King George V would keep the horses and the new Free State would get the land. But, like many intractable arguments, it took both sides a long time to shake on the terms of a settlement that had changed very little in the 21 years it took to thrash out.

At the end of the 1920s, the fledgling Free State Government had wised up to the value of bloodstock. Money was scarce. Smaller studs had closed. Hundreds of grooms and labourers were laid off in the process. Yet there were still up to 1,400 horses racing and significant money had been spent improving the quality of Irish thoroughbreds. The greatest stallion of the time, Blandford, had been born and reared at the National Stud. He produced seven winners of the Derby. This was all to the benefit of Britain.

Despite the success of Blandford, and particularly his offspring, Westminster considered closing the Stud down. There were profitable years, but overall the Stud was losing money. In the early 1930s, its Public Accounts Committee was out to wield an axe.

The Stud survived and the Anglo-Irish brinkmanship continued until May 4th, 1943. By then London was distracted by more pressing matters. General Montgomery was a few days off beating General Rommel's army in Northern Africa. In Ireland, the terms were agreed for the handover of one of the last hangovers of the War of Independence. After 21 years spent digging its heels into the lush meadows around the crumbling remains of Black Abbey, the British Government packed up and walked away. It took the most valuable assets with it: 30 broodmares. Ireland got the empty stables, the farm equipment and an opportunity.

The ambition to continue the business was not universally popular. In the summer of 1945, newspaper editorials opened fire. In the Dáil, opposition deputies lambasted the notion of letting private individuals spend public money. They demanded to know exactly how the new venture would help small breeders.

The well-connected Agriculture Minister, Dr James Ryan, was vicious in his defence. He said it was a despicable issue to make political capital out of and stressed that he urgently needed to pass the necessary laws in time to buy horses in the autumn. Dr Ryan said the Stud's accounts would be the subject of scrutiny and the staff, although not civil servants, would be "treated humanely".

Preparations lasted three years. The legislation was passed and £250,000 was found to allow the Stud to re-stock. Three hundred tonnes of lime were spread across the grounds and paddocks to kill off a worm infestation.

The Irish National Stud eventually came into being on April 11th, 1946. In August, it paid £80,598 to take possession of the outstanding crops and livestock. In November, it moved its offices from Merrion Square in Dublin to Tully House and registered its new telephone number, "Kildare 26".

Then it got down to business. In May 1947, it bought its first stallion, Royal Charger, for £52,000 and sold 20 opportunities for mares to be covered by him for 198 guineas each. Its manager, the Oxford-educated creator of Windsor Forest Stud near Ascot, Major Cyril Charles Hall, boldly sought to enhance the Stud's reputation. A course for the rearing and training of horses was inaugurated. A couple of two-year-old fillies, Cnoc Gorm and Ceol Srulla, were leased to President Sean T. O'Kelly. The President was a budding horse-racing fan. For the first time, jockeys wore the national colours of St Patrick's blue with gold sleeves.

However, the company suffered from the usual ailments of a speculative start-up business. Those already in the trade were suspicious of it. At the same time, its privileged position in the market did not sit well with some of the people it was intended to serve.

The ultimate purpose of the Stud is to improve the quality of racehorses in Ireland. It is supposed to do this by bringing in high-calibre stallions that cottage-industry breeders cannot afford, and selling access to these horses at a price which smaller studs can manage. Some saw the new venture as interference, an example of the Government trying to take over.

In February 1948, Lord Fingal, then a Board member of the Stud, had to address a gathering of the country's suspicion-filled breeders. He told the group that the Stud would have mares, as well as stallions, and these would be bred with. But crucially, he said, the foals born to the Stud would not be brought to sales' events. This was to allay fears that the Stud would exploit its position by competing directly with private operators. The State breeder would lease the foals, Lord Fingal said. This account was featured in an *Irish Field* report of the time. The promise was not kept. But, by the time it was broken, the industry was back on side.

The company's growth was badly hampered by the post-war shortage of quality horses. It did what it could and, in 1948, bought three sires: Black Rock, for £8,465; Whitehall, for £6,890 and Preciptic for £15,131. The same year, £33,633 was used to bring in five mares. Still, there was a dearth of talent in the thoroughbreds available for breeding. The problem was so great that the two countries who had fought for ownership of Tully for 21 years decided to come together to produce some winners.

The new and strong-willed Irish Agriculture Minister, James Dillon, and his counterpart in Westminster, Tom Williams, negotiated an effective stallion-sperm swapping arrangement. Ireland would get to send one mare to the new British National Stud at Gillingham, to be covered by its headline act, Big Game. In return, the British would choose to have one of its own mate with Ireland's finest: Royal Charger, Black Rock or Whitehall.

It was an innovative scheme, but it was no magic bullet solution. Losses rose and, by 1950, it was scouring, but struggling, to find more quality stock. All the while, the President's two new race horses proved to be duds. It was an anxious wait to see if the first progeny of its £52,000 star sire, Royal Charger, would make an impression on the race track. The Stud knew it had to bide its time.

Confidence in the wider industry was improving. Meanwhile, a horse called Tulyar was proving how Irish breeding could beat the best. Owned by His Highness, the Aga Khan, and bred at his Kildare stud, Tulyar ran rampant across the flat tracks throughout 1952. This had delivered ordinary punters a bonanza victory over doubting bookmakers.

The Government liked the sense of success that Tulyar helped bring to the young Republic. There was a feeling of ownership in him. Even the Department of External Affairs got involved. The diplomats did not like loose descriptions in the British press which claimed that Tulyar had been born in England. Kevin Rush, first secretary of the External Affairs' trade section, wrote a departmental memo to say he wanted something done.

"In view of our hard-fought campaign of the past two years to have outstanding thoroughbred horses born in Ireland recognised as 'Irish bred' instead of being called 'English' or 'British' or worse still 'English bred'.

"And in view also of Tulyar's outstanding importance as a winner of this year's Derby and Eclipse Stakes, we should be very glad if you would make every possible endeavour, in collaboration with Miss Ryan on the publicity side, to have Tulyar recognised as a 'Decent Boy from Ireland'," Mr Rush said.

This was particularly touchy because Tulyar was the advance party for a combined Irish crop that would win £1.3m in 23 countries around the world during the next season. Given this level of affection for Tulyar, it may have been expected that his home nation would make a bid to own him outright. The Stud had been looking for a quality long-distance runner. He was the celebrity of the hour.

So nobody expected the uproar when the Stud went ahead and offered the Aga Khan £200,000 to buy Tulyar in January 1953. It even had to up its bid by £50,000 to land the stallion. The company was spared further controversy by the Aga Khan's generous decision to reject an offer of £331,000 from America.

The public had kept faith in the Stud throughout the difficult early years. Now their patience and acceptance of the State's most speculative enterprise was about to buckle. The three stallions of 1948 had arrived for a total outlay which came to a little more than £30,000. It now wanted to spend eight times that amount on just one animal.

Ireland had seen unemployment grow by 22 per cent since Tulyar began his successful seven-race campaign to win the Epsom Derby and St Ledger a year earlier. Moreover, Tulyar was not a horse that ever acted like he deserved the attention. The *Cork Examiner* at the time labelled him the world's best advert for laziness. He would doze off while being groomed and was happiest when asleep. "He believes in taking things easy," the paper said.

Those who focused on his race record were more complimentary. The emigrated Tipperary jockey-come-trainer, Michael Beary, sent a telegram to the Minister's office when he heard of the deal.

"Congratulations on the purchase of Tulyar for Ireland. He is the best horse in the world from five furlongs to five miles, and will increase the value of Irish bloodstock by several million pounds," he said.

It was estimated that 75 per cent of his progeny would stay in Ireland. This, the Government hoped, would add speed to the Irish thoroughbred herd, even if the eventual product introduced a slightly dopier posse to the country's paddocks.

It was the price, rather than his ability or his demeanour, that rankled people. The prospect of the Stud spending half of its money on a single horse provoked a terrific outcry across Ireland. News spread quickly.

The international impression of Ireland's post-war woes added to the fascination overseas. Around the same time, America's racing bible, the *Daily Racing Form*, glibly reported that the Stud had agreed to sell its most lucrative asset, Royal Charger, for £106,324, "only because the Government needs the dollars".

Households had seen the price of butter rise. Milk producers were on strike. The Irish Medical Organisation was battling plans to introduce free health care for poorer families. In the midst of this, and not for the last time, the Government was seeking to change the law to allow it to channel money into the Stud. A legislative amendment was needed to permit the Stud to buy Tulyar and, to do him justice, improve on the standard of the 10 mares the Stud had at the time.

"The people cry for milk, the Government gives them a horse," came the protests in the Dáil, where TDs said it was a luxurious gamble Ireland could ill afford.

"It is a simple choice between the people and a racehorse," said critic-in-chief Sean Dunne TD. "Should we take a gamble with £250,000 of taxpayers' money on a racehorse, which may be good or which may be bad?

"Should we take that step or should we invest that £250,000 for the purpose of improving the living standards of the people or providing work for them."

On this occasion, the horse remained the priority. Industry Minister, Sean Lemass, faced down angry Fianna Fáil members at a meeting in Cavan. Ireland needed to make a statement, he said. The Government stood firm.

A month later, the cheque was handed over. A £9,000 annual insurance premium was agreed. Tulyar was on his way. At 11.20pm on April 23rd, the dark-brown stallion stepped back on to his native soil after a short sailing from Holyhead on the Slieve Bloom steamer. He was happy and placid when he moved in next door to Royal Charger the following day, unaware of the furore which his move from Newmarket had whipped up across a country suffering after a spring of severe flooding. It turned out that his new owners did not really know what to do with their new toy. He was still able to race, but could also earn £400 from each mare who visited him. A meeting to decide his fate took place at the Stud on February 9th. It broke up without a decision being reached.

It was eventually agreed to bank his ability to breed. In doing so, the Stud ignored the potential winnings that keeping him on the track for another year offered.

Tulyar was expected to generate at least £16,000 in annual stud fees during a time when the average agricultural worker earned £4 a week. His first year's take of £14,400 fell short of expectations but, because of his exploits with the Stud's own mares, he was still a cash magnet.

However, the syndication process used to decide who could nominate their mares to be covered by the world's best horse was a botched job. There were widespread allegations of corruption involved in the supposed random selection of breeders. Lucrative rights were passed off under a shadow of suspicion. This, and other dubious decisions, fed major misgivings about how the Board was running the company.

A horse, Whitehall, was bought for £6,890 and almost immediately leased out to a Kildare farmer, Charles Rourke, for £140 a year, only for him to earn £1,039 in stud fees. The company's best performing asset, Royal Charger, was sold for £106,000 to an American syndicate that reaped a world record £142,840 in fees from him the first year he spent away from Ireland. Fianna Fáil, now in opposition, had appointed the majority of the Board but, still, its TD Donagh O'Malley demanded a complete clear-out.

"I am not interested in who appointed them but if I were the Minister for Agriculture I would put out the lot of them very quickly, if they are responsible for the appalling state of affairs of the National Stud at the present time," he said.

The Board was a network of relics from the British horse establishment and the politically well connected. It was chaired by the former IRA combatant in the War of Independence and creator of the Army's show jumping school, Major General Liam Hayes. At this stage its manager, Major Hall, had already cashed in on the contacts he had made while buying Tulyar from the Aga Khan and had been recruited to run His Highness's stud farm down the road.

The Irish National Stud needed hands-on experience to fill the space left by the strong presence of Major Hall. A young, quietly-spoken, stocky Cork vet, David Hyde, was singled out. The Fermoy native was steeped in bloodstock tradition. But he had none of the political expertise required to deal with the chaos about to unfold.

First, Tulyar was sold. The Stud had let the word circulate that it was willing to sell and a powerful American syndicate, led by Arthur B.

Hancock, stepped up with an offer of £240,000 and brought him to Kentucky. It was a loss on the value of the horse but, in his three seasons in Kildare, his activities had yielded a crude 200 per cent profit.

Mr Hyde immediately travelled to France and bought an underwhelming replacement, Vimy, for £105,000. This deal pitched the Stud as a quick-sale horse trader while it was working to improve the drainage and fencing around Tully. Those notions were no long falling asunder.

In June 1955, the Stud phoned the Minister for Finance and said it wanted an extra £45,000 to buy a cut-price stallion called Panaslipper from the country's most prominent businessman, Joe McGrath. The politician-turned-sweepstakes operator could have got £75,000 for the horse on the open market. The animal was intended for stud but, instead, was sent out to race three times in the President's colours in England, and once in America, with no return. The next year, he had still to get near a mare. But the Stud went on a solo run. Without Government knowledge or consent, it gathered for a Board meeting on March 5th, 1956 and decided to sell Panaslipper again.

The next day, Mr Hyde sent a telegram to a Beverly Hills-based billionaire, Neil Steere McCarthy, offering him first refusal. Two years earlier, Mr McCarthy had led the 10-member syndicate which prised Royal Charger from the Irish people on St Patrick's Day, after his burgeoning stud career had made him a sensation. Mr McCarthy read the March 5th message with more than a passing interest.

On the same day this telegram clipped its way across the Atlantic, Mr Hyde wrote to the Government, but made no mention of the decision to flog the Irish Derby winner. Word eventually reached the Cabinet by way of a newspaper report on March 15th.

The Government was furious with the Stud's "ill-advised" correspondence with Mr McCarthy and the decision to sell the horse before it had even covered a mare. Returned Agriculture Minister, James Dillon, hauled Mr Hyde to appear in front of his officials. The Government was determined to block the sale, but was afraid it did not have the legal power to do so. Mr Dillon summoned the Board together to get answers, but he was snubbed.

"We did not receive from the Board any explanation that appeared satisfactory to us of the circumstances in which it had been decided to sell Panaslipper without consultation with us," he told the Dáil.

The Government made its feelings known but was hamstrung in what it could do.

Then one of the directors, A. P. Reynolds, made matters worse. On April 10th he resigned from the Board. Mr Reynolds released a statement to the *Irish Press*, the *Irish Times* and the *Cork Examiner* notionally biting his tongue but actually casting doubt on the truthfulness of the Government's position.

"A director of a company, and particularly of a government company, cannot disclose confidential information and consequently I cannot make a statement except to say that I resigned from the Board this morning.

"I think in fairness to the Board that the ministers concerned should permit the directors to publish all the facts concerning the purchase and sale of Panaslipper," he said.

The suggestion was that Minister Dillon had been on the phone to the Stud the day before the March 5th decision to sell Panaslipper and, at that stage, had expressed no objection to the trade. The turnaround only came when Finance Minister, Gerard Sweetman, got wind of it and put his foot down. It had become an unnecessary international mess.

Mr McCarthy was so desperate to get his hands on his horse that he flew from Los Angeles to try sort it out. The day before Mr Reynolds' resignation, the American met Mr Dillon and Mr Sweetman and was told that they would not fight him in the Four Courts, but they really wanted Ireland to keep the horse.

"Mr McCarthy made it clear that, in his view, he had bought the horse and that he was anxious to have him," Mr Dillon said. The ministers knew they were in a legal quandary and were not willing to take on the man who had made his fortune as the trusted lawyer of the media and airline mogul Howard Hughes. They leaned on the trim and brash Irish-American to show a bit of goodwill to a country which had suffered an exodus of its top-quality thoroughbreds. Reluctantly, he withdrew his £80,000 demand. The stallion the Cabinet had taken such an unusual interest in stayed at the Stud well into the next decade, with little more said about him in political debates.

In a convoluted exchange, Mr McCarthy left for England after buying another stallion, Artarsula, from the original owner of his first target, Panaslipper. Mr McGrath, who, on top of his many business interests, ran the country's oldest stud farm at the Curragh and had re-invented Waterford Crystal, had sold Panaslipper cheaply and felt short-changed by the Stud's antics. But Artarsula was a horse with limitations. He finished third to Panaslipper in the Irish Derby. Artarsula also hated flying and had to be taken off the plane at Shannon just as it was preparing to wing him to his new home in California.

The Beverly Hills lawyer was not the first or last American to arrive in Ireland with a limitless cheque book and an offer to boost the Stud's coffers. But, even after Mr McCarthy showed generosity to the country of his ancestors, in the Dáil, Deputy Donogh O'Malley was on his feet again and was livid.

"It is about time the National Stud woke up to the fact they are there for the purpose this House decided under the Act of 1945 [to assist breeders] or else they might as well disestablish themselves and open up as 'tanglers' and horse-dealers. Certainly their only purpose is to obtain the best stallions for the benefit of breeders of this country. I would even go as far as to say that they have no business acquiring mares for breeding themselves," he said.

Mr O'Malley, who would go on to become Ireland's most influential education minister, also said the version of events put forward by Mr Dillon and Mr Sweetman did not stack up. He felt the entire affair had made a disgrace of the country and the Stud.

"[Mr Dillon] must have been the only individual in the country to have to wait until the 15th of March to hear of the intention to sell the horse when every man, woman and child knew of the deal which Mr McCarthy contemplated.

"The Government Information Bureau praised the attitude of Mr McCarthy in agreeing not to exercise and enforce his lien on Panaslipper. In my opinion that put the nation in a very embarrassing situation.

"It is embarrassing to think that we should have to kow-tow to Mr McCarthy, or any American, or indeed any individual for that matter and say, 'We are sorry. The National Stud definitely did agree to sell, but we would ask you not to go through with it'," he said.

Mr O'Malley said that, while Mr Reynolds' resignation was welcome, it was a pity he did not go in advance of the Stud's decision to sell Tulyar. The Fianna Fáil TD said the rest of the Board should follow Mr Reynolds out the door.

Mr McCarthy's abandoned bid for Panaslipper did not mark the end of American syndicates' interest in the Stud's stallions. Over the years, such advances presented various managers and boards with cyclical crises of conscience. On each occasion, they had to decide whether to cash in on an asset or retain the best thoroughbred stock for the indigenous breeding industry. Despite their experiences with Royal Charger, Tulyar and Panaslipper, there remained no obvious way in which they could side-step future furores. However, immediately after each controversy, life would soon settle down around Tully and mundane, day-to-day concerns would take over.

By the end of the decade, the sprawling complex was split into 72 paddocks, 143 loose horse boxes and 7 isolation units for birthing. It had a modern veterinary hospital and covered riding school, in which a metal shoe belonging to each winner to pass through its paddocks was hung as testament to their successes. There were indoor and outdoor exercise yards. And 10,000 people were paying to visit the Japanese Gardens between early spring and late autumn each year. The State had acquired full ownership of the remaining lands from the heirs to Lord Wavertree.

Profits were small, but steady. Happily, the French replacement for Tulyar, Vimy, had three times more people wanting to breed from him than there were opportunities available.

But just as events settled down, the Stud was about to lose the man who had overseen its development from an empty, worm-infested meadow in Kildare to a shopping centre for speculative American play-boys.

On February 11th, 1959, the long-time chairman of the Irish National Stud, Major General Hayes, took leave of a friend at the Clarence Hotel. They had been chatting about the Cheltenham festival over two whiskeys. The 66-year-old former Adjunct General of the Irish Army and Stud chairman was a pioneering force in Irish breeding. After leaving the hotel, he drove up Grafton Street and suffered a suspected stroke. He lost consciousness and crashed into an oncoming car. The force of his own steering wheel stopped his heart. Major General Hayes died immediately.

The Stud had lost its chairman and, in a sad moment, a colourful and chaotic period of its history was brought to an end. This set the tone for what was to come.

CHAPTER
2

Innovation and Ambition

The job description for the manager of the Irish National Stud has changed little in 65 years. The interpretation of it has varied widely among the five men who have filled the post. There has been a retired British army major; a quiet vet; an innovator of the same profession; an experienced horse trader; and a dealer in young horses, whose father held the same position 27 years before him. All five have bedded down in times of particular turmoil.

At some stage, each struggled to keep the business running while the company rattled taxpayers for more money. They managed animals that were the envy of an industry that cyclically forgot its failures and leapt at the prospect of the next big-ticket win. The Stud, and those who run it, have forever been pulled between the forces of popularity and prudence, tenacity and transparency. It is politically dependent. So it flirts with public opinion. Yet it remains central to an industry that hates to conduct its affairs in public.

Gamblers do not like to broadcast their business. At its core, bloodstock is a high-stakes game of pitch and toss on the unpredictable consequences of pedigree and performance. Over the past 65 years, the industry has climbed to excitable highs and hurtled to deeply depressing troughs. History shows that, despite its unique responsibility, the Stud fell foul of fads, forgot to bank its winnings and routinely turned to its parent department for more pocket money.

When recessions hit, it struggled badly, hamstrung by laws that limited its ability to get its hands on extra revenue and confused about what its priorities were supposed to be. Six times it has succeeded in having the law changed so that the Government could shunt cash its way. On other occasions, it juggled with more elaborate schemes to find quick and loose change in the public purse. Grants were provided for expansion projects and, at times, the Government waived the rent the Stud was supposed to pay for its massive plot spread across four townlands. It has sold off assets. With its farm, it has tried to be self-sufficient. And it has leant on tourism to bankroll bad times. But the company has suffered from forgetfulness. When it hit on bounties, it neglected to squirrel away for the future. It wrongly believed money and patronage would always be forthcoming.

After the boom of interest in its infancy, the Stud's progress pulled up. Through the early 1960s, it spent £300,000 investing in bloodstock. Twelve new stallion boxes, and a hexagonal shed for mares to meet their maters, were built. Meanwhile, the cost of maintaining and insuring the place was rising. Americans had poured billions into improving their own infrastructure and bloodlines. In Kildare, the Stud was trying to compete with them with a facility designed by Col. Hill Walker before World War I. It was struggling. A stallion had not been bought in five years and the number it owned fell to just four. Stables that housed visiting mares were falling down and were too scattered to make sense.

The product was a poor draw for breeders and not enough cash was being squeezed from its few resident stallions. In 1968, the Stud ran out of money. It had already stopped buying horses. The directors took stock. It was estimated it would take between £500,000 and £600,000 to catch up with privately-owned competitors.

The Survey Team of the Horse Breeding Industry had assessed the situation and said the company needed more than that. For the sake of the Stud, and the quality of bloodline available to Irish breeders, a top-class stallion should permanently stand at Tully, the team said. The Stud agreed. It just did not have the wherewithal to buy such a superstar.

The 1945 National Stud Bill had capped the amount of money it could borrow. So, to get fresh funding, it had to convince the

Government to allow it to create new shares and sell these back to the State. Every time this was done, the original Bill had to be tweaked.

In the summer of 1969, a swashbuckling young Finance Minister came to the rescue. Still jubilant after his party's return to power a month earlier, Charles J. Haughey said he was happy that the case made by the directors stacked up. Moreover, the public needed to invest in order to ensure that Tully had the freedom to track the tenuous trends deciding which sires and bloodlines were in vogue.

"'Fashion' is very important in this business. Many high-class young horses have been acquired by private studs over the last two or three years," Mr Haughey said. "The National Stud should clearly be in a position to provide the services of comparable sires."

It was an easy time to be generous – Mr Haughey was flush with finances from 1968. His budget speech shortly before the National Stud Bill inspired the *Evening Herald's* front page headline, "'The best year of our lives', Haughey".

While the Minister conceded that bidding for the best horses was a risky business, as they did not always perform to expectations, he felt the Stud needed to get into the market for a "prestige" stallion. To facilitate this, he bought, on behalf of the Government, an extra £500,000 shares in the company. The State's stake was doubled. Simultaneously, he allowed another one million £1 shares to be created on the strength of the taxpayer's goodwill. It meant that, if the Stud identified the right horse, it was just a phone-call away from claiming another £1m. The hassle of getting a new law drafted was parked for the time being.

Unlike the Tulyar controversy, the extra investment won broad support. The short Bill raced through the Dáil before a summer break that was to be dominated by a deteriorating humanitarian situation in Northern Ireland.

The State's wager on the stallion farm was, in contrast to events in Northern Ireland, a feel-good and frivolous venture. Money was available and horseracing had renewed its popularity.

The country had spent the past six years egging on its hero, the jump-racer Arkle. He dominated Cheltenham. He flew over fences. He breezed past opponents, despite punishing weight handicaps ladening him down by as much as three stone.

Tall tales swept the country of his fondness for Guinness. And the horse who people reverentially rechristened "Himself" was a headline item on television's fledgling evening news bulletins.

There were no guarantees for Mr Haughey's investments in the Stud. But even if bloodstock was reckless, the suggestion of giving taxpayers a share in a notional ticket to the titillating theatre of winners' enclosures and parade rings was fun. Fine Gael's Liam Cosgrave accepted that, no matter how energetic and alert the Board and its advisors were, investing in unproven sires was a blind bet. It was still a hunch worth chasing, he said.

The consensus was that the outcome was not as important as the promise. Besides, Mr Haughey liked horseracing. This meant the 1969 Bill was not his only significant intervention into the Stud's, and the industry's, future that year. Two months earlier, he had made the profits from all breeding between Irish-based stallions and mares free of any tax burden. For almost 40 years, this tax vacuum attracted the cash-rich from all quarters to invest in bloodstock as a way of keeping their earnings away from the Revenue Commissioners. It helped keep quality stallions in the country and retain international financiers. It also strapped the stability of the bloodstock business to the fortunes of other excitable endeavours, such as construction and banking.

In 1969 this was not a concern to the Stud as it looked ahead to the promise of a new decade. Fermoy man David Hyde was leaving the manager's position. So, in May 1970, the Stud brought in AIC recruitment specialists to find a replacement. They head-hunted a well-respected and charismatic vet based in Naas – Michael Osborne. An interesting choice, Mr Osborne was diminutive in stature with a thin smile and a cheery demeanour. He had worked as a vet since qualifying from UCD and he had an instinct for horses and an eye for an attraction.

With difficulty, he tracked down the remains of Arkle, which were buried on the grounds of the Stud in 1970. In May 1977, the horse's skeleton was reassembled and put on display as a morbid, but fascinating, anchor item in the Stud's new museum, which was opened by Taoiseach Liam Cosgrave and which displayed exhibits donated from the Duchess of Westminster.

Mr Osborne's background made him sensitive to the importance of the horses themselves. There were times when this ran contrary to the increasingly cut-throat activities in the industry.

Stud farmers continually sought to breed sooner in the year, so that their foals would have a four-month head-start when their racing careers began two years later. But, at a time when its stallions only covered 45 mares a season, Mr Osborne never forgot the effect such stunts could have on future fertility.

"It has evolved over millions of years that foaling should take place when sunshine and grass are at their best, i.e. around May," he said.

The money given to the Stud in 1969 allowed it to act on its ambitions. The six-month bloodstock breeders' course, which would gain world renown, was established in 1971. Old buildings made of recycled railway sleepers were torn down. The Sun Chariot yard for pregnant mares rose up around a new, bright white fountain. Proper drainage was installed in the stables to keep the animals healthy.

Interesting experiments were undertaken in an attempt to allow nature to take its own course. The low-grade stallion, Tapukei, was allowed to roam free in 1976 and had a 100 per cent success rate with mares. This was in contrast to the stage-managed, and astonishingly brief, attempts at romance arranged for the rest of the roster.

Tapukei had a knack for playing it coy. He stood off until a mare was at her keenest. Oddly, his techniques were not always appreciated. His broody harem bit and kicked him so often that the free roam was not tried a second time. Mr Osborne said it was never a trick to use on expensive stock, but it showed that the conveyor-belt breeding regime was not sacrosanct.

As these innovations carried on, the market improved. This meant that the Stud benefitted. Between 1971 and 1974, the company made an annual profit of £34,000. Using these profits, it made its best effort to re-open its dusty cheque book and begin buying stallions again. But the nature of the trade had been revolutionised. And the Stud's 1946 model was not coping.

Throughout its first two decades, the company bought stallions outright, stumping up the full cost and, inevitably, taking the full hit for junk charges. This was not the style of increasingly contorted financial arrangements being used to fund bloodstock. There was hostility outside the industry to the idea of the Stud syndicating its stock and wheeling and dealing behind closed doors. But, from 1974 onwards, the emerging domination of the relentless Coolmore Stud changed the game. By the end of the decade, the Stud had joined a syndicate to manage a new arrival, Tap on Wood. The Board was not happy to be joining the syndication circus, but a share in the horse was as much as it could afford.

The bloodstock trade is not just about the scramble to pay high prices for proven winners. In the lucrative world of flat racing, top-class stallions show form at two years of age. They race like the clappers in their third year, win all they can, and the best are retired to stud to spend the next 20 years trying to produce future three-year-olds. If they are already winners, especially of the big money Group One and stakes races, they cost more and their stud fees rocket. The shrewder operators are those who can measure the best early, based on a gut instinct and the animal's shape, muscles and temperament. Flashes of inspiration can have phenomenal consequences.

The Stud bought Sallust early in the 1972 season for £250,000. Had it waited until later in the year, after he had won the Prix du Moulin at Longchamp, his cost would have doubled at least. But, if you strike gold in one seam, you can hit on gravel in another.

A stallion called Calcas was bought for £50,000 and sold quietly for £5,000. Crash Course was bought for £30,000 in 1976. Royal Match arrived the same year at twice the price. Twenty years later, Crash Course was still spoken of as one of Tully's great national hunt success stories while Royal Match was a relatively forgotten beast.

In 1973 the Stud dug deep to bring in the high-profile, but temperamental, African Sky. "He's the best looking horse I have ever seen," Mr Osborne declared as the Stud handed over £331,000. Despite initial hopes for African Sky, he was successful, but volatile. Wealthy breeders were happy for the stallion to do some business. Smaller ones could not justify the fee.

In 1980 Ahonoora was bought to offer the Stud's customers a cheaper option. In his first season, a nomination to breed with Ahonoora cost £2,250. Among the foals of this cut-price crop was Princess Tracey, who broke the European record as a three-year-old in 1984. After Princess Tracey's siblings finished their dash to that summer's finishing posts, Ahonoora's fee multiplied four-fold. By 1987, a breeder was paying for one turn what nine breeders combined would have paid in his first season.

The discovery of Ahonoora marked the end of a good decade for the company despite a market crash six years earlier. Its stallion roster included the stars African Sky, Crash Course, Lord Gayle and the Stud's top-earner, Sallust. Together they were covering between 700 and 800 mares a year.

Mr Osborne and the Board had continuously stretched themselves to do more. They drew up a five-year plan and brought it to the Government in the spring of 1976. This asked for money to increase the number of stallions and to build extra stables, a laboratory and research facilities. There were ideas for a health farm for horses and an extension of its training programmes. It also wanted to make the most of Mr Osborne's dream to open the horse museum.

Fine Gael's Finance Minister, Richie Ryan, was called on to sponsor or sink the blueprint. Squeezing cash from the man lampooned as

"Richie Ruin" was not straightforward. He was cutting spending, inventing new taxes and trying to keep the country running in the midst of the Oil Crisis. Still, he found some money for Tully.

A new law was prepared which gave the Government permission to invest another £3 million whenever it saw fit. The Stud was also allowed to borrow a little more in case it needed fast funds to buy a stallion.

The Bill would have galloped through the Oireachtas with little debate. But Mr Haughey, plonked back in the opposition benches, was not having it. He said the ethos of the Stud's shareholder was all wrong. The farm side of the enterprise was not being run well enough. The Board did not have the clout to protect its interests from bodies like Kildare County Council, which wanted to seize part of its land. In addition, the investment proposed by Mr Ryan was not near enough to allow the company to compete for the top lots in the stallion sales.

"There are two different approaches to the finances of the National Stud," Mr Haughey announced. "One school of thought suggests that the National Stud should become commercial in its activities and should seek to build up its own resources and its own funds and to have these at its disposal for the purchase of suitable stallions when they come on the market.

"Another school of thought says that the primary purpose of the National Stud is to provide services for the small breeder at very reasonable costs. In other words, the company should not be too commercially oriented in its outlook." He wanted the company to serve both masters. Mr Haughey said allowing the Board to borrow bigger sums would keep it keen in the main markets, but realistic in the prices charged to Ireland's smattering of small breeders. Most of all he yearned to see a top-class stallion of international calibre standing in the yard at all times. His argument claimed it was a simple solution to generate easy money.

"One can pay £1 million or £2 million for one of these horses and be almost certain that one will recoup that money over a four-year period.

"One can insure against fertility and all those things. The Board of the National Stud, in 99 cases out of a 100, could certainly go out with the Minister's blessing as a straight-forward commercial proposition and borrow £1 million or £2 million to get for themselves a prestige stallion. I cannot understand why the Minister will not agree to that," he said.

Mr Ryan knocked him back. He said it was not right for taxpayer-owned businesses to be borrowing large sums and paying hefty interest rates. Mr Haughey kept pressing. He looked for the Board to have nine members instead of five. His fear was that when the Stud manager brought requests to make big purchasing pitches, a small pool of decisions-makers was more likely to stall and split. He wanted more independence and freedom within the company to go after the best bred horses.

Mr Ryan said no. A compromise was reached. Spaces for two extra directors were created. It was not the concession the Fianna Fáil stalwart was after. But it was a small victory.

Minister Ryan did not budge on the borrowing and told the future Fianna Fáil leader to stop meddling. The tetchy exchange lasted most of a day and struck at the heart of the dilemmas continually facing the Stud. Mr Ryan said the Board was largely getting what it asked for, it could be trusted to decide its own direction and Mr Osborne was a better judge of the company's needs than Mr Haughey.

"A lot of Deputy Haughey's criticisms might have been valid several years ago but in fairness to the existing Board and to the manager we should put on record our admiration for the great progress in recent years. The National Stud has been opened up in more ways than one to stimulate the interest and involvement of people who are concerned with the bloodstock industry and they have also excited interest in other people who previously had not a direct involvement in this industry," he said.

Mr Ryan's stated agenda was to plough down the middle of the road and this won out over Mr Haughey's exercise in exuberance.

The outcome was still good for the Stud. It had more directors, more support and more money. But there were always complications.

On May 4th, 1973, Olive Alexander of Milford Stud in Carlow paid £1,600 for her mare, Chip, to be covered by Sallust. Chip arrived in the stables but by the next month several efforts at consummating the business deal had floundered. On June 10th she was put in a restraining harness called "the hobbles", which workers in the covering shed had used for 70 years to protect stallions and contain reluctant mares. But Chip was not having any of it. She pulled her head away violently when Sallust got near. Then she broke through the door and rushed headlong across the yard. She was still caught up in "the hobbles". After a long and awkward run, the mare met with a wall headfirst. Chip died instantly. Mrs Alexander headed for the High Court. In June 1977, she was awarded damages of £15,000.

This was a dangerous precedent and one the Stud could not live with. The case was sent to the Supreme Court. The superior judges' panel reviewed the evidence and, in November 1978, ruled that there had been no negligence, so there was no wrongdoing.

Vindicated and refinanced, the Stud refocused on its business. It tried many tricks to keep pace with the exploding bank accounts of rival Irish, French, American and Arab operations. In autumn 1980, it launched a small share ownership scheme to entice punters to invest minimal amounts for a stake in a hobby horse.

"Tie a message to the tail and give a racehorse to the one you love," ran the advert. Coolmore tried something similar. Both failed.

The Stud had built small natural buffers for the erratic markets. It had the size of its farm and the quality of the land on its side. Each year it was producing 1,500 tonnes of silage, 200 tonnes of hay and 50 acres of oats to supply its horses. It also kept a large herd of cattle to help improve the land and steady its income. The Japanese Gardens and new museum were a growing tourist attraction. But this all meant that the complex had become a confusion of disciplines. For this and other reasons, staff relations at the Stud were never straightforward. Divisions existed between the stud farm and the rest of the business.

To bring it all together, it was decided to set up a musical society: 'The Staff and Friends of the Irish National Stud'. After its first production of *Mikado*, it put on four more shows throughout the 1980s. Mr Osborne went to great lengths to kit out the Japanese Gardens for the occasions and to foster a sense of camaraderie. He also decided to build a new recreation area for the workers, which chairman, Larry Ryan, later nicknamed "The Osborne Arena". But, behind the staging of the *Mikado* and the *Pirates of Penzance*, the same financial problems kept surfacing.

The State has always been the Stud's banker. However, the fact that the law needed to be changed every time it required more money slowed its pace incredibly. The 1976 pot had been all but emptied. The Board tried to cajole the permanently slow civil service into action. It just did not wield sufficient power to crack a proper whip.

In April 1981, the Board asked for cash. Mr Osborne, and chairman, Larry Ryan, had a mind to buy a multiple winner called Runnett. But a general election campaign was being fought. It was an era when public servants were being tossed back and forth between political masters.

The Department of Agriculture came back to the Stud three months later and said "no". As a compromise, it suggested the company's right to borrow could be increased. On August 17th, the Stud wrote back and asked for permission to look for a lender.

Letters crossed back and forth between the Stud, the Department of Agriculture and the Department of Finance for a further 11 weeks. The Department of Agriculture said the delay was necessary to carefully examine the company's proposals for repaying the money. Agriculture Minister Alan Dukes eventually agreed. At that stage, the horse was already ensconced in his new home of Cleaboy, Co. Meath. The Stud had, not for the first time, missed its chance.

A year later the situation deteriorated. The star stallions of the 1970s were ageing, and replacements were not forthcoming. Chairman Larry

25

Ryan's 1981 report said that, while it had been the best-ever year for stallion revenues, it was a dismal one otherwise. A lack of cash meant that it had to close two satellite studs, which had been opened to make life easier for dispersed mare owners. Nomination fees charged to breeders were hiked up to cover investment on the farm. This was still not enough to buy new horses or even replace casualties.

"This situation is a grave one," Mr Ryan said and complained that his persistent pleas to Government had been ignored. The racing press supported him completely. The then editor of the *Irish Field*, Valentine Lamb, ran a front-page article demanding the Stud be given proper attention.

"Certainly it would be a terrifying scandal if the National Stud, now an international showpiece due to the tireless work of resigning manager Michael Osborne, was allowed to disintegrate owing to the lack of interest by civil servants," he said. By that stage Mr Osborne had been head-hunted to become vice president at one of America's largest operations, Franklin Groves's North Ridge Farm.

The former vet and father-of-five was fêted from all quarters and finished up at Tully on September 10th, 1982. The Irish Thoroughbred Breeders' Association gave him a bronzed mare and foal to thank him for the outstanding job he had done in the industry. His chairman lauded him for revolutionising the business in the 12 years he worked at Tully.

"Under his enthusiastic and imaginative guidance with total dedication, and some considerable personal sacrifice on his part, the Irish National Stud has renewed, expanded and diversified and become a unique national asset," Mr Ryan said. Fifteen years later, he was still being name-checked by politicians looking for proof of the inherent promise in the investment in the National Stud.

However, the custodians along the corridors of power were not always as generous to Mr Osborne. The 1976 law which gave the Stud a brief financial respite had a sting in the tail for him and his successors.

A 44-word caveat Minister Riche Ryan included in the Bill took control of the manager's pay level back from the Board. It cut Mr Osborne's salary dramatically and left future wage scales at the mercy of ministers. *The Irish Field* branded it an "immoral and extremely underhanded" action by "power-seeking civil servants". Such prudence was quite a distance from the lavish life he was witness to in the lush pastures north of Lexington, Kentucky.

His new boss was the owner of The Bart, who was within a nostril of winning the Arlington $1m in 1981. A year earlier, Mr Groves was involved in the world record-breaking syndication of Seattle Slew. And, while Mr Osborne was in Kentucky, the North Ridge Farm smashed records for the value of foals it sold. The operation dwarfed the annual turnover of the National Stud with single syndications of horses like the $16m Saratoga Six.

In the 1980s Michael Osborne had access to a near limitless pile of money. His old employer was now scraping for savings. Trouble was taking root. The Stud's supporters were losing interest. Problems were starting to flood the foundations.

A new foreman was on-site. The Board wanted help to buttress the Stud's books. In the middle of their project, three decades of rebuilding and renaissance were about to be tested by an almighty quake.

3

The Collapse

Since the time of The Crusades, the evergreen pastures surrounding the Black Abbey have been used to support superior stallions. These beasts were never expected to pull ploughs or drag carriages. Instead, generations of these horses were nurtured to be the embodiment of pedigree and purpose.

In the early years, military-minded men relied on the stallions' progeny to help raid far-off battle fields. Later, the cavalier owners would send the horses' offspring to plunder richly rewarding race tracks.

With this goal in mind, hundreds of breeders, large and small, have opted to make the costly journey to the Irish National Stud every year since its inception. Each has pinned their hopes on a magical match-up between their mares and the Stud's stallions.

The mare-owning legion was not the only group with an embedded interest in affairs around the Abbey. Tens of thousands of tourists travelled here each summer to get as close as possible to some of the most expensive heartbeats on four legs. Taxes, paid by millions of workers, sponsored and secured the Stud's survival. And, at all times, a few dozen local employees depended on the success of the business to provide for their families.

To please all of these people, a clique, drawn from some of the most powerful networks in Irish life, had swapped seats around the boardroom table. These directors enjoyed privilege and endured pressure. Various senior staff have always helped to shoulder the directors' responsibilities. Much of the burden fell on a handful of stud managers who moved into Tully House. Michael Osborne had been a most formidable figurehead. Predictably, the company did not have an easy time finding his replacement.

In April 1982, the Board had gone looking. It was six months before he was due to emigrate, but nobody of the required standard was biting. A shortlist of four candidates failed to impress. So the search started again.

The salary on offer was upped from £16,500 to between £19,500 and £22,000. This hike reversed the unpopular cutbacks that had been slapped on Mr Osborne five years earlier.

In late September, the improved salary attracted a 31-year-old bloodstock manager, John Clarke. He was a tall, slim and fastidious man who had been working in Dublin, with Ballsbridge Sales International, since 1975. The Dublin 4 company was originally established to fill a void in the RDS, created after Goffs moved its sales operations to Kildare.

It started modestly, generating its deals from point-to-point horses and show-jumpers. Then, in 1977, the British giant Tattersalls took it over. This was a strategic ploy to break Goffs' monopoly in Ireland. Tattersalls did not want to give its rival a free run at the increasingly deep pockets of Irish-based breeders.

Long before Mr Clarke moved to Tully, the start-up sales venture had developed close ties with the National Stud. Since the new company had opened, the chairman of the Stud, Larry Ryan, had been one of Tattersalls Ballsbridge's directors. Another was Kevin Frost, the son of Mr Ryan's immediate predecessor as chairman. The Stud had also made some very healthy trades at the Simmonscourt venue since Tattersalls had got involved. Mr Clarke would have known a lot about the operation he now agreed to take charge of.

The title of manager of the Irish National Stud sounds grand. In reality, though, the job of running it was not the best in the business. The initial salary scale was only a little above the average industrial wage. Even this increased offer was fixed, despite a culture of rampant inflation. However, along with the enviable access it gave to the industry, the company was able to attach juicier perks.

"Fringe benefits include an excellent rent-free house, in which the successful applicant will be required to reside and a choice of company car or suitable mileage allowance," the recruitment advert said. This was particularly lucrative. Interest rates for home loans were racing north of 15 per cent. A State job was also secure.

Tattersalls Ballsbridge was in difficulty. One of its main investors, the RDS, had written off the entire value of its £30,000 stake. The management had to re-jig the enterprise. This worked. Tattersalls fought off its critics. Ultimately, it survived.

By then, Mr Clarke was helping to cultivate another revival at the Stud and settling into what would be a 27-year stay at Tully House. When he arrived on January 1st, 1983 the most pressing task was to try to save money.

It was a pressured period, but Mr Clarke did, at least, have some cover from premature publicity as he bedded down. Five weeks after the new manager's arrival, the outstanding Shergar was kidnapped by the IRA from the Aga Khan's Ballymany stud farm. It was the international news story of the moment. The horseracing community was transfixed.

For a time, this also distracted attention from the wider problems at Tully. These had put the most unique, and underperforming, feature of the Stud under serious threat.

The Japanese Gardens had blossomed for 80 years on a marshy bed, sodden by the same sparkling source that enriched the fertile fields around Black Abbey. The crystal clear, calcium-rich stream bubbled up from a giant reservoir under the Curragh. It gurgled steadily and peacefully to feed the plants and help the gardens become a flowering fixture for wedding albums, photo-shoots, Communion celebrations and annual Rose of Tralee outings. This spring-water flowed into the garden from the stone-encased St Bridget's Well behind the site. It snaked around rocks drawn from the Wicklow Mountains, listing bamboo shoots, black maple trees, and under the symbolic, and iconic, arched red footbridge.

But the gardens and the horse museum lost £12,930 in 1983. This was on top of £31,321 the year before. Chairman Larry Ryan could not continue to finance them as a charitable exercise. So he placed the gardens on probation. Costs had to be cut aggressively for it to survive.

Nobody really wanted to uproot generations of care and growth. Unsurprisingly, a decision to bring the excavators in was dodged when problems in the rest of the business steadied. Both the stallions and the farm even turned a profit.

Yet, the Board remained consumed by the fear that its books were not sustainable. Directors saw a massive weakness in how the company was funded and the room available for them to manoeuvre was getting tight. Worse, tragedy was intent on once again visiting the boardroom.

Company director, Sean Doyle, who owned the Baroda Stud in Newbridge, was exercising a horse in his own yard on a Sunday. A qualified vet, Mr Doyle was aged 40 and was married.

Mr Doyle was appointed to the Board on July 13th, 1983 to fill the seat vacated by Mr Osborne. He was cut from a similar cloth to the man he replaced. He was a determined buyer at auctions and driven to make a difference in the industry. In the summer of 1984, he was responsible for the attendance record at the Phoenix Park being smashed. This was because he sponsored the event and, along with his staff, distributed 18,000 tickets free of charge. Earlier, he pocketed a nice profit by orchestrating the £1m sale of his stallion, Lyphor, to Japanese buyers.

But, on Sunday December 16th, 1984, Mr Doyle was thrown off the mount he was exercising and was killed. The Stud closed its doors for two days as a mark of respect and looked to fill yet another void.

Notwithstanding the tragedy, Mr Clarke's tenure as stud manager had started well. In an otherwise erratic economy, the horse industry was booming. This helped to quell the gnawing anxiety at Tully.

Bloodstock was employing 10,000 Irish people full-time. Another 10,000 had part-time jobs because of it. The expansion was fuelled by a far-flung spending spree and rising prices in the world at large. At the same time, there was a scrap for supremacy in the sales rings between Coolmore and the recently arrived Arab armada. These battles and bubbles always fizzled up into a big boom for bloodstock. The impact of the busts and butchery that invariably followed were in direct proportion.

Stallions and mares have no concrete value. Their worth is based on breeders' and speculators' belief that past successes may repeat themselves.

When fashions change, prices can catapult or collapse. This has frequently been a source of gripes and grievances. It also landed the Stud back in the High Court in October 1983.

George Williams, from the Carrignaveen Stud near Iniscarra in Co. Cork, arrived late for the November sales at Goffs in 1977. He had travelled in the hope of finding a horse with a similar pedigree to his Cheltenham Gold Cup-winning Captain Christy. Mr Williams was with a group in the bar when he met a Kilkenny woman, Amanda Cayley. She had just bought a filly from the Irish National Stud that looked, at least according to the catalogue, as if it oozed the pedigree he was after. So he offered to give her £295 for the horse, £50 more than she had just paid.

Three years later, the registration body, Weatherby's, wrote to him and said the animal he owned was not the one he thought he brought home. A printing mistake had confused her pedigree. Mr Williams felt aggrieved. He looked for £6,466 in costs from the Stud and compensation for the economic loss he felt he had suffered from buying the wrong filly.

Michael Osborne flew back from Kentucky to testify. He said the heritage Mr Williams was looking to attach to the horse, to increase its value, was tenuous at best. Mr Justice Keane agreed. He said any horse was only worth precisely what people were prepared to pay for it on

32

the day it was sold. Furthermore, the courts could not be expected to arbitrate on the industry's intricacies.

It was a logic that helped the Stud win the day but, in the long-term, these quirks of concocted commodity also caused it to suffer severely.

An entire portfolio can be written off because of a trend in a single sales' season. Similarly, a selling spike can deliver beautiful bounties. One of those happened in 1987.

By then, 5 out of Europe's top 10 stallions were standing in Ireland. Sheikh Mohammed of Dubai brought his family's oil wealth to Ireland in earnest. He enticed Mr Osborne home from Kentucky to manage his affairs. Once home, the Kildare man organised the purchase of the Kildangan Stud near his home to help get the Sheikh established.

After his arrival, Sheikh Mohammed and the hawkish Coolmore started a frenzied buying war that pumped up the price of horses. Cash was flying around. Every breeder was taking stock. Meanwhile, in the National Stud's own sunlit stallion boxes, its gem, Ahonoora, was shining. After his crop of 1984, which was shockingly successful, speculators had begun to take notice. The Board did not know what to do with its jewel.

Ahonoora's abilities had helped make the Stud the second biggest in Ireland, in terms of turnover. Only Coolmore trumped it. Thirty years before, Deputy Donogh O'Malley had slated the Stud for pioneering this path. He said the 1945 law, passed to establish the company, was not drafted to open a horse-trading venture. His view was shared by many others, who felt that, above all else, the semi-State enterprise was set up to help small breeders get access to good stallions at affordable prices.

The Board of the late 1980s took the Donogh O'Malley philosophy more seriously than any other before, or since. A priority was placed on helping others to produce better horses.

Traditionally, the Stud charged less than the market rate for its stallions. Demand usually exceeded supply. Generously, it gave money back to breeders if a foal died more than three months before it was due to be born. It was viewed as a public service for the owners of mares, not a chance to make a quick buck from a market able to look after itself.

The company could point to a long history of successes from owners who visited it. The winner of the 1989 Prix de l'Arc de Triomphe, Carroll House, was sired at the Stud. His father, Lord Gayle, was the grand old warrior of the farm, after a career during which he was shuttled over and back across the Atlantic to race. Lord Gayle kept running until he was a five-year-old and, against the bookies' best calculations, he retired on a winning note.

The Stud had bought him with the new cash given to it by Charlie Haughey's law in 1969. Still, not much was expected of the animal. Quickly, Lord Gayle got down to proving people wrong.

Twenty years later, as the sire approached retirement, there were more than 580 winners placed on the next row of his family tree. The Stud proudly reflected on his impact on the bloodline of Irish thoroughbreds as its justification for existing at all.

Apart from breeding, the Stud had another role to fulfil. It was responsible for finding and putting forward horses to race for the President of Ireland. During this period, it also delivered on the track in this regard. The winning horse was called Seskin Bridge.

Bought for nearly Stg£9,000, Seskin Bridge slugged it over the fences for a few years in the colours of the President, Paddy Hillery. She had successes, despite the likes of Dawn Run dominating the era. Mr Hillery's filly still won the Leopardstown chase in 1985.

Back at Tully, Ahonoora was not a racer. Neither was he a cheap destination for mares. To the Board, Ahonoora was a dilemma. It felt that if the company kept him, at the expense of its ideals, ordinary breeders would have to be priced out of the market.

Yet, at the same time, Ahonoora's neighbours in the stallion boxes were getting old and unattractive for many customers. The then chairman, renowned trainer and son of a former director, John Oxx, told the Oireachtas the company could not afford to leave all its money hinging on one big asset. A quick peek at the Stud's finances revealed this to be an obvious truth.

Six years of depending on the success of one great stallion was taking its toll. On top of that, where once the Government had seen the Stud as its dependent, it had now begun to view the farm as a cash machine.

Between 1976 and 1981, the Department of Finance had provided fresh funding annually to help the company enhance its stock and improve its facilities. First, this lifeline was pared back. In 1982, it was withdrawn altogether.

The Stud panicked and its chairman, Mr Ryan, pleaded with the Government not to make this a habit. It tried to curry favour. At one point, the Stud dutifully paid the Finance Minister, Alan Dukes, a share dividend on its meagre profit.

"As rare as hens' teeth," Mr Dukes described the arrival of such envelopes into the Department. The Stud was taught a lesson. After it sent a dividend of £75,000 in 1984, the Government hiked up its rent. The Board subtracted the extra rent from its gift to taxpayers the next year. Automatically, the boffins responded and increased the rent again. So, the Stud stopped sending dividends.

The Government did not stop fiddling with the rent. By the time the game of landlord–tenant chicken reached its peak in 1989, the company's rent had risen six-fold in five years. Times were changing. The status of the industry was shifting. The Osborne era was drifting from view and demands on the Stud were more complex.

Over the same period, Mr Clarke had also become more established. In February 1987, he was advertised in London as the headline speaker at a conference in the Royal and Lancaster Hotel on the subject: "Investment in bloodstock, tax and financial planning." However, like his predecessor, his rhetoric may have convinced potential financiers in Britain to start spending, but there was no squeezing money from the single investor in the Irish National Stud – the Government. Whatever long-term hope there was of extra cash coming, money was never on hand when he needed it most.

Part of Mr Clarke's job was to scope out stallions and bring a report on these prospects to the Board for approval. But, while he succeeded in eliciting enthusiasm among directors, the Government of that time did not want to know about it.

The Stud argued that it just wanted to borrow money on its own, not snaffle a hand-out. Plus, it did not need a massive mortgage. It just wanted a short-term, but big-budget, overdraft to allow it to pounce on potential early in the year. Having this bit of credit would have allowed it to pony up the full cost of a horse as soon as an owner was willing to sell. The ideal series of events would have the Stud spot and secure winners before they went to race. This way an early stallion investment would pay dividends even before he began his covering career. In these circumstances, the company would repay the loan quickly by bringing in other investors in a broader syndicate.

The 1986 report of Lord Killinan implored the Government to allow this borrowing to take place. But the pay-masters did not budge. All manner of accountancy theatrics had to be performed to get by.

The Stud organised with the Bank of Ireland for it to provide a guarantee in a convoluted, delayed repayment deal. This allowed it to buy horses, almost on the basis of a hire purchase, and pay off the bank's claim with the stallions' earnings over the next three to five years. It was the type of bewildering bureaucratic loophole that allowed State agencies to side-step laws to get by in a far from desirable fashion. The result was similar to a medium-term loan. Legally, it was far more complicated. Still, necessity overruled complexity and three stallions arrived in Kildare under such bank-backed deals.

Then, Ahonoora started attracting suitors. Immediately, the Stud spotted an even quicker fix to funding failures. First, it worked out an £80,000-per-share syndicate arrangement in Ahonoora. The partners brought in cash and it kept hold of the majority stake.

In 1986, these profits paid for the £500,000 122-acre Maddenstown Stud complex alongside Tully. This provided a potential containment area after an outbreak of disease in mares had scared the international breeding community. But the once-off, half-a-million pound pot was not enough. Internally, pressure grew to sell him outright.

Not a lot was required to win the argument. The Stud gave in to the advances of Coolmore, who shared the deal with an Australian syndicate.

In July 1987, the 16.1 hands-high Ahonoora was sold for a record £7million. It was 29 times the price the Stud had paid for the chestnut horse eight years earlier.

The State-owned business was entitled to a £5.3m share of that. It took its money and went out and bought three younger, and lesser grade, stallions. It believed these would better serve the tighter wallets of its target market.

Money was also thrown in the bank's direction to end the deferred payment juggle. The sale bought a bit of time in an era when there was rarely any respite. Shortcomings were not just of the Stud's own making. Nothing was being done to cool or control the economic hysteria the company was contending with. The cost of horses was inflating unchecked.

In early 1987, Charlie Haughey bounced back into power. Within a month, he poured more petrol on the bloodstock prices. His Government put up money for the Goffs' Million. All 250 yearlings sold at Goffs' premier sales in October would race off the following year to try and win £1m at the Phoenix Park races.

The competition was heralded as an effort to break the stranglehold of big buyers. There was a staggering response from a community happy to believe prices could just keep rising. The trick showed scant concern for tempering the market. It did, however, reveal the tell-tale signs of a political leader rewarding a sector that helped him back into power.

Fine Gael had run into the 1987 election promising to sell off 49 per cent of the Irish National Stud, to bring in new investment. The party also wanted to revolutionise the structures of the horse industry. Mr Haughey was not having it. He told the Irish Congress of Trade Unions he was dead against the privatising plan and other reforms. The industry stuck by him. But, for what they were worth, the rival election manifestos did not improve the lot of Irish racing.

Successive governments in the 1980s did little beyond throwing out headline grabbers like the Goffs' Million. At the time, the race tracks were in dismal shape and the betting regime was ill-equipped to take in the scale of revenues that people hoped it would. Ultimately, because they did not act sooner, politicians could only watch on when the market collapsed in the late 1980s. It was a chaotic political climate and it became a desperate economic one. The struggling semi-State Stud again fell well down the list of priorities.

In 1982 Lord Killinan had been hired by the Department of Agriculture to lead the Commission to Investigate the Thoroughbred Horse Breeding Industry. His team was made up of 13 of the most powerful names in the industry.

Four years later, he delivered his report. It said consideration should be given to merging the Stud into one super horseracing body. But, if the company was kept independent, it needed a better way to access cash. He said its capacity to work off credit from the banks would have to be increased to £5m. The Government "noted" its findings and put the report out to pasture. It took a year before the issue was even aired in a low-key Seanad debate.

Agriculture Minister Michael O'Kennedy said he did not want to diminish the status of the Stud and he accepted it should be allowed to borrow more readily. Back in his office, however, he did not deliver. On multiple occasions in that period, negotiations to buy foals were fatally compromised by an inability to borrow money in the short term.

In the meantime, the mixture of recession, short-sighted strategies and procrastination from the company's patron started to bite. The only shift in scenery was the fall-out from the well-trampled Fine Gael plan to part-privatise the Stud.

A high-profile Dáil committee was established to talk about its future. This was the Joint Oireachtas Committee on commercial semi-State bodies. In 1990, it killed the sell-off suggestion dead. It said the

Stud should remain the State-owned star around which the Irish industry orbited. Small breeders needed the institution to protect them from the selfish interests of the private operations. The committee also urged the company to do more to help itself.

The Board did not have a statement of corporate goals or a long-term plan to find a way around its troubles. The committee said it urgently needed a roadmap for the future. This five-year plan was eventually delivered to the Department, which did not like it. The document was sent back for revision.

More than any other Board before or since, this group of directors adhered rigidly to the mantra of the original small-breeder service. Yet, it was snidely denigrated because of it. The ethics-based arguments made by the chairman, John Oxx, certainly did not win support at the State Assets' Committee. In his report, its head, Deputy Dick Roche, asked why the company had ignored repeated calls for it to invest in the type of mare magnets which were the mainstay of its rivals.

"With one or two exceptions in its four decades the company has not purchased what might be termed 'top stallions' or 'prestige stallions'.

"Since the acquisition of top stallions has been officially recommended on a number of occasions, both before and after the establishment of the Stud, it is surprising that Tulyar is virtually the only such acquisition the company ever made," he said. It was largely true.

Except for African Sky, the Stud had stumbled on the successes of all other stand-out stallions to stay at Tully. Mr Roche accepted this had as much to do with the State's failure to support the Stud as the Board's belief in its original ethos.

"The apparent unwillingness of the Government to make adequate capital available, and the limits it has placed on its borrowing power, has meant the purchase of top stallions has usually been beyond the company's capacity," he said.

The lesson from all of this was that, politically speaking, generating profits would win the Stud more friends than prioritising its principles ever could.

The Stud was told it should have a prestige stallion. And, with space for 14 sires, it could easily cope with one money-earner while keeping cheaper options available for cottage-industry breeders.

This was as good as fairy talk around the Japanese Gardens, because the truth was that the Stud was now juggling its assets just to stay afloat. When Ahonoora left, Mr Clarke told the press his sale would put the Stud on a firm financial footing. The premature sale also spared taxpayers a massive loss. Ahoonora died two years after he moved home, when the gruelling seasonal shuttle between Australia and Ireland took its toll. He broke his hip in an accident and was destroyed.

While this news was winging its way around the world, so too were the advancing clouds of a major recession. Quickly they engulfed the industry.

In the financial fog, the Stud soon realised that, despite occasional windfalls, its core business was not sound. Through the earlier bidding battles of the 1980s, and the Ahonoora bonanza, the Stud had only lost money twice in 10 years. From 1988 onwards, it forgot what a profit was.

By 1992, the stallion business was costing the company £1.6m a year to run, but it was only generating £610,000 in income. This was despite a record 590 mares visiting its stallions that spring season. Prices had plummeted. Since the peak in 1987, the value of all farm products, home bred yearlings, stallion services and tourist tickets that were sold by the company fell from £815,000 to £353,000. Over the same time, the Stud had siphoned £6m from its savings.

It had maxed out its borrowing. It had exhausted its winnings from Ahoonora. The value of its horses had dropped by £1.9m with one considered stroke of a pen. It was losing an average of £63,471 per month. The Government had pumped in an extra £1.3m, by buying up all remaining shares. This had merely helped to cover the growing losses.

The then chairman, Sean Collins, signed off on his 1991 accounts on a depressing note. If left alone, the Stud's recovery prospects were poor, he said. Lord Gayle had retired. Ahonoora had departed and died. For the first two years of the 1990s, the Stud again did not have the money to buy a single horse.

Dancing Dissident was supposed to be its star stallion but he generated none of the revenue of his predecessors. His next-door neighbours were risks rejected by less desperate competitors.

The Stud tried to change. It decided to buy more cattle. It submitted a revised five-year revival plan to the Department of Agriculture. It brought in independent consultants to revolutionise the farm side of the business. The recommendations were trialled for two years and abandoned when they failed.

The Comptroller and Auditor General checked the accounts and said it was safe to keep trading, but only because of the emergency cash arriving from Agriculture House. The company argued for more support. But patience in government quarters ran out.

In October 1992, Agriculture Minister Joe Walsh took a broom to the Board. He brought in five new directors, including bloodstock breeder, Pat O'Kelly, trainer, Dermot K. Weld and career civil servant, Jim Beecher.

Foxrock resident David Shubotham, a partner at Davy Stockbrokers, was installed as chairman. The idea was to bring business sense to a virtually insolvent company. Mr Shubotham said its plight could only be understood in the context of an international breeding crisis.

"[The Stud] is a barometer of the Irish bloodstock industry and reflects the prosperity or otherwise of breeders in general and Irish breeders in particular.

"In the face of the worst bloodstock recession in living memory the results for 1992 reflect the difficulties which breeders have had for the last five years," he said.

This logic won scant sympathy. When the Government reluctantly brought forward another bail-out Bill in 1993, it came with a serious slap-down.

The rules of the company were changed to allow it to borrow up to £5m. Crucially, the amount the State could invest directly was doubled to £10m.

In the Dáil debate, Deputy Dessie O'Malley took up where his uncle, Donogh, had left off 40 years before. Mr O'Malley said that the haphazard habits of the Stud were such that it had lost the faith of breeders. He said, apart from the financial results, there were deeper problems with its conduct and these had been well-circulated within the industry.

Fine Gael's spokesman and Wexford bookmaker, Ivan Yates, said the quality of the horses at the Stud was atrocious. He begged the company to spend its newly-sanctioned money wisely.

Minister Walsh said his opponents were spot-on. He claimed the flowers in the once-again blooming Japanese Gardens were better bred than the progeny of the stallion roster.

"We must produce very high class stallions. When I called to the Stud last year and observed what was taking place there, including viewing the skeleton of Arkle, I came to the conclusion that they were better at breeding plants and rare species of flora than breeding horses.

"The only money-making activity there was the Japanese Gardens. The core activity was in a shambles," he said.

He said that whatever about the thoroughbred recession, the failure to make money given the rest of its land and assets was inexcusable. He was giving the company, and its new Board, a chance to recover.

Political inertia and internal inadequacies had brought the company to the brink. Taxpayers were once again called on to save it. In the years that followed, the Government signed over a series of cheques to replace bad buys and cover poor bets.

The fresh faces in the boardroom and the new hooves in the paddocks provided promise. But they could not save the people who suffered and struggled with the Stud.

Before Christmas 1992, the outgoing chairman, Sean Collins, sent a letter to all staff telling them the company could not survive in its current form. The Board felt too many people were employed given the level of business it was now doing. There were going to be casualties. He asked for volunteers to take a redundancy package. Workers were not impressed with what was on the table. They argued with the company about their entitlements. The longest and most loyal servants would be the hardest hit, because a decision was taken to cap the redundancy payment in line with Department of Finance demands.

The Stud gathered together £352,889 in compensation. By the end of 1993, twenty people had walked out of the gates of Tully to an uncertain future. Some had spent night and day keeping watch throughout the breeding season and toiled in the fields to harvest feed for the precious bloodstock. But sentiment was not a consideration the Stud could afford. Directors were removed. Breeders had turned their backs.

The politicians, who were the mouthpieces for taxpayers, had shown contempt for what was happening. Meanwhile, a third of those who worked at the Stud were joining the 290,000 other souls signing on in 1993. It was a grim time when the best prospect for anybody taking a place in the dole queue was an airline ticket and emigration.

With fewer friends, poorer pedigrees and debilitating debts, the Stud had one last chance to rebuild the edifice that had caved in around the ruin of the Black Abbey.

CHAPTER
4

Rebuilding with a New Generation

Nobody expected a hobbling and demoralised Stud to recover quickly. It had lost staff, haemorrhaged money, angered its sponsor and weakened its prestige. Such was its sorry state, the target was survival more than revival.

For over 45 years the Stud had been winched up. Sometimes the pace was frustratingly slow. At other stages, it rose so fast it was foolhardy. But Tully, the old Irish name for a small hill, kept rising. Ultimately, the farm mixed with the bloated billionaires who ruled the international industry. Then the cables suspending the Stud's status snapped. It fell fast and it landed hard.

By the beginning of the 1990s, the company could barely prop itself up. Rescuers had no choice but to respond. Help came from all quarters.

The Board had been removed and replaced. A new chairman with a business background was installed. In the financial fields some favourable winds were whipped up. The market experienced a dramatic pick-up. August 1993 showed the first sign of strong demand for young horses since the beginning of the recession. The farm turned a profit.

The Department of Agriculture waived a demand for four years of rent that should have been paid. This was worth £304,000. The live-for-free arrangement continued for another three years. Finance Minister Bertie Ahern bought £1.5m extra shares, with a promise of more of the same. Bord Fáilte delivered £302,000 towards a new visitors' centre.

This was opened in 1993 and straightaway increased the Stud's ability to tap into the buying power of tourists. After some sad goodbyes, the workers who left the Stud helped to ensure a more stable future for their former colleagues. Those 20 people who accepted the voluntary redundancy package saved their former employer £176,000 in 12 months. It would transpire that fortune was blossoming on all fronts, even if the Stud was oblivious to some of the long-term benevolence Lady Luck was planting along its path.

In late 1993, two horses, who would one day graze in adjoining fields at Tully, emblazoned their names on a pair of the most prestigious trophies in the world of sport. Separately, each animal was to leave an indelible mark on horseracing and, for very different reasons, attract incredible international interest in the Stud.

Urban Sea was the first of these two to make a move. She found a burst of speed around the sweeping turn at Longchamp to defy the bookies' scornful odds and win Europe's most coveted prize, the Prix de l'Arc de Triomphe. The Stud was not to know it, but one day she would deliver its most complete son.

Seven days after Urban Sea's win, an old warhorse, Vintage Crop, brushed aside 12,000 miles of travelling, negotiated confusion and quarantine, and powered home to win Australia's revered Melbourne Cup. He was the first northern hemisphere horse to withstand the perilous journey and arrive in good enough condition to win the race. Vintage Crop's trainer, Dermot Weld, was one of the new breed of directors at the Stud, and he had masterminded the gelding's victory. In time, the horse's relaxing retirement would see the champion and his trainer reunited at Tully. But the Stud did not simply sit back and rely on charity and chance – it tried to steer its own course by beginning to buy horses again.

In 1993 a broodmare, Athens Belle, arrived. That October, two fillies were snapped up at Goffs to race for President Mary Robinson. Elsewhere, a strong stallion prospect was pinpointed. This under-appreciated horse, Indian Ridge, did not just offer hope of a new beginning. He also provided a direct link to the most lucrative moment in the Stud's history.

Indian Ridge had been conceived at Tully. He was but one of 281 sons and daughters of the last great stallion to live at the farm, Ahonoora. The young stallion was the result of his dam, Hillbrow, visiting the Stud's sire in 1984. This was at the start of the seminal season for Indian Ridge's father, when his progeny's winning streak led to a surge in demand from breeders.

The fee for mating with the sire, Ahonoora, rose and the price his offspring achieved at the sales soon went in a similar direction. His scrawny yearling, later to be named Indian Ridge, was sold at Goffs in 1985 for £22,000. The prices that week were a fraction of the jaw-dropping sums spent the previous year. Neither was bidding as hectic as it had been at the Newmarket sales a month before, when Shiekh Mohammed and the Maktoum family exhibited early clout to snap up 80 per cent of the lots. Still, on the week he was first sold, Indian Ridge only achieved 5 per cent of the event's top trade. The fee was a good £50,000 below more reasonably priced prospects.

Two years later, he began racing for Anne and Sean Coughlan during a mixed career that spanned three seasons. He had three wins from seven starts. The Coughlans earned Stg£105,000 from his campaign.

When he retired in 1989, a 40-share syndicate took him over and sent him to Britain to stand at stud. Just like when his father began his covering duties, the softly-toned and powerful five-year-old was not thought of as a product for the upper end of the market. His price dropped from £5,000 to £3,000 before the Irish National Stud received the cash it needed to buy him in early 1993. Then, as the summer unfolded, early indications of the punt's true potential emerged. In the first 28 races that Indian Ridge's progeny completed, there were 17 winners. After a decade drifting towards decay, the Stud could not believe the jackpot it had struck.

It was "an important first step in positioning the Stud for the future", said the new chairman David Shubotham in his reflection on that season's racing. Indian Ridge had a rare ability. His failings stopped with him and he liberally passed on his talents to the next generation. His offspring almost always emerged better than either of their parents. He was just one of many new faces bedding down at Tully.

Six new directors had settled in around the boardroom table. In the chair was Mr Shubotham. Around him, the bright and fresh posse brought a measure of success and diversity. Together they would largely shape and control the development of the business for the next two decades.

Jim Beecher, a career civil servant living in Killiney, came straight from the Department of Agriculture. The then 46-year-old was familiar with the ins and outs of the industry's politics and the Stud's relationship with its paymaster. He was also accustomed to the N7 road from Dublin into the heart of horse country, having been appointed by his Department to be a member of the neighbouring Irish Horse Board.

Pat O'Kelly, born over Christmas 1931, carried the most impressive reputation for breeding. Diminutive in size, she brought immense weight in buying power. She had inherited the 200-acre Kilcarn Stud farm at Navan from her father, Major Ned Kelly, and had shown a consistent ability for producing exceptional horses.

The honorary title of company secretary passed from Lorcan Mooney to Kildare accountant, John McStay. Mr McStay became a more hands-on presence than his predecessor. The accountant also had pedigree and professionalism, which had already seen him become one of the country's foremost liquidators.

In the early 1980s he was as much a celebrity as any accountant could wish to be. Less than a year after he was made a partner at Ernst & Whinney, later to become Ernst & Young, the High Court appointed him as the liquidator of the *Sunday Tribune* after it catastrophically collapsed owing £3.5m. It was an acrimonious affair and a brutal brief to be in charge of. Over the 144 days he spent salvaging the company, he put in 1,850 hours' work. He earned £42,500 and, more importantly, an immensely enhanced reputation. The profile earned him a right to have his voice heard. In a speech, he warned of the dangers of "cowboy" company directors exploiting antiquated fraud laws.

With increased status came muscle. Mr McStay earned six times as much from the fractious liquidation of Kerrigan Investments, which he was put in charge of a short time after the *Tribune's* rescue. Nine months before he joined the Stud, he made a bold break and set up his own accountancy business. The liquidator had again been in the news for successfully steering a struggling Dublin animation firm into the arms of a Hong Kong buyer. He felt the market was right for smaller, specialised firms. So, when Lorcan Mooney retired on November 4th 1993, Mr McStay was appointed to the honorary and unpaid position of company secretary.

Mr McStay already had connections with Tully. He was a life-long friend of Stud manager John Clarke. Their children had grown up together and Mr Clarke was godfather to one of the new company secretary's sons. Their independent and steeply-rising careers had almost run in parallel. Two years after Mr Clarke joined Ballsbridge International Sales, Mr McStay was hired by Ernst & Whinney.

Exactly 12 months after the 31-year-old accountant was made a partner at the firm, the 32-year-old Mr Clarke became manager of the Irish National Stud. They found themselves under the same umbrella when Mr McStay's new business began providing accountancy services to Tully.

Despite the liquidator's work, wading through the flotsam and jetsam of assets in many different businesses, Mr McStay was steeped in horseracing. He and his wife, Clodagh, ran the Oaklawn Stud. Many people would also have known him as the son of Michael McStay.

For a long time Michael McStay was one of Kildare's and Ireland's most famous and powerful businessmen. A trained barrister-turned-accountant, he was the first non-Dutch national to become managing director of the electronics multinational Philips. He was chairman of numerous boards, companies and agencies. As chairman of Unidare he worked with Michael Osborne and the Irish National Stud for programmes to help the industry. He sponsored the apprentice jockeys' championship. With Mr Osborne, he worked to secure the facilities for the truly visionary RACE training academy beside Tully. He was also the chairman of Stallion Investments.

This was a speculative creature of its time that grew from nothing in the late 1970s to announce it was listing on the stock exchange with its booty of two fully-owned stallions and shares in another four.

Such a move was an unprecedented, and ultimately unrealistic, show of faith in the value of stallions. One of the animals it owned was Indian King. It had bought this horse in early 1983 in a 50:50 deal with the Irish National Stud. Indian King was the first major stallion purchase of Mr Clarke's tenure. It would not have been possible without the backers from Mr McStay's Stallion Investments.

Michael McStay died suddenly at his home in Kildare in 1987 at the age of 69. His funeral was a check-list of the elite power brokers in politics, business and bloodstock. His son, John, was already carrying forth the family's business reputation.

A year after he joined the Stud as company secretary, he also followed his father's path into the divisive policing body for the horseracing industry, the Turf Club. Politically, the Stud's new company secretary, the Department of Agriculture nominee and its quick-moving chairman were significant and experienced arrivals. But in that era, the real star appointee was Dermot Kenneth Weld.

As a youngster, Mr Weld was a mix-disciplined globe-trotter. He travelled as far afield as Australia as a jockey. The Kildare man worked as a vet in vaunted venues such as New York's famous Belmont Park. Travelling in his twenties banished the fears many other Europeans had about competing in America and Down Under. As a trainer, he made good use of the experiences. Then, a year after he replaced Denis McCarthy on the Board, his talents were broadcast to the world.

It was November 1993 and he had been training Michael Smurfit's five-year-old, Vintage Crop. The horse, who had a chronic bad back and persistent stomach ulcers, had notched up an impressive stakes' win at Newmarket in 1992. But this was an entirely different season's preparation with a single goal in mind – the Melbourne Cup. The cost of the journey meant that the challenge could only be realistically contemplated by exceptionally wealthy owners. The Smurfits could foot the bill. Notwithstanding the expense, Vintage Crop spent weeks in quarantine. The flight alone had been enough to fatally handicap every other overseas aspirant. Mr Weld prepared Vintage Crop to withstand the arduous journey: by cushioning his back problems and treating his stress-affected stomach. In Australia, Vintage Crop did something no other northern hemisphere-trained horse had managed. With the line in his sight, he accelerated from the crowd, charged forward and won the great Melbourne Cup.

Immediately, Vintage Crop became a sensation. It was regarded as racing's most incredible feat of preparation and training. D. K. Weld became a star, and justifiably so. And the Stud had him at its disposal. He, and the rest of the fledgling directors, began to develop a sense of ownership over their new roles. It was the company's policy to encourage the Board members to spend money at the Stud and to share in its investments. Pat O'Kelly donated one of her mares, Dark Hyacinth, to the farm and straight away it was carrying a foal by Indian Ridge.

Mr Weld began to train Moy Water, one of the fillies that arrived in October 1993. She won carrying President Robinson's colours in 1995. In January 1994, a late recruit to the Stud's boardroom revolution, Chryss O'Reilly, paid £55,000 for one share in a newly-formed syndicate. This was organised for a recently retired stallion, Catrail, who had won at Ascot and Newmarket during the season.

The Catrail joint-venture did not work out at first. His price was set too high. Breeders turned their backs and Catrail only had 31 foals in his first year. But soon Mrs O'Reilly, the Stud and the other shareholders began to see a return. Australia's Arrowfield Stud bought a significant minority stake in the stallion. His first foals had yet to hit the track and already he was splitting his time between New South

Wales and Kildare. While the wait was on, the Stud kept activity ticking over on Catrail's books by using its own mares.

In 1996, the mare Ms O'Kelly had signed over, Dark Hyacinth, was in foal to him. That year, 4 of the Stud's 13 mares were covered by Catrail, the same number as were sent to the superstar Indian Ridge.

Catrail never really made it consistently at the mating game. But he helped the Stud develop a useful strategic partnership with Arrowfield. Its horse, Flying Spur, was later sent to Kildare while two Tully residents were flown south to stand for the season.

Flying Spur was the son of the spectacular stallion, Danehill, who pioneered the successful seasonal shunt of horses across the equator. After her arrival, Catrail was the first, but not the last, breeding partnership Mrs O'Reilly became involved in with the Stud. Later, she was party to some of its most significant and successful ventures, and played a powerful role in the company's progression.

Mrs O'Reilly was born Chryss Goulandris in New York in 1950. She first came to Tully, with an immense reputation, the month after Vintage Crop's famous win. She was the daughter of Greek shipping merchant, John Goulandris. Her grandfather had pioneered steamboat shipping in the Mediterranean and the family was extraordinarily wealthy in an archipelago country where marine transport was floating gold.

John Goulandris died of a heart attack when Chryss was three years' old. She was raised on New York's Fifth Avenue at the Savoy Plaza Hotel. Chryss Goulandris was part of a strong family network and earned her pocket money going to race meets with her stable-owning uncle, George. In the 1970s she went to university at the Sorbonne in Paris. She made her first feverish foray into ownership at the Keenland sales in 1976. Two years later, she took over the La Louviere stud in Normandy when another uncle, Constantine, died.

With a soft American twang and long, dark hair pulled back from her face, Ms Goulandris proved to have a wonderful talent for selecting and breeding horses. By the time she met divorced media mogul Tony

O'Reilly in the late 1980s, the deliberately low-profile Goulandris network was expanding its billion-pound portfolio. Meanwhile, Mr O'Reilly was making a pitch for the family to invest in the business of Waterford Crystal.

The Goulandris clan liked the idea. But this did not mark the start of their eventual romance. A year later, Mr O'Reilly, the owner of *Independent Newspapers* and head of the Heinz corporation, asked the shipping heiress to a horse race his company sponsored in Ireland. By 1991, they were married at a ceremony in the Bahamas.

The new Mrs O'Reilly had a reputation for being bright, considerate and always splendidly dressed. Along with her husband, the Goulandris family had also bought into Waterford Wedgewood and she was appointed a non-executive director of its UK operation. But, of more interest to the National Stud was her involvement with breeding farms in America, France and Liberia. She brought expertise and contacts.

The Stud had to act while conditions were ripe. Bloodstock had come through its recession with a typical exuberance. Japan, in particular, was back in business.

Between 1991 and 1995, Japanese breeders had cheque books out to snap up every single Derby winner. This kept prices hot. Ireland's breeders were warming their toes. International figures were starting to look at the Irish industry with more than a degree of jealousy. There was bitterness about the amount of action top stallions were getting. An overwhelming majority of owners believed they should only be allowed to cover 80 mares a year.

In Britain, voices from various sectors were especially critical of the benefits a few large Irish stud farms got from lucrative tax breaks. Coolmore, the biggest winner from the breaks, fought back. It commissioned economist Paul Tansey to examine the situation. He said if the Irish industry was to compete, it needed a tax-break from government, a lot of mares to be covered and sustained investment.

This suited the Stud but it was still playing catch-up as others stretched their stride. Its situation was helped by one resident who worked harder than any other – Indian Ridge. By 1995, the stallion was already being hailed as "possibly the greatest sire to ever stand at the Stud".

He was a simple guy. During the off season, he would wake, get fed, be taken out to his five-acre paddock and chill. In winter, his handlers would work on his fitness. Come breeding season, he would have a short walk after his breakfast, cover a mare, exercise in his paddock in the late morning and meet another mare in the afternoon. He never struggled to perform. Once a mare was willing, he succeeded.

At the turn of the century, the Indian Ridge syndicate, which was controlled by the Stud, was offered $50m by Americans who wanted to buy him. Shareholders refused. He was Tully's own four-legged mint. The Stud was happily cashing in on him and his stable mates.

At the time, Mr Clarke described the yard as being like Clapham Junction; "mares in and out all the time". It was paying off.

At the end of 1995, its trading loss was effectively little more than £86,000. This was almost six times lower than the previous year and more promising because the value of services it was trading in leaped from £455,829 to £1.8m. It was the first time in five years that it had hit this height. There were signs of over-exuberance.

In December 1995, it decided that the bloodstock were worth far more than they were given credit for. So they cranked up the value by £442,709. On paper, this swelled the sum in its savings account. The next year, the Stud reversed this decision and wiped the exact same amount off its books. It then reconsidered the whole practice, stopped using a reserve savings account and put all its money into one pot to trade from year to year. There was growing optimism.

"The financial revitalisation of the company has been a difficult process. The ground work has been done and I believe 1996 will be a turning point," said Mr Shubotham at the end of 1995. He said he lived out the next year in trepidation. His prophecy started badly.

On January 15th, 1996, Castleblaney Garda station in Monaghan was tipped off about a planned cattle-rustling operation; it was said that the target was a State-owned herd. The Gardaí immediately scoped out the Department of Agriculture's farm on the outskirts of Dublin.

Forty cattle had gone missing from that facility a year before and were never seen again. Gardaí never thought to put the Stud on alert. The raiders had sussed the place out. They waited until the security guards had finished their routine final check at 1.30 am. A trailer was driven in. Eighty-three cattle were rounded up. The only trace of the missing herd was a pile of balaclavas, gloves and boiler suits flung into the Japanese Gardens. It cost the Stud £56,614. Fortunately, at that stage, it was better able to deal with such hits.

Another £1m shares had been bought by the Government to increase each taxpayer's stake in the project. The company happily ploughed it into improving its roster.

Sean Coughlan, who had sent Indian Ridge out to race, approached the Stud and asked if it wanted to buy a part in the super stallion's son, Ridgewood Ben. He was a big, strong and good-looking specimen who was snapped up and moved to Tully for the 1996 season. Ridgewood Ben came at a great time.

The Stud was awarded the Irish Thoroughbred Breeders' Award for having the top sire, Indian Ridge. The prize was accepted by Stud manager, Mr Clarke. At the same time, Vintage Crop retired and took up life in an accessible paddock where throngs of tourists could get close and take pictures. The presence of the darling underdog helped attract a record number of visitors to Tully. Money was free enough to build a new porch, bathroom and bedroom onto Mr Clarke and his wife, Monica's, home at Tully House.

On the track, Desert King was winning the Irish Derby and Irish 2,000 Guineas, two parts of the elusive triple crown. He was the son of Sabaah. She was the queen of the Stud's band of broodmares, bought at the tail-end of the company's trip towards oblivion in 1992. Desert

King's success helped attract interest in her other son, later to be called Wadj, who was sired by Indian Ridge.

For Wadj, the Stud was paid its highest ever price for a yearling, £330,000, by Sheikh Hamdan's Shadwell Estate company. More footfall, more foal fees and more frenzied finances culminated in the inevitable. The Stud returned a profit for 1996. It made £189,505. This was after wiping a hefty chunk off the value of its horses.

"Success has been attained, progress has been made and we will set ourselves more exacting targets for the future," the chairman pronounced.

Each milestone helped the company gain more kudos from its peers. Mr Coughlan was just one of a number of increasingly successful friends the company was making. But it also kept nurturing its home-grown links.

Director Dermot Weld bought a filly born at the Stud in 1997. As a yearling, the chestnut Caumshinaun was brought to a sales event in England by the Stud. She was a daughter of Indian Ridge and had a very good pedigree. It appears she went lame the morning of the sale so no buyer was interested. Mr Weld stepped into the breach and purchased the filly from the Stud for his mother, Gita's, stable. The deal was private and the fee was not disclosed. Caumshinaun was to race 16 times, winning 5 and earning €129,856 for the Welds.

When she retired, Caumshinaun became a truly outstanding broodmare. Her son, with star stallion Galileo, was called Nighttime. He won the Irish 1,000 Guineas in 2006, delivering €228,000 for the Welds.

Caumshinaun's other offspring were also lucrative. Her son with Green Desert was sold for €140,000 at Goffs in 2005. In 2006, a filly was sold by the Welds for €110,000. Her colt from Refuse to Bend was sold by the Castlebridge Consignment for £200,000 in England in 2008. The same year, her second son with Galileo, Olympiad, was sold at Tattersalls for more than £650,000.

Each new trade and event has always brought fresh assets and new opportunities. But, in 1998, when Caumshinaun changed hands, there was no let-up in the Stud's effort.

It made its first significant attempt to expand overseas. One of its stallions was sent to Italy on a lease. The horse, Dancing Dissident, was a problematic beast. Nobody knew what to do with him. After he was emigrated, just one of the maligned pre-1993 posse, Magical Wonder, remained among the seven stallions living in Tully. Magical Wonder's first two seasons were good. Then he developed an allergy to straw. This affected his ability to perform and he only produced two foals the next year. Other national hunt horses of that era were farmed out to the likes of Bert House and Knockhouse studs.

The Irish National Stud was focused on its more recent acquisitions and was making the most of a buzz in Irish breeding. At Goffs, the average 1996 price for a yearling (£21,000) jumped 50 per cent over the next two years. In England prices had remained static.

The summer of 1998 was the wettest on record across the country. But there was an inescapable feel-good vibe in the Stud. Before the flat racing season was in full throttle, it had bought two of that year's would-be stars, Croco Rouge and Desert Prince.

James Wigan of London Thoroughbred Services had orchestrated the Desert Prince deal. The Stud was delighted.

"I am thrilled that at this stage in the season we have virtually completed the acquisition of two quite outstanding prospects," Mr Clarke said. Desert Prince turned out to be the real star.

Fortunately, the Stud had worked out a little profit-sharing perk to make sure it got hold of him early. Although he was 100 per cent owned by the Stud he raced in the colours of his original owners, Lucagan, and the two parties split his winnings. In addition, a promotional deal sponsored by Mr Wigan meant that he handed the Stud £1,000 every time the stallion crossed the line first. These purchases did more than show good fortune. They also revealed the renewed respect the most powerful players in breeding were affording the Irish National Stud.

It bought Ashkalani from the Aga Khan and he stayed involved with a sizeable minority stake. The fabulously wealthy Wafik Said allowed the company to split the ownership of Croco Rouge with his Florida-based Addison Racing operation. The Stud cemented its stallion-swapping synergy with Arrowfield Stud. Also, Australia's mammoth Woodland Stud joined it in the syndication of Desert Prince. Progress was frantic. Smaller things suffered.

In July 1996, the Sheriff of Kildare and Carlow issued a warrant to collect money after the Stud did not pay its tax for two months that year. The letter threatened to impound goods if it did not hand over the £2,430 due and £75 in expenses.

Again, in 1999, the Stud failed to pay its annual tax bill to the Revenue Commissioners on time. The delay cost the Stud £16,672 in interest charges. Running parallel to that was a dispute over the VAT it should pay for work done on its behalf.

An agreement between Martin O'Reilly, who worked for Mr McStay's firm, and the tax collectors was eventually agreed in February 2001. It resulted in Mr Clarke sending a cheque for £32,305 to settle the affair.

Some matters were a bit chaotic at the Stud. It did not file mandatory annual reports for 1996 and 1997 with the Companies Registration Office on time. They were handed in with its 1998 accounts in August 1999 and paid for with the same cheque. This was despite the 1996 account being laid before the Oireachtas in September 1997. Ironically, these delayed accounts would have afforded the Stud its first opportunity to boast about a profit in years.

However, just as the Stud returned to positive finances for the first time in a decade, Mr Shubotham shipped out. Ahead of the AGM of June 1998, he decided he did not have the time to devote to a third term. Chryss O'Reilly moved up to take his chair. She was hailed, by restored Agriculture Minister Joe Walsh, as a "unique asset to the horseracing industry", who the Stud was fortunate to have at its disposal. Because of her promotion and Mr Shubotham's resignation, there was space at the boardroom table.

John Osborne, the son of the famous former Stud manager Michael, arrived in to the director's spot. He had grown up at Tully House and offered a direct link to the most vaunted time in the Stud's history.

Mrs O'Reilly's first job in the chair was to shepherd in the long-threatened carve-up of Tully. Even before her arrival in 1993, the Stud had been in a protracted dispute with Kildare County Council over plans to drive a by-pass through its farm. The outcome had been inevitable from the start, but the Government had never delivered the money to act on it. Meanwhile, there were fights over rare snails and protected habitats elsewhere on the route. The Stud's concern was that it would split the farm in two and make it impossible to run a coherent operation. It was the beginning of a deeply antagonizing battle between the two state bodies that continued long after the motorway was finished.

The council ended up taking 11 acres for the road. Another 22 acres on the far side of the new motorway was severed. In time, 17,000 cars a day were diverted away from Kildare town where, during that rain-drenched summer of 1998, the five-mile lines of traffic filed past a stretched-out sign: "The National Stud for the fillies and the Sam Maguire for the lilies".

The company felt like lifting the mood and supporting the famous revival of the Kildare Gaelic football team under Kerry legend, Mick O'Dwyer, whose arrival had been orchestrated by none other than Michael Osborne. When the cash from the compulsory sale eventually came to the Stud, it was most welcome.

Crucially, the Government had brought in a new law to allow the Stud to sell off the land and keep the profits. This was a subtle, multi-million-pound sweetener which otherwise would have gone directly into central funds. The necessary Bill was introduced by Minister Walsh.

Since taking the sweeping brush to the Stud's Board in 1993, Joe Walsh had briefly left government with his Fianna Fáil colleagues. In 1997, they were voted back in and he returned to the same desk in Agriculture House. The Cork south-west politician was heavily involved in horseracing. He had also become an increasingly absorbed patron of the company. He visited Tully so often it was joked that he was mistaken for one of the stable hands. He clearly liked the improvements in this complex after a period when he was caught up in a series of controversies over the control of the horseracing industry. He campaigned on behalf of the Stud against the Department of Finance to allow it to keep the money from the sale of land for the Kildare by-pass.

In October 1998, he introduced the quick-fix law to allow the portion of the Stud to be offloaded. In his speech, Minister Walsh's rhetoric was reverential, whereas five years earlier it had been closer to ridicule. He specifically praised Mr Clarke and his assistant, Annette Boland.

"I take this opportunity to pay tribute to and thank the Board of the National Stud, particularly Mr David Shubotham, whom I appointed chairman a number of years ago.

"He and the Board did a superb job in building the Stud, getting quality stallions and giving it international recognition. They also improved the financial structures of the Stud," he said.

By law, he was the most powerful influence in the company. But the amount of business directors were doing with the Stud showed those around the boardroom table shared his confidence.

In 1997, directors spent £81,500 on keeping mares on the grounds of the Stud and paying to use its stallions. This was an increase of £52,828. A year later, this figure jumped to £240,500. In 1999, it rose to £336,500. By 2000, the value of the company's trading with its own directors had jumped to £651,774.

The facility benefitted from the goodwill deals with its directors and the flow of business with its Board. This was showcased in the £800,000 creation of the Lakeland attraction, St Fiachra's Gardens.

Designed by Professor Martin Hallinan, the island was sculpted to accommodate cascading waterfalls in order to make the place more pleasant for the swelling seasonal demand from tourists. At the garden's heart, was a re-created small stone monastic cell complex. Its centrepiece was a nest of Waterford Crystal ornaments buried under a glass panel.

Mrs O'Reilly was part of the family network which controlled the crystal factory and said its involvement in the ode to St Fiachra, the patron saint of gardeners, had particular significance.

"On a personal level I am delighted that a centrepiece of the garden is a magnificent interpretation in Waterford Crystal created and generously sponsored by Waterford Crystal.

"The combination of the Irish National Stud and Waterford represents a natural link between two of Ireland's internationally recognised centres of excellence," she said.

The sponsorship of the garden was part of a business relationship that glistened over the next 10 years. By the time the O'Reillys and Goulandris investors wound down the Waterford plant in 1999, the Stud had spent €93,646 on its crystal products, mostly for sale to tourists in the gift shop. But, even before her acceptance of the chairman's brief, the Board wanted more than a quaint six-acre island garden and a stream of tourist buses filling its car park. It wanted independent recognition of the revolution that had occurred. At the time, the most prestigious stamp of approval was the coveted Q-Mark for quality.

The drive to attain a Q Mark would inspire those involved in the Stud to make exceptional efforts in pursuit of their goal. Nobody realised the internal enmity that would come with it.

1st Baron Wavertree

Invincible Spirit in his paddock

Indian Ridge

Japanese Gardens

The stallion's stables

Mares and foals at Irish National Stud

Sea the Stars winning the Prix de l'Arc de Triomphe

Above: John Osborne

Right: Pat Mallarkey

Pat Mullarkey and Eileen Kavanagh   *Mrs Ling Tsui*

© Healy Racing Photographers

© Courtpix

John Clarke   *Julie Lynch*

A young Christopher Tsui in his red blazer watches on as his father, David, celebrates his mare's (Urban Sea) surprising win at the Prix de l'Arc with trainer Jean Lesbordes and jockey Eric Martin

© Healy Racing Photographers

Sea The Stars With L-R: Monica and John Clarke; Michael, Sinead and Catherine Kinane and John Oxx.

*Above: Tully House, the
home of the Stud manager*

*Right: The €22,258 patio at
the rere of Tully House.*

CHAPTER
5

Heartache in the Quest for Quality

Pat Mullarkey and John Clarke used to get along just fine. One managed the stud business. The other looked after the 1,000-acre farm supplying it and the tourist trade which helped soothe the shocks during rough times.

Mr Mullarkey arrived in 1979, for the final years of Michael Osborne's era. Mr Clarke joined four years later, to replace the popular front man. Long before either manager came through the old gates of Tully as young men, a history of low-level conflict had existed at the Stud.

The flashing steel of the stud stallions occasionally struck off the stone-solid support of the farm. All the while, the temperamental tourism trade brought an additional measure of scrutiny and stress to the semi-State business. This all tended to spark more than ignite.

Cattle, tillage, tourism and thoroughbreds were all at their busiest at different times of the year. There were distinct cultures and disparate demands involved in pleasing the various customers.

At Tully each section was expected to hold its own rhythm, earn its keep and ensure its seasonal cycle was in harmony with the corporate concert the company was trying to conduct. Yet, understandably, inevitable mishaps and misfortune meant there was often the din of discord irrespective of who was involved.

During Mr Osborne's time, he encouraged the establishment of a musical society to help unite all the factions into the one chorus. Mr Clarke's work involved a lot of time in the office arranging coverings for clients, or travelling to hunt for horses on the company's behalf. Mr Mullarkey worked around the yard to ensure the sprawling campus was able to meet the Stud's needs and that it generated whatever profit possible.

There were times when it worked well. When it did, it moved with metronomic ease. On other occasions, both managers had seen their side of the ensemble slump badly with seasonal set-backs and structural problems.

Consultants and assessors came in to try to figure out what was going wrong. Often it was nothing more than yet another cycle in topsy-turvy trade. Generally their sections bounced back. Invariably, they were soon called on to carry the tune for the rest of the operation.

Mr Mullarkey and Mr Clarke had lost equal numbers of staff in the cutbacks of 1993. Ten permanent workers left the Stud: the farm lost four, the tourism section fell by one and the maintenance yard was reduced by five employees. The two managers had also seen the nature of the business they were involved in change utterly. Over time, so did their working relationship.

Mr Mullarkey was broad. He was strong. He got things done. However, he would later tell the High Court he was bullied by the manager of the Stud, John Clarke. It got so bad, he said, that he no longer believed he had a safe and sound place to work.

In 1994, Mr Mullarkey was appointed to take control of the tourism side of the business, along with his farming responsibilities. The new visitors' centre had opened a few months earlier and there were plans gestating to renovate and expand the horse museum.

The Board, under David Shubotham, set demanding profit targets. It entrusted Mr Mullarkey with ensuring these were reached. Inside a year, tourism turnover more than doubled to £569,967.

Record visitor levels the next season saw another £100,000 put on top of that. The Board heaped praise on all involved, for smoothly, successfully and significantly supporting the company's business plans. The Japanese Gardens were a constant attraction. The retired

Melbourne Cup winner, Vintage Crop, became a further draw. At the end of the decade, the new, Professor Martin Hallinan-designed St Fiachra's Garden was opened by President Mary McAleese.

The combined complex routinely drew in more tourists each year than the likes of Newgrange, Clonmacnoise and the Rock of Cashel.

"Balancing the running of a successful public stud whilst operating a significant and profitable ancillary tourist attraction is a challenge which faces the company," Mr Shubotham admitted in 1997.

Yet the shoots of success in Tully and across the country had seen a certain ambition sprout. The Board decided it wanted more for both the tourism trade and the stud farm.

It set its sights on the Q Mark for quality. Mr Mullarkey and office manager, Eileen Kavanagh, were charged with delivering it.

The effort required to qualify for the Q Mark placed new rigors on the entire outfit. There were internal audits and unannounced spot-checks. Paperwork had to be kept in a way which neither the Stud, nor the industry, was accustomed to. This jolted and jangled all aspects of an enterprise used to ticking over in a more improvised fashion.

Over many months, Ms Kavanagh had to cajole her colleagues into scrapping bad habits, which had been acquired through years of theatrics the company had relied on just to stay in business.

"Pat and I would never have envisaged the amount of work… There wasn't anything to copy. We had to go it alone," she said.

Still, just before Christmas 1998, their prize came in the form of a glistening golden Q Mark to hang on the wall. Balloons and banners were pulled out to celebrate the achievement. The two project leaders were given a £7,500 bonus for their efforts. Minister Joe Walsh made the trip down for the presentation. On that night, he said the commitment of the Stud was an exemplary credit to the country.

The chairman he had appointed six months earlier, Chryss O'Reilly, said the framed testament of its progress set a standard the business would have to live up to on an ongoing basis. Ms Kavanagh said the place was all the better for having reached for, and been reformed by, the Q Mark.

"The systems improved enormously. It will keep us all on our toes. And we certainly don't do anything lightly anymore. We document everything," she said.

But, with quality came controversy. Mr Mullarkey later told the High Court that his work coordinating the exercise was made particularly difficult by Mr Clarke's attitude towards it. He said the relationship between the pair had broken down after he accepted responsibility for tourism in 1994. It had not recovered.

The farm and tourism manager said he was accused by his colleague of not pulling his weight to get the Q Mark. Mr Mullarkey considered this outrageous and groundless.

A lot of what the Stud did and how it operated evolved in a functional, if not always logical, fashion. Little was written down or formalised over the years. Even the stature of the stud manager was not enshrined. Mr Clarke was the chief executive. But Dáil records from the time were careful to include the caveat that his title was stud manager, not chief executive.

Two of Mr Clarke's predecessors had been particularly prominent. Their status provided his position with a public prestige. The Stud was there primarily to breed horses. And Mr Clarke's stallions had always provided the pulse for the entire operation. This all ensured that his role had a senior status. Yet both managers still answered to the Board. That habit created confusion in the chain of command.

As the years drifted by, the structure was never properly defined. Periodically, that shortcoming would cause low-level friction but, in 1999, things became particularly unpleasant.

All summer, sheets of rain had swept across the town lands of Curragh Farm, Tully West and Tully East, which combined to make up the National Stud and Japanese Gardens. These torrents kept visitor figures down. It was time for the rest of the company to pick up the slack. After six years of focusing on improving the quality of its band of horses, the Stud was finally reaping its rewards. The stallion section was back with a big profit.

Arabian investor, Wafic Said of Addison Racing, and the Stud teamed up for a $4m evenly-split purchase of the racer, Croco Rouge. Within 12 months, Mr Said had gone on to pay more for a yearling from the Stud than any buyer in history: £500,000 for a horse which had been born to the mare, Sabaah, in 1999. All the while, the presence of the Addison operation and other international heavyweights attracted additional breeders. The *Irish Field*, the newspaper for Irish horse racing, was enamoured by the Stud's evident ambition and said the success was a "credit to the nation".

"Gone are the days when a successful Tully sire was tagged as 'too dear for our clients' and was sold on to further glory with better class mares.

"Now the company is taking on other top farms and if a stallion is successful, it stays," it said.

The *Irish Field*, made this assessment when reflecting on the 1999 accounts published by the Stud. A few paragraphs later, it reprinted a comment Mrs O'Reilly made in them. She had complained about the problem of rising wages and private competitors poaching the best workers.

"It is becoming increasingly difficult to recruit and retain the high quality staff that are so essential to its business," Mrs O'Reilly said.

Yvonne Mullarkey read the article a month before she celebrated her 22nd birthday. Mrs O'Reilly's comments struck a chord with her. Two months later, Ms Mullarkey had reached the point where she felt she had to write to the chairman on the strength of those words.

The young woman said there was a good man, a good worker, on the payroll of the National Stud who was being driven out.

"Mrs O'Reilly, I recently read an article of yours in the Irish Field newspaper on September 9 in which you commented on how hard it was to find and hold good, reliable staff in the present economic climate.

"I would ask you not to overlook my dad or the situation he now finds himself in . . . if at all possible, please try to find a fast and effective solution to this problem."

The young letter-writer was referring to the distress her father, Pat Mullarkey, said he felt because of his treatment by the stud manager.

Skirmishes between the two men were sometimes subtle, but were striking nonetheless. Stallions were moved away from the entrance road for a more peaceful life. This did no favours for the curious crowds piling out of tourist buses every day to try and take pictures. Ms Mullarkey watched on as her father's situation deteriorated.

Shortly after the letter had been sent, father and daughter sat down with Mrs O'Reilly. They were joined by John Osborne, who had arrived on the Board as a director around the time Mrs O'Reilly was made chairman.

Later, in sworn testimony, Mr Mullarkey said Mr Clarke had accused him of not doing enough to help maintain the company's Q Mark status. The farm and tourism manager said the tenor of the chairman and Mr Osborne's arguments were similarly dismissive of his efforts to maintain the quality standard, which he helped bring to Tully in the first place.

Mr Mullarkey claimed that, at that meeting, Mrs O'Reilly said it was the first time she had heard he had responsibility for the tourism side of the business. Annual reports released by the Board had listed him as the person in charge of the farm and tourism operations since 1994. Mr Mullarkey pointed to photographs of him with her and Minister Walsh taken two years before, the night the Q Mark was presented.

It was not the first time Ms Mullarkey had tried to intervene on her father's behalf. The Stud had always enjoyed its strongest support from Fianna Fáil ministers and Ms Mullarkey was part of the Fianna Fáil family. She was a member of the Kildare Cumann and, in 1999, she had used her contacts to secure a meeting with local TD and Finance Minister, Charlie McCreevy. Ms Mullarkey had told him everything.

The Minister had close friends involved in the Stud and was very familiar with the business. He arranged for the Mullarkeys to meet the then Taoiseach, Bertie Ahern.

Yvonne Mullarkey and her dad drove to the infamous terracotta-bricked converted house on the banks of the River Tolka on April 10th, 2000. It was a dry and mild spring evening and horse racing was already on the Taoiseach's radar. Earlier that day, the Flood Tribunal had heard how builder and racehorse breeder, Thomas Brennan, bankrolled the former Dublin Assistant City and County Manager, George Redmond. Mr Brennan said he did this by placing bets on races and passing on the winnings to his golfing buddy.

On a lighter note, Kildare was abuzz. The previous day saw the return home of the father-and-son success story, Ted and Ruby Walsh. Together, they trained and rode Papillion to win the Aintree Grand National. The Walshes and Papillion drew hundreds of well-wishers, a battalion of banner wavers and a smattering of international media for the celebration in the village of Kill. The mood was much darker in Drumcondra.

"We met in St Luke's. Dad and I cried. Bertie said he'd talk to Joe Walsh. Bertie rang me afterwards and said he'd spoken to Joe. But after that, the situation at the Stud only got worse," Ms Mullarkey later told the *Sunday Times*.

Whether the Taoiseach actually spoke to the Agriculture Minister or not remained a question of Cabinet confidentiality. But, regardless of what was said in St Luke's that evening, it failed to alter the Minister or his colleagues' opinion of the company.

Separately, the Cabinet agreed to give it another £1m towards new shares. This obviously helped. With this additional support from taxpayers, the Stud turned a £625,140 profit during the 12 months when the Mullarkeys were bringing their plight to the chairman and the leader of the country.

It was the second time in two years that the Stud had hit this height and it meant the venture passed the psychological milestone of extinguishing the debt it had racked up at the beginning of the 1990s. This quest had been successful in no small part because of the two men at the centre of the seething antagonism. Despite everything, they had done a good job in their respective areas while the dispute was going on. The books showed that each side of the business was pulling its weight. There was a slight decline in the earnings of both the bloodstock business and the farm, but this was due to the revaluation of animals and not the performance of the men involved.

Mr Clarke's horses brought in £3m and the progeny from the star stallions had an outstanding year on the track. As a result, the Stud had relied on three times more of Mr Mullarkey's home-grown barley, rather than selling it to other farms for money.

Meanwhile, tourist figures hit a record level. This arm of the venture took in €1m in revenue, a jump of 13 per cent on 1999, which helped to pay for sprucing up the facilities. In the middle of this, Mr Walsh was so impressed by the company's performance he wanted to give the Board an even freer hand. If he had been made aware of the Mullarkeys' meeting with Mr Ahern, it was not reflected in his policy decisions. Apart from an extra £1m share options, he proposed a Bill that attempted to free the Stud, insofar as possible, from political interference in how it spent its money.

"I have always placed great trust in the Board of the Stud company. This Board is appointed by the Government and such boards must be given flexibility to do their job and not have their hands tied.

"I have a high regard for the current and previous chairmen and the Board of the Irish National Stud," he said.

This was just seven years after a decimated and demoralised Stud was accused by the same minister of being better at breeding plants than horses. As he brought forward the potentially bountiful National Stud Bill 2000, he appeared to have forgotten his historical concerns.

"The Stud has been very successful in operating its business on a sound and profitable basis.

"This is because successive Governments ensured it was given the resources and freedom it required," he said.

Politicians of all hues queued up to support the additional independence that Mr Walsh proposed. This was in keeping with a traditionally bipolar relationship between Oireachtas members and the Stud.

In particular, TDs have tended to tap to whatever tune was popular at the time, without looking under the surface to see if the company was sound or not. Political party colours have often had a lot more to do with Oireachtas analysis than genuine scrutiny. When the prevailing mood or press commentaries have been critical, the Dáil dispatches have been scathing.

In the 1950s, the Fine Gael front bench lined up to lambast the decision to invest in Tulyar. Three years later, Fine Gael was in Government vociferously defending a similar involvement in Panaslipper. Across the floor, Fianna Fáil's Donogh O'Malley was calling for a clear-out of the Board after his party was responsible for installing it.

In the 1960s, Charlie Haughey lauded the Stud and its potential. Seven years down the line, he was in opposition claiming that the structure was not fit for purpose.

In the 1970s, the Fine Gael Government was pledging support to improve the Stud and praising the asset. Soon afterwards, it cut the company's funding and procrastinated on requests to increase its ability to borrow.

At that time, Fianna Fáil bemoaned the lack of investment in the company. While in power at various stages over the next 10 years, it silently wrung its hands of responsibility when faced with report after report calling for proper financing of the farm. The harshest comments coincide largely with the times of most difficulty. Praise was well-lathered when the books looked rosier.

In the 1990s, the two opposing parties joined forces with a public flogging by Joe Walsh and Fine Gael spokesman, Ivan Yates. In 2000, they came together again with Alan Dukes taking the place of Mr Yates. This time, the two teams were competing to trumpet the Stud and its structure.

In a press release, Mr Dukes claimed that he had strong-armed the Government into boosting the Stud's borrowing ability from £5m to £30m. He sought kudos for a potential taxpayer investment of £20m.

Mr Walsh had already proposed slightly smaller figures. Furthermore, he supported Deputy Dukes' request that the threshold of public funds available to the Stud be increased from £10m to £30m. Mr Walsh said that during the 1990s the taxpayers' investment had been used to buy top-class stallions. It had. With the extra money he committed in 2000, the Stud went and bought a major shareholding in the top-class sprinter Indian Danehill – the son of the hemisphere-hopping sensation, Danehill. The Stud bought its stake from Baron Rothschild before Danehill won the Prix Ganay, a victory that brought about a nice increase in his value. It was the third get-in-before-they-win purchase the Stud had made in three years.

It was not the only big move or major money deal affecting Mr Clarke's specialist section of the complex that season. Most profitably, there was the quick resale of Croco Rouge. He was sold off to a Japanese syndicate for $7m. He had completed his first season at Tully earlier that year and delivered a healthy return on a $4m half-in-half investment by the Stud and Wafic Said. Catrail, the under-performing stallion whose syndicate Mrs O'Reilly had first joined, was sold off to the Wafare Stud in Kentucky in the belief he would be better suited to American bloodlines.

Mrs O'Reilly herself made a significant boost to the Stud's coffers. She bought its yearling filly called Desertion, who was a full sister of the winning son of the Stud, Desert King. Desertion cost her £650,000. She said she had known the filly since she was born and wanted it for her broodmare band. Good press was coming fast.

Mr Mullarkey's patch also got help in the ongoing effort to coax in more customers. This happened because the Melbourne Cup hero,

Vintage Crop, got a companion in the grazing paddock with the arrival of the "people's champion", Danoli. The Stud only found out about this additional attraction by accident.

Tom Foley, the trainer of Danoli, let it slip in an interview on RTÉ's Pat Kenny show that he wanted the horse to be available to the public. He suggested the Stud would be a great retirement ground for him. It took Tully by surprise but it was happy to work out a deal with his owner.

Mr Clarke said the animal was an immediate success. "He's a real crowd puller and the nicest horse you could have anything to do with."

The company as a whole also had some good news. In September the ink finally dried on the contract to build the £60m Kildare by-pass.

During an acrimonious planning process the route was tweaked and sent slightly askew by a desire to keep the hurtling traffic away from the Stud's horses. This would not have been an issue had another section of the by-pass not run over a protected marshland fen. Mr Clarke irked the environmentalist lobby when he said horses were sensitive and "the fen is not my concern, the Stud is".

However, construction went ahead. The rare snails living along the route, the protected fen and years of broken promises to pay for the project were overcome. This, coupled with a commitment in the 2000 Bill to vest the land in the company's name, promised a windfall of National Lottery proportions.

But the Stud did not have time to sit down and savour the success and start settling on a shopping list. The Mullarkey–Clarke affair was rumbling towards a costly conclusion. The company was back-tracking to find a strategy to bring a modicum of peace.

All the while, two key directors were drafted in as foot soldiers in a bitter civil war which had erupted in the small and intertwined bloodstock industry.

Shortly after Ms Mullarkey had petitioned Finance Minister Charlie McCreevy to help with her father's situation, he had kicked off hostilities with the racing community in typically blunderbuss style.

Mr McCreevy and Joe Walsh wanted to centralise racing the regime. To do this they had to force a merger between parts of the Turf Club and the Association of Irish Racecourses. The two biggest racing fans at the Cabinet table proposed a new body: Horse Racing Ireland. The AIR resisted giving up lucrative media rights. Turf Club members did not want to cede power. Because of their private responsibilities and interests, the Board of the Stud could not remain neutral.

Jim Beecher, the Assistant Secretary General of the Department of Agriculture, had been the de facto ministerial ambassador for the bloodstock business. He was appointed a director of the Stud in 1992, when Mr Walsh was cleaning the Board out. When the ministers were faced down by the Turf Club, Mr Beecher was one of two negotiators appointed to seal the deal.

His chairman at the Stud, Chryss O'Reilly, played an even more public role. She became the figurehead of the self-titled Industry Group. This was a powerful alliance of individual interests from the top to the bottom of the trade.

Views became more entrenched as the months went by. At one stage in mid-October it looked like Mr Walsh, Mr McCreevy and their array of allies were destined for defeat. Mr Walsh casually threatened that a proposed £18m prize fund for racing would be pulled. Pressure mounted. The animosity took to the streets.

Hundreds of breeders, owners, trainers, stablehands and jockeys from Mrs O'Reilly's group made the solemn trek up the sloping rise of the Curragh and handed in a letter to the Turf Club demanding that it surrender. A "high noon" meeting was called for members of the Turf Club. Just a week after it appeared the ministers had messed up, they emerged triumphant. It was brinkmanship at its most public.

Mr Walsh, Mr McCreevy and Jim Beecher sat opposite Turf Club chief executive, Brian Kavanagh, Senior Steward, Gerry Scanlon and their advisor, the former Fianna Fáil minister and European Commissioner, Ray MacSharry. Mrs O'Reilly was in London the day it all came to a head.

"I had already said I wouldn't join the march. I am not Irish for a start and I held the American view that marches in Ireland can become unruly.

"But in retrospect I think it was a good demonstration of what the industry represents," she said.

The Ministers, Mr Beecher and the Industry Group had won the day. Horse racing was reformed forever.

The day of the march was not the only trip Mrs O'Reilly made to London at that time. There was also a visit with her husband to accept a knighthood from the Queen of England. The former Irish rugby international and media magnate became Sir Anthony O'Reilly. Accordingly, his wife became known as Lady O'Reilly.

Back at Tully, the new Lady O'Reilly and her Board decided the bitterness between its two senior managers had gone on too long. In early 2001, the Stud tried a new approach to sort out the situation. It brought in a facilitator, Mr O'Connell, to investigate the breakdown and see how it could be resolved.

Mr O'Connell looked under the lid of the Stud's management structure and delivered a report to the Board, which said, that because of the animosity that had existed since Mr Mullarkey's promotion in 1994, Mr Clarke had tried to avoid dealing with him.

"As a result, Pat Mullarkey has suffered complete loss of morale and thus ceased to co-operate positively with John Clarke.

"For this reason the CEO has tended to bypass Pat Mullarkey when matters relating to tourism are being discussed or implemented," he said.

The facilitator's report also said that the situation could not continue without damaging the Stud and the health of Mr Clarke and Mr Mullarkey.

"This history of error and misunderstanding has resulted in the total loss of mutual respect and confidence on a personal level between John Clarke and Pat Mullarkey. As it cannot continue without potential damage to the good management of the Stud and not to mention the health and well-being of the men concerned, it remains to be seen if means can be devised which will eliminate the impact of the mutual antagonism and possibly in time heal the rift."

Mr O'Connell made a series of recommendations. But the antagonism continued and the situation did not improve. In the middle of it, the favourable winds which had been blowing were replaced by a darkening sky.

Plumes of smoke, billowing from burning pyres stacked high with the corpses of slain animals, dominated the newsreels on both sides of the Irish Sea. The dreaded foot-and-mouth disease had struck and had sent the entire agricultural sector into lock-down. Movement was restricted. Farms were put in quarantine. Overseas travellers were confronted with decontamination mats at every entry point and gate post. The Stud, like every other farm in the country, was effectively shut down. More woe was to follow.

This time the images of thick black smoke were rising from the previously iconic World Trade Centre towers in New York. It was September 11th and terrorist hijackers flew the aircraft into the skyscrapers. A global war on terror was declared by America. Air travel, which had already been greatly curtailed by foot-and-mouth, went into lock-down.

Tully's tourism team did what they could. But a lot of money was lost in a tumultuous 12 months. The two disasters at either end of the year wiped more than €300,000 [24 per cent] off its tourism income for 2001.

When the tumult died down, the company set about acting on the report of the independent facilitator. But there were no signs of any urgency.

A policy for preventing and dealing with bullying at work was drawn up in November 2002. The health and safety committee also decided that staff needed to be trained on how to deal with bullying. The plan was sent to Mr Clarke for his approval. Two months later, his imprimatur was still not forthcoming. There was a dispute about the wording of the final section of the policy. The committee felt its phrasing was less ambiguous and more positive. Quick action was urged of Mr Clarke.

"With the new season now upon us we believe it is imperative that the policy is finalised and implemented immediately," it said.

However, it was a full 12 months before a final draft was agreed. It committed the company to providing all of its employees with an environment free from bullying. A formal procedure for reporting and investigating allegations was established. Managers would inquire first of all to see if disputes could be resolved peacefully. If this did not work, a proper investigation would take place. Failing that, the next step was a formal complaint to company secretary, John McStay, who would refer all issues to the Board.

The plan threatened disciplinary action and the dismissal of any employee who violated it. It was to be a template for the future and a commitment to avoid the bitterness which had been dogging the small group of staff.

The plan and other measures came much too late to repair the relationship between Mr Mullarkey and Mr Clarke. By then, the Stud had had enough of the years of recrimination between its two senior managers.

On March 5th, Mr McStay and the civil servant director, Jim Beecher, called Mr Mullarkey into a meeting. They discussed his job and proposed changes to the management structure, including formalising a chain of command.

Mr Mullarkey said the proposal was effectively a plot to demote him without touching his salary. He left the meeting distressed. He got into his car and began to drive home. It was a showery day across Kildare, but otherwise bright and warm considering it was so early in March.

On the way, Mr Mullarkey felt pains in his chest. He turned off and made his way to his GP. A heart attack was suspected and he was sent straight to Portlaoise hospital, 45km away. Yvonne Mullarkey picked up the phone and rang Bertie Ahern's St Luke's office.

He was busy, she was told. Among other things, Fianna Fáil had the razzmatazz of its Ard Fheis kicking off that evening. Ms Mullarkey left a message.

"Please tell Mr Ahern that, if anything happens to my father, I'll hold him personally responsible."

6

A High Price to Pay

Pat Mullarkey survived. But he could not continue working in the place he blamed for causing his illness. Initially he stayed at home on sick leave. He tried to recuperate. The company watched the weeks go by.

During those months, John Clarke was tied up with trips to Florence, the Epsom Derby, the Newmarket sales and a spell on Japan's rural island of Hokkaido. This took in racing in Tokyo and unsuccessful negotiations to buy into a six-year-old stallion called Falbrav, a former winner of the prestigious Eclipse Stakes.

All the while, Mr Mullarkey's absence was aggravating an open sore. He felt he had the right to keep his salary until he was well enough to return to work. After three months, the Stud believed it could legitimately stop paying him. The farm and tourism manager could not afford to take the financial hit. After a quarter of a century working at Tully, withholding his wages was a step too far. Four years of plámásing and peace-making had failed. Even before the decision to cut Mr Mullarkey's sick pay, it had become inevitable that the dispute would have to be settled in the High Court.

Such cases cannot be prepared for hearing in the Four Courts overnight. They must wait their turn to get a proper airing before a judge.

The farm and tourism manager argued that his employer should not take any drastic action on his salary, at least until each side got to plead their case. The Stud disagreed. It was up for the fight.

When Pat Mullarkey's sick pay was about to be stopped, he did not take it lying down. On June 9th, 2004, his legal team went into the High Court and sought a temporary injunction. This was designed to stymie the Stud's solo run until a full trial could be arranged. The company did not buckle.

Mr Clarke, his wife, Monica, and director Pat O'Kelly were heading to Royal Ascot. They were booked in for a week at the plush Pennyhill Park Hotel snuggled into 123 acres of Surrey's rolling countryside. On the way to the airport, Mr Clarke's driver took him to the offices of McCann Fitzgerald solicitors, the firm handling the defence. The Board felt its chief executive could not deal directly with the case, because he was involved in it. Responsibility was passed to his friend and company secretary, John McStay.

Ascot finished under a sweltering sun and Mr Clarke returned to Kildare. But, two days later, racing was already banished from the minds of the directors in Tully. It was Monday, June 21st, and Mr McStay sat down at the same solicitor's offices and swore an affidavit on the Stud's behalf. This claimed that the company had done all it was supposed to do for its farm and tourism manager.

Mr McStay said he had asked Mr Mullarkey's co-workers, and the man accused of bullying him, about the practice for paying sick leave. On the basis of this, nobody would have been expected to have been paid for longer than three months.

"From my inquiries of long-standing staff members, including the chief executive, this policy of 13-weeks sick pay is and has been notorious amongst staff members for in excess of 20 years," he said.

Bluntly, the company secretary said Mr Mullarkey's salary claims were "untrue". He said an internal Health and Safety Committee had met in February 2002 and decided that the three-month rule applied to everybody. This was the same winter that the independent facilitator had told the company that either Mr Clarke's or Mr Mullarkey's well-being would suffer if their fraught situation continued.

Mr Mullarkey responded two days after Mr McStay's statement with his second affidavit. He rejected what was said about him. The farm manager had no memory of such a sick-pay discussion ever taking place at the Committee. He said he had never even seen the minutes of the meeting which Mr McStay referred to.

"No similar document has ever been furnished to me or, to the best of my knowledge, to any other member of the management team.

"I repeat my previous argument that at no time was I ever informed by the defendant, its servants or agents that my entitlement to be paid sick pay was to be limited to a period of 13 weeks."

Throughout the third week of June, letters carrying the coarse arguments crossed back and forth. These contested the staff rules supposedly laid down two years earlier. The friction fuelled revised affidavits as each side honed their argument.

The rest of the country was on high alert. The unpopular American president, George W. Bush, was visiting for a summit. There were pitched battles with protesters in Clare. Gardaí dealt with these in a swift fashion. The Stud's simultaneous stand-off was not as straightforward.

The Board gathered for its annual general meeting with the result of a small profit to celebrate. In her report, Lady O'Reilly pondered the smooth, seasonal cycle between the various sections of the Stud. She discussed how each discipline gripped for different months to help drive the company through the year.

At that stage, the breeding season was about to slip into idle mode and the tourists buses were already revving up in the car-park. Lady O'Reilly thanked Mr Clarke and his staff for all their work the previous term. She committed the company to building up its international reputation.

That was a Friday. The volley of argument and counter-argument between the Stud and its farm manager had reached end-game. The directors gathered for that AGM aware that the Stud's valuable reputation was in danger. They knew there would be serious scandal if the weekend did not bring an emphatic change of heart. It did not.

On Monday, June 28th, Mr Mullarkey and his erstwhile paymaster stood before Mr Justice Peter Kelly to plead their competing cases. The judge heard the arguments over two days.

Mr Mullarkey said that, since his promotion to the tourism post, Mr Clarke had taken a turn against him. At two different times, he said he was accused of not co-operating with the quest for the Q Mark.

On Wednesday, Mr Justice Kelly announced his verdict. He said Mr Mullarkey had joined the Stud 25 years earlier with a letter explaining the job. There was nothing to outline what he was entitled to if he became ill. Mr Justice Kelly said the dispute between Mr Clarke and Mr Mullarkey was not new. The warning signs, picked up by the independent facilitator two and a half years earlier, had come to pass. Now, Mr Mullarkey was in the care of a GP and a consultant psychiatrist.

"Both doctors express the view that his illness is directly related to the situation which obtains at his place of work," Mr Justice Kelly said.

Mr Mullarkey wanted the entire affair to go to trial. His legal team argued he should be paid until that hearing could be arranged. Mr Justice Kelly said Mr Mullarkey did not have a right to his salary simply because he felt the Stud was responsible for his illness. But this did not mean his employer should stop paying him. The Judge lashed the semi-State company for being lax with its efforts to even write down what its workers could expect, especially in times of distress.

"It is rather astonishing that a body such as the defendant operating in the semi-State sector and with 82 employees does not appear to have terms and conditions relating to sick pay entitlement documented in crystal-clear fashion," said the Judge. "That, however, appears to be the case here."

He said Mr Mullarkey's plea had six strengths underpinning it. Nothing in his contract dealt with such a situation. There was no evidence to support the Stud's claim to a 13-week sick leave policy, except for the minutes of a meeting which Mr Justice Kelly did not believe had power to change anybody's job specification. Never before had anything like this happened at the company.

The Stud appeared to have flouted the 1994 law governing an employee's right to contractual information. Furthermore, he said a semi-public sector employer would be expected to be more generous with its rules.

Mr Justice Kelly also summarised the Stud's case. He said it was based on a sworn statement which described what it believed to be standard practice going back 20 years. On this basis, the Judge granted the injunction and said the company could not stop paying Mr Mullarkey. He considered the payment of upfront damages as an alternative, but he did not accept they would be suitable. Mr Mullarkey's family situation meant that he could not wait for a sum to be settled on. He had bills to pay and these could not be stalled if his salary was suspended. The judgement said the inconvenience for the Stud having to pay Mr Mullarkey, until a trial could take place, was far outweighed by the hardship the man would have to endure by living without an income.

The Judge said it was not his place to rule on whether Mr Clarke had bullied his co-manager. The injunction had only been sought to stop the company cutting off Mr Mullarkey's sick pay. However, Mr Justice Kelly said the former farm and tourism manager had made enough of a case to justify a full hearing. This fact had been the main hurdle his legal team had to overcome.

"I am satisfied that there is a serious issue for trial in that regard," he said.

It never did go to trial. There were five more mentions in Court as both sides prepared a full defence throughout the next six months. Then, in November, the company decided to settle before it risked any further exposure.

On December 6th, 2004, the High Court was told Mr Mullarkey's claim for personal injury damages had been settled. A sum of €142,109 was paid to its long-time manager. Another €220,741 went towards paying its legal and professional bills. Mr McStay, who had stepped in to represent the company because Mr Clarke had been compromised, was also rewarded. The company paid the accountancy firm run by its secretary, McStay Luby, €48,400 for its work on the case. As far as the company was concerned, Mr McStay was left to carry out duties which would otherwise have been the work of the chief executive. The Stud felt it did not have the legal expertise to fight the case properly. Mr McStay was at its disposal and the Board felt he was a knowledgeable man who "knew the industry inside out".

"Cost and time were involved. The idea was Mr McStay would act on behalf of the company at the time and he was paid for that service," Mr Clarke's successor, John Osborne, later explained.

Mr Mullarkey walked out of Tully. As far as the Stud was concerned, the door on the protracted and problematic matter closed after him.

There is no evidence that Mr Clarke's role was affected by what went on. His work continued as normal. He travelled to Paris for the race meeting at Longchamp and New York to try and buy a stallion called Grey Swallow. There were trips across the Irish Sea, one of which ended in hospital when he received a serious head injury at the Newmarket sales event. In her annual report for 2004, Lady O'Reilly thanked him and Mr McStay for their work throughout the year.

Within 12 months of the settlement with Mr Mullarkey, money was found to renovate sections of Mr Clarke's house, which the Stud had responsibility for. A new carpet was bought for €1,500. Furniture and a fireplace also arrived at a cost of €2,434. A dishwasher and lights cost more than €4,500. This was after a €1,200 safe was installed. The settlement marked the end of a highly disruptive spat for the company. It also came at the end of a frighteningly difficult 12 months for the company.

The seasonal cycle at the farm was organically regimental. That meant diaries changed little from year to year. Foals were born to the broodmare band during starlit frosty nights. Stallions got down to breeding on February 15th. Their antics continued through the spring and summer. The Japanese Gardens would bloom as the trundling traffic of horseboxes receded. Chugging coach-loads of tourists came instead.

Half of all visitors arrived in June, July and August. Of those, 42 per cent were Irish, mostly on weekends and bank holidays. The midweek bus tours carried a split of nationalities. The largest contingent was from America.

The summer also brought the flat racing season, a reminder to everybody why the horses they were breeding were so important. Just as these races reached their peak, the combine harvesters turned on the crops at Tully.

In autumn, the entire operation focused on the yearling sales and the effort to secure sires for next year. Simultaneously, the push was on to confirm as many bookings as possible for the upcoming season's stallion roster. By December, the generation of foals born the previous spring was strong enough and old enough to court buyers in the sales.

The routine had varied little in more than 50 years. The results fluctuated wildly. A €379,483 profit in 2001 turned into a loss of €401,485 a year later. In that time, the total amount of business the Stud did fell by a quarter.

It had borrowed €2m on its bank overdraft and wiped 66 per cent off its savings. Then, by December 31st 2003, the results shot back up to show a small, but welcome, €54,104 profit. Smiles were short-lived. At the end of the 2004 cycle, the books were brutal.

The company was increasingly seeing itself less as a small semi-State agency and more as an international competitor. With this came a quest for more freedom, and an acceptance of greater responsibility.

It stopped using the services of the State-appointed Comptroller and Auditor General and hired Deloitte &Touche to verify its accounts.

A tender process was carried out and Deloitte charged €17,000 per annum for a three-year contract. In synch with growing aspirations across the Celtic Tiger society, the Stud's ambitions had let loose. They had moved well beyond permanently pandering to small Irish breeders.

Lady O'Reilly said the Board wanted to find horses with international appeal, even if many were well outside the company's price range. She said the cost of stallions was so high it needed partners to help with nearly every purchase. There were wealthy overseas breeders the Board wanted to see involved.

"We are extremely grateful to the range of international breeders who have supported us by acquiring shares in stallions retiring to the National Stud.

"Their support, both in acquiring the stallions and in sending top quality mares, is an essential cornerstone of our activity."

The Stud's long term financial success was dependent on this, she said.

The Board had become a more international creature compared to what it was originally intended to be. By 2002, almost half of all its stallion customers [47 per cent] were from foreign studs. The majority of these were based in Britain, followed by Italy and then France. The Stud was "moving more and more towards the upper spectrum of the commercial market", Lady O'Reilly said. The chairman also said the company had to strive to compete at the very top of the international arena.

In five years, since it returned to a healthy profit in 1998, the average stallion fee it charged jumped 77 per cent. The figure was standing at €15,779 per-covering for the Stud's six sires. But that year, 2002, the number of mares covered was the lowest since these prices started rising.

The Stud's medium-term plan, produced at the same time, said it wanted 10 stallions. Ideally, two of these would serve the very pinnacle of the market. This was more in line with the historical argument of Charles J. Haughey in the 1960s and 1970s, rather than the view of his Cabinet colleague, Donogh O'Malley. The Stud argued its case.

"The upper sector of the market is more resistant to economic downturn as breeders, and yearling and mare buyers, focus on quality in times of uncertainty," its plan said.

However, riding with this global gang carried the risk that it would hurtle at speeds the Stud could not sustain. Despite its market analysis, it was not prepared for 2004. The year was close to catastrophic. Despite living it large for a few years, the Stud had carried debts into the crash.

When it was forced to wipe millions off the value of its horses, the company was left with a loss of €4.2m. A year earlier, it had considered inflating the book value of these animals even more, but had decided against it. Coupled with these losses, the Stud felt handicapped in its bid to compete.

Customers were getting offers of free transport and cheaper rates to bring their mares abroad. Compounding the dismal figures was the money it spent trying to fight Pat Mullarkey in the High Court.

Lady O'Reilly sought to put it all into perspective by highlighting the irrationality of the industry. She echoed the assessment of Charlie Haughey 38 years previously, by stressing that the effort to stay in vogue was an inherent trait of the trade. As a result, the cycles could not be judged beside more reasoned endeavours.

"Comparisons with the fluctuations in taste within the fashion industry would not be out of place," she said.

Buying a foal or a yearling was a luxury expense for those who can afford it, she said.

When the final accounts came in, the new Agriculture Minister, Mary Coughlan, visited the boardroom and backed up the chairman.

"Stud farming is no ordinary business. It operates in a marketplace, which is ruthless in its search of winners. Its volatility is legendary.

"While in Ireland we regard the breeding sector as a traditional farming activity, the purchase of foals and yearlings for racing forms part of discretionary spending for many in Ireland and overseas as well," she said.

In the privacy of the directors' meeting, Ms Coughlan also committed to supporting the Stud. This came in the form of millions of euro in extra shares.

"As far as the future of the Stud is concerned the stallions are everything," Ms Coughlan said.

As a result of the hype in the early part of the decade, the market was flooded with animals yet again. Too many no-good yearlings appeared on the sales catalogues and there were too many working stallions to go around. The pain was felt across the industry. Customers were ducking out of debts. In 2004, the Stud was owed 50 per cent more than it had been the previous year.

It had also increased the amount it had borrowed from the bank to €6.5m, more than twice the sum it had borrowed in 2003. At the same time, the Stud had also bought a large slice of land at Strawhall, near its largely unused Curragh farm. This €3.2m tract was viewed as a potential isolation facility in case disease broke out. It would replace the land annexed by the Kildare by-pass.

In 2005, the situation improved a bit. More than €350,000 was still lost, but there was not a repeat of the seven-figure hole it had got itself into 12 months earlier. The partial recovery in 2005 was also boosted by a few silver steroids.

Kildare County Council finally paid compensation for the land it had used to build the motorway by-pass. The payment of €1.2m came after a protracted and bitter dispute with the local authority. The company and the council argued over damage done to one of the paddocks, the €317,434 contribution towards VAT and the effect that building work had on the supply of water.

The Stud had expected €2.9m from all sources to cover the cost of replacing facilities. According to a letter sent by Mr McStay to the Department, Minister Joe Walsh and the then Stud chairman, David Shubotham, had negotiated that the by-pass payment would be inflated above the basic value of the land. This was agreed in 1998 to compensate for the loss of sections of the stables in the

Minoru, Black Cherry and Kildare yards, and to help restore the property.

Two years later, the matter was still being pursued by John Clarke. He told the Department "while under the laws" the Stud had been paid in full, there were still fees outstanding to two professionals who represented the company in the negotiations.

"In the meetings, Kildare County Council have hidden behind the law and have been most unreasonable.

"This has been an issue for approximately 10 years and we have had a lot of correspondence as well as meetings on the matter," he said.

Behind the scenes, he was ensuring everybody involved kept the maximum amount of pressure on the council. He said his preference was to go down the legal route.

"The issue with the water is the flow and I am dissatisfied with our expert as he is not firm enough with them [the council].

"I gave him a huge bollocking on the phone today on foot of a letter he sent to me and I have firmly stated that I want the matter handled by our solicitors who could force [the council] to increase the flow," he said in an e-mail to the Department.

If the Stud felt aggrieved, unwittingly the Irish public lent a hand. Finance Minister, Brian Cowen, agreed to give the Stud an extra €1.1m. This additional share option more than covered the bills the company had clocked up defending itself against Mr Mullarkey.

On top of that, the Department of Agriculture signed over ownership of 322 hectares of land to the Stud for free. This generous gesture had a long-term goal, but, more immediately, it meant there was no longer an annual rent bill to pay.

The Stud's chairman explained the second year of depressing results. Lady O'Reilly said the business fell victim to the mêlée in the international markets which it increasingly sought to be a part of.

"Stallions are the core of our activities. In recently examining some old company records I noted that some of my predecessors, even 50 years ago, were bemoaning the difficulties in acquiring suitable stallions.

"The position today is no different and... it is exacerbated by the concentration of high-class racehorses in the hands of two of the most financially powerful groups, each of whom operate commercial stud farms with seemingly unlimited means and enormous budgets," Mrs O'Reilly said.

The Stud looked at providing alternatives to Darley and Coolmore. Indian Ridge, for example, gave owners exposed to inbreeding in the unparalleled Northern Dancer line an outcross. It sought more money from the Government to increase its band of broodmares to 25. The company also strived to use all the resources available. This included its directors.

This group brought much to the Tully table – experience, skills, buying power, contacts, breeding options and interests. As Mr Haughey envisaged in the late 1970s, different directors adopted different roles.

In the area of international sales, Pat O'Kelly was the point person. She had pushed the idea of scouting American markets for mares to add value to its internal breeding operation. As she had been particularly successful in this area, she was nominated by the Board to travel to sales events on its behalf. It covered €71,157 of her expenses over eight years as an investment in her ability to spot a prospect.

She was joined on the advance party excursions by chief executive, John Clarke. Between 2003 and 2007, the pair advised on the purchase of three mares in America and seven through British markets.

At this time, the directors' pool also included the steadily rising heir to the Smurfit Kappa empire, Tony Smurfit. His family owned the Forenaughts Stud. It was a young Mr Smurfit who had led the victorious Vintage Crop home after his legendary burst at the 1993 Melbourne Cup. That day, Mr Smurfit and his family's horse shared the winners' enclosure with trainer, Dermot Weld.

For five years the trio of horse, rider and owner were reunited at Tully because both Mr Smurfit and Mr Weld sat in a boardroom that was a stone's throw from the now-retired Vintage Crop. In the midst of this, the gelding's owner and trainer also hooked up to prepare a fresh horse selected to re-trace the 1993 expedition.

Media Puzzle made the 12,000-mile journey to Melbourne in autumn, 2002. He endured the same arduous journey as Vintage Crop had. His race was particularly poignant, though, because of the heartbreak suffered by his rider.

The Australian jockey who boarded him, Damien Oliver, lost his brother Jason in a fall from a horse the week before the great race. There was a doubt over whether he would still be entrusted with the ride. But Dermot Weld's son, Mark, said if Mr Oliver felt able to board Media Puzzle, his judgement would be trusted.

A grieving Mr Oliver took the saddle. He kicked Media Puzzle towards the line a little early. It did not matter. The horse kept cranking up his speed in the final 500 metres. He pulled clear of a tightly-bunched pack with track to spare. Media Puzzle claimed the title in a time of 3 minutes, 16 seconds.

As he rode back towards the cheering crowds and the waiting Dermot Weld, Mr Oliver pointed to the air and famously admitted to a television reporter.

"Mate, Melbourne Cups don't mean a thing to me anymore. I'd give it back right now to have my brother back."

Minutes later, he met the horse's trainer, quickly gripped his hand and hugged him. Then Mr Oliver embraced Dermot's son, Mark, and told the crowd what both meant to him.

"Dermot Weld, what can you say about him? Truly one of the greatest trainers in the world."

The Stud believed this long before Mr Oliver proclaimed it. Where it could, it made use of the trainer who twice defied the belief that truly global racing was impossible because the animals would not be able for it.

Mr Weld's colleagues on the Board were particularly keen to see what he could do with a colt called Cairdeas. He had been born on

February 11th, 2001. And if Col. Hill Walker had been around to read the horoscope of the bay-coloured Aquarius, he would have taken an immediate shine to the foal.

There was one dominant star in his family. At that time, she was as bright as anything in the business. Sabaah, who was born in America, endured a poor racing career. By the time she delivered Cairdeas, she had already spent nine years in Kildare.

Unlike stallions, who can cover more than a hundred mares in any year and are judged on a selection of the best, broodmares get few opportunities to prove their worth. The potential of many is never realised because their owners cannot afford the right stallion or make bad choices chasing the wrong pedigrees. If she is fortunate, a broodmare will have one foal every year. Then, should she be very lucky, this will be with the right stallion, and their foal will get the right run to the races. If all of this happens early in her career, her owners can sit back, do their best to repeat the success and add zeros to the windfall from their investment.

Various classes of broodmare have grazed at Tully since the Stud first opened. Some were shocking. Some were superb. None struck the elusive jackpot as often as Sabaah.

Herself and Indian Ridge came to Kildare in the midst of the mayhem and misery of 1992 and 1993. Space was made for her from the sale of Friendly Ann. A reasonable Stg£37,000 was made from the sale of her first colt in October 1994. That yearling was to become Bigwig. He hit the market twice more in his life. There was little interest in him. His disappointing career could have defined Sabaah and capped the prices her progeny demanded. However, since April 9th that year she was back in foal. This one, Desert King, ensured she became an incredible income earner.

"The doyenne of our mares, the classic producer of Guineas and Derby winner and successful stallion, Desert King, and other illustrious progeny, Sabaah is the yardstick by which our other mares will be judged," Lady O'Reilly said.

Desert King was conceived in 1994 at Sabaah's visit to the internationally regarded Danehill. The record of the colt's father helped the Stud to sell him as a yearling for £175,000.

When the chance came, Desert King sprung to life. In 1997, his five race wins included the Irish Derby and revealed a stunning synergy between his sire, Danehill, and his dam, Sabaah. Unfortunately for the Stud, it had not predicted the debut success would be quite so good. Before Desert King showed his form as a three-year-old, Sabaah had already given birth to a foal from the Stud's less than stellar stallion Catrail. The Catrail colt, Admire Cat, made £120,000 at the sales. He earned roughly the same amount on the track when he grew a bit older.

A year earlier, Sheikh Hamdan's Shadwell company bought Wahj, Sabaah's son from Indian Ridge, for £330,000. That horse did not come to much. Three years after the Shadwell deal, the horse, Wahj, was sold for just 4 per cent of what Sheikh Hamdan originally paid for it. The Stud at least got to keep all the profits from them, along with the added bonus that it did not have to pay a nomination fee, because it used its own stallions.

However, once Desert King let loose, forking out to send Sabaah back to Danehill could be easily justified. So Sabaah was shuttled back to the sire.

In 1999, Wafic Said's Addison racing bought the first yearling to be born from their reunion. He called him Chianti and gave the Stud £500,000. Twelve months later, it was Lady O'Reilly who got in on the act. On October 4th, 2000, she bid £650,000 to buy the next foal the pair produced.

"National coffers filled by filly's sale," the *Irish Times* headline read the next day.

At Goffs, Lady O'Reilly said it was a beautiful filly who she had been watching since she was tiny. Lady O'Reilly called the horse Desertion. She did not get to keep her exclusively. When Desertion went to track for the first of her six races on June 28th, 2002, the Irish National Stud was again involved in the ownership structure.

Despite the trade being registered in the yearling sales, and the purchaser named as Castlemartin and Skymarc farms, the Irish National Stud was subsequently listed as a co-owner for Desertion's racing career. When Desertion retired a year later, the Stud said it had a 50 per cent stake in the mare. She was eventually sold in 2006 for Stg£400,000. That trade was organised by Castlemartin.

All the while, buyers were hungry for Sabaah's potential. Bright Morning was still in Sabaah's womb when Sheikh Hamdan's brother, Sheikh Mohammed, used his Godolphin operation to buy the unborn animal. Godolphin owned Bright Morning's father Dubai Millenium.

"An unusual and once-off opportunity," Lady O'Reilly recalled.

This early in-utero sale meant it was 2002 before another Sabaah foal appeared in the sales ring. He was later to be called Cairdeas. Brian Grassick, a former director of the Stud and, subsequently, an astute advisor to it, was listed as having bought the yearling for £300,000 at Goffs.

However, at some point, the Stud decided to hold on to him. The decision was taken to race him in the colours of Her Excellency, President Mary McAleese.

Eight weeks after his triumph with Media Puzzle, Mr Weld began to train Cairdeas. The semi-State company did not tender for the training contract, which was to be worth €90,713 over three years, because it said the policy was to match each horse to the most suitable trainer.

There were high hopes for Cairdeas. His father, Darshaan, was costing £50,000 per nomination when Sabaah went to him. Darshaan's progeny were on their way to winning well in excess of £4m. Cairdeas was thought of as a potential Derby-winning horse. This did not come to pass. Over his career he earned just more than €150,000.

There were 15 starts and three wins, reaching a peak when he beat three other horses at the High Chaparral European breeders fund Moorsbridge Stakes at the Curragh. This was on heavy ground in early May 2005.

That summer the Cairdeas team could not repeat the success. A second place at the Curragh was his best in five outings. Twelve months later, he raced for the last time. It was an evening meet at Leopardstown – the 7.30pm on May 31st, 2006.

Eight horses went to post in good conditions over one mile and six furlongs. Cairdeas preferred softer soil under him. The eventual winner of the race, a prized relic from Mr Weld's incredible career, did not have such worries. This aging horse had achieved more than could ever have been dreamt for Cairdeas. His name was Media Puzzle and he was in his penultimate race.

The Melbourne Cup winner had been plagued by injury since his most famous victory in November 2002. He had raced only five times after that afternoon. In Dermot Weld, Media Puzzle shared a trainer with the President's horse. The Smurfit-owned gelding had even taken Cairdeas' long-time jockey, Pat Smullen, for the night.

The eight-horse Leopardstown field started slowly. The jockeys sat high. Long shadows swept across to their left. Cairdeas hung back, and was paddy last with six furlongs to go. Then things quickened. Turning for home, Cairdeas made his move. There were three out in front. But the President's horse was making the most of the final 200 metres. He looked to be reeling in his foes. But the nine-year-old horse out in front, with six wins and £1m banked, had too much composure. Going for the line, Cairdeas had slipped back and was pressed to hold on to fourth. The winner was Media Puzzle.

The victory fostered renewed hope for the Melbourne Cup winner and he was given another shot at cementing his legacy.

One month after Leopardstown, Media Puzzle was sent to try for the Ascot Gold Cup. Mr Clarke and Ms O'Kelly were in the crowd.

The gelding never looked comfortable during his comeback. His head bobbed and he spent most of the race struggling to stay with the field. With a mile to go, they started a steep climb towards the grandstand. Media Puzzle tried and tried. With a furlong left, his front leg appeared to catch. It flicked to the side; he veered the same way.

Still he hobbled on. It was no use. Yeats, the horse Cairdeas had defeated in his career-defining win a year earlier, burst past the line with four lengths to spare.

Media Puzzle was assessed by the vet. He had shattered his leg. He was destroyed at the track. Cairdeas, too, never raced again. Hopes for him faded and the Stud switched Mr Weld over to train another horse, Sualice.

Racing has never been just about one event or even an entire career on the track. There has always been an industry to sustain and money to make. The Irish National Stud had this to consider when it parked Cairdeas and reflected on his satisfactory career.

Meanwhile, its directors were about to be given a chance to put all the woes of in-house fights, debts and unrealised dreams behind them. One stallion was about to transform a "solid if not spectacular" first year into an incredible and nigh-on invincible one.

7

Unbeatable in a Boom Time

"The Invincible Spirit stallion has been a great anchor for the finances of the company. His heartbeat is significant to our finances."
Chief Executive of the Irish National Stud,
John Osborne, June 11th, 2010.

Death, disease and debt swept over the Stud in brutally quick succession. At other times such a torrent could have wreaked irreparable havoc. Yet, when all of the above were visited upon Tully in the space of 36 months, the Stud did not struggle to recover. It rose up and ran rampant.

There were different reasons why it emerged standing so proud. Dominant among these was a single stallion. His name, Invincible Spirit. Dark brown, with two white socks, this was a sleek and strong horse.

His fractured racing career was salvaged because of a fleeting, yet incredible, burst of speed. Still, he was never able to get a proper run at the big time. Whatever opportunities he lost, because of injury and misfortune, were distilled and delivered in the dozens by his progeny.

This power and talent turned a €700,000 pitch by the Stud into a stake worth €19.9m in just six years. Controversially, he also handed three of the Stud's most senior figures a multi-million euro bonanza of their own.

The way this deal evolved irked many inside and outside the Stud. But the process by which these three parties – Lady Chryss O'Reilly, director Trevor Stewart and, especially, company secretary, John McStay – profited from their shares so spectacularly has been staunchly defended by the company they oversaw.

The Stud points to a history of hits as well as misses in such partnerships. It argues that, whether these directors were involved or not, their custom as breeders was as valuable as any other investor's. Better again, the Stud said, the fact that Board members were involved at all was a sign to other breeders that they had faith in the product being peddled.

As far as the Stud was concerned, Invincible Spirit was not the first or the last joint venture it operated with members of its Board. So, the fact that one stallion they shared became such an outrageous success should not tarnish the increasingly intertwined businesses of the State-owned stud and its directors.

Throughout everything, the most connected of all in the boardroom was its chair, Lady O'Reilly. After her £55,000 purchase of a share in the mediocre Catrail, in 1994, she dabbled with minor holdings in various stallion syndicates managed by the Stud. Any syndicate would always have been delighted to have her involved.

While she raced colts, she tended not to keep stallions herself. Her band of broodmares, spread across studs in Ireland, France, England and America, held promise for any stallion owner looking to create a winner.

Some of Lady O'Reilly's investments were small and strategic. More carried an element of emotion. Others had both. Wisely, she kept a stake in the aging and almost unwanted Verglas when others lost interest. Before Invincible Spirit revealed his prowess, Verglas had become the most prominent partnership involving her and the company.

Ten years earlier, the pale grey stallion campaigned for Lady O'Reilly and her husband Sir Tony. He won the 1996 Coventry Stakes at Ascot, with his owners cheering at the television at home. For the next two years, he tirelessly tried to top his outing at Ascot. He never quite got there.

He impressed, but his ambitions were thwarted by an unstoppable season from a son of the Irish National Stud's Sabaah, Desert King. Verglas still earned the O'Reilly family more than €150,000 in 14 races. He took second place in the Irish 2,000 Guineas and landed another runner-up spot during a short-lived bid for glory in America.

At the end of 1999, he was retired and syndicated. The O'Reilly operation kept a token interest. The next few years were to be a lot messier for Verglas.

Initially, he stood at the Haras de la Haie Neuve in Normandy, where it was costing just €2,290 to visit him. Even with a bargain price tag, he did not attract much more than curious interest. French breeders had a special grá for his father, Highest Honor, who was bred by Lady O'Reilly and was routinely among France's leading sires. Yet, while Verglas's genetics may have garnered conversational attention, he was not getting a lot of customers. He had only 68 foals in his first two crops, not even half what he could have delivered. His managers moved him to Australia to put in a winter season's work at the Alywn Stud. The wait was on to see what his first crop would do.

Then, in April 2003, Veri Star came home at the Maisons-Laffitte in France to become the grey stallion's first two-year-old winner. Another of his progeny, Blackdoun, claimed a group two race in America months later.

Thirteen wins came in the first 32 starts by Verglas's offspring. It was not incredible. It was respectable. It was also enough of a prompt for owners to upgrade him.

In August 2004, it was announced that he was to be moved to Charles-Henri de Moussac's Haras du Mezeray. The Mezeray operation had controlled the original Verglas syndicate and, nine months before the planned move, the French stud had set up a dedicated company to manage him.

But then, just as the grey horse was about to relocate to the de Moussac yard, the arrangement appeared to fall apart. Within weeks Haras de Mezeray let its dominant interest go. The Irish National Stud speedily stepped into the breach. It picked up one-fifth of the shares in Verglas and brought the 10-year-old to Kildare. Their interest was lower than the controlling 25–45 per cent stake the Stud usually looked to secure in younger horses.

As far as Verglas was concerned, Lady O'Reilly had always retained an interest. When he arrived in Ireland, she ensured he was not left standing idle. As a syndicate member, she had automatic nominations for mares to be covered.

In 2005, his first season at the Stud, Verglas covered 121 mares at a cost of €9,000 for each one. Of those, 12 came from stud farms owned by Lady O'Reilly and her husband.

Tully also saw broodmare benefits in Verglas. He introduced a different bloodline to a yard ruled by the almighty genes of the father–son duo, Ahonoora and Indian Ridge. Three Tully mares Abyat, American Queen and Moy Water were sent to Verglas that first season.

Each sire at the Stud was always treated like a separate company and the likes of Verglas showed how a director's private practice could help secure a future for these enterprises. These directors also offered a chance to open connections with markets and money with which the company had no natural relationship.

Pat O'Kelly knew America. She was able to discover good mares across the Atlantic to boost the Stud's band. Lady O'Reilly knew France. She and the Stud shared an appreciation of some of the undervalued prospects in that market. Both parties appeared to have a fondness for Verglas's illustrious father, Highest Honor.

When a syndicate behind one of Verglas's siblings, Take Risks, fell apart in France during 2004 the Stud tried to exploit the opportunity. It was rare for a working stallion to be laid at the mercy of bidders in a sales ring. However, the 15-year-old Take Risks was paraded in this way and John Clarke was among the keenest to have him. Mr Clarke tried hard. But the travelling chief executive backed off the final bid of €460,000. Take Risks was let go to his former part-owner, Marc de Chambure.

The Deauville auction indicated the value the Stud attached to stallions born of Highest Honor. This routine tit-for-tat to secure Take Risks also showcased the chronically inbred network of breeders and businesses driving the bloodstock markets. Players can pair as partners for one lot and be pitched as rivals in the next.

At the time, the buyer of Take Risks, Mr de Chambure, had a nephew, Nicholas, studying at the breeders' course in Tully. Within a few years, they had teamed up with Lady O'Reilly on a four-person strategic committee to manage Capital pur Sang – thoroughbred capital.

This was a French-based investment machine launched in 2010 to attract money from outside the racing set to plough into broodmares. The Irish Stud was to go a long way towards establishing its own version of this scheme, before it backed off at the last minute.

Lady O'Reilly's competitors and contacts had always been considered a great asset for the Stud. The ability of the semi-State enterprise to ride along on her elegant coat tails endeared her to political patrons of the company. It suited the Stud to have big breeders involved in stallion syndicates.

Much later, chief executive, Mr Clarke, explained that, as a general rule, it wanted to control stallions in a team with horse owners who had mares to offer. If nothing else, it helped make life more straightforward for Mr Clarke and his stallion nominations' team, who each season had to fill the spaces on their sires' diaries.

"What we want are breeders who are going to use their nominations," he told Australia's Thoroughbred Times, "because if they own a one-fiftieth share in a stallion they will have two nominations a year.

"If you have 50 breeders who all send two mares, then you've got 100 mares already booked to your horse."

Director-breeders had also become good customers. Over the first eight years of the new century, six directors and Clodagh McStay, the wife of the company secretary, had spent a combined €235,200 for their mares to be kept at the Stud while they were being covered. Tony Smurfit's family spent the most (€57,535 in four years); Mrs McStay spent €55,196; Pat O'Kelly spent €44,114; Lady O'Reilly spent €39,798 and John Osborne spent €30,620.

Their increasing desire to visit the Stud's stallions since the late-1990s, and their appetite to join its syndicates, reflected the fact that Tully's product had become more attractive. In the wider breeding circles, the Stud's prestige had improved no end. Since the era of its post-1993 recovery, it had nurtured international clients with bulging budgets and better broodmares.

By 2005, despite the multi-million euro hole in its accounts, it was well and truly soaring with the jet set. It had significant stature in the sales' rings. Moreover, it continued to be second only to the behemoth, Coolmore, in terms of the value of its Irish nominations.

But if the country required a more tangible testament to its National Stud's prominence, proof was provided with the Stg£6m syndication of the Epsom Derby winner, Motivator.

The 50-share syndicate arranged in October 2005 read like a roll-call of who mattered in the breeding business. It cost Stg£120,000 per share and was managed by a genius within the sector, John Warren.

The Highclere Stud, which Mr Warren ran with his wife, Lady Carolyn, was the ancestral base for the Earl of Carnarvon. Mr Warren started as a stable worker and, over time, his obsessive eye for a good horse put him on a steep and fast escalator to the top of the trade. As an agent, he counselled and bought for the richest buyers in the business. He also became the stud advisor to Queen Elizabeth II and the manager of her bloodstock interests.

Mr Warren had the contacts and reputation to put the unusual Motivator offer out to his illustrious peers. In doing so, he secured an 80-fold increase for the original 250-member Royal Ascot Racing Club, who bought into the animal before his racing days. Mr Warren told the *Racing Post* the syndicate was a uniquely transparent one: "Everybody knew who was in it, everybody knew who was invited."

So, everybody who was anybody accepted. Even Coolmore and the United Arab Emirates ruling Maktoum brothers allowed themselves to be seen under the same umbrella.

The Maktoums used it like a ceasefire in hostilities which, in the months leading up to the deal, had seen them boycott any lot offered by Coolmore in the sales' rings. This was a tactic to keep a lid on the Tipperary outfit's earning ability.

Other members of the Motivator ensemble included extended members of the British royal family, the Hong Kong Jockey club, American heavyweights, Lady O'Reilly's brother, Peter Goulandris, the Smurfit family, and the same Marc de Chambure of Haras d'Etreham. The Irish National Stud was invited. The Irish National Stud accepted.

The Queen kept hold of a number of shares and Motivator went to stand at her farm at Sandringham. Here, her band of broodmares was like nothing in the business and a treasure for any syndicate she got involved in.

The benefit of such deals, like Team Verglas, was that members of the syndicate had quality mares to ship into the stallion's yard. It is simple sums and basic branding.

When better mares visited stallions the odds of getting a competitive racehorse multiplied. The more good mares – the more contenders.

Motivator had 10 individual winners of stakes' races in his first crop. High numbers of winners in a family tree eased anxiety among investors skulking around a seam of progeny. Buyers react to the genetic branding and they normally start to bid against each other.

With the right results, and a steady flow of stock, it can become a self-feeding frenzy.

With the Motivator deal, the original club that campaigned him was disbanded. The new 50-member Stg£6m was born. Mr Warren explained that on top of the mare mathematics, the profile of the club members was a strategic asset. Most of the select owners kept their own foals and put them directly into training. Such a habit automatically restricted the proportion of every crop being put up for sale.

So, for those that did decide to sell, smaller supply plus greater demand equaled healthier prices. As far as Mr Warren was concerned, there had never been a more diverse and secure syndicate.

"By syndicating a horse you secure his future. If a horse isn't in his prime, once he has missed his moment, he's lost his best chance of doing well at stud.

"I think one of the great beauties of this syndicate is that the high percentage of foals will never come on the market," Mr Warren said.

As an investment strategy, it paid off. Despite a depressed 2009, ten of Motivator's yearlings were sold for more than €100,000. The top lot made €350,000.

There is an obvious flip-side to Mr Warren's and Mr Clarke's independent arguments for having the heavy-hitters involved in syndicates. If a stallion is split among speculative shareholders, the likelihood of these carting in mediocre mares or flogging nominations into poor quality bloodlines increases. Custom from such quarters would help to improve the standards across the wider national herd, but can serve to devalue the value of the stallion involved.

The magic moment Mr Warren spoke about with Motivator came in his third year. He had won what was on offer and he was young, virile and in the public eye.

Year one of retirement has traditionally been the fashionable season. In the second year, investors start to have doubts. They wait to see how much was paid for the first foals. These December sales help to decide whether it is wise to fork out for a second season's nomination fee.

By the third year, trainers and agents will have had a chance to assess yearlings and make an initial judgment on a crop of progeny. At this stage, owners are nervous about whether their initial exuberance will be justified.

Finally, the pitch is trumpeted or torpedoed after the stallion's fourth year at stud, when his first colts and fillies finally get tested on the track. The older the horses get, the less attention they will attract. The more shuffling and shifting that goes on in his career, the more investors can look on a sire as damaged goods.

So the Irish National Stud could spend all its money chasing the likes of Verglas and Take Risks for bargain basement prices. But it also had to have an eye to the future for the younger, long-term prospects. These naturally cost more.

A couple of weeks after the Motivator deal, it was announced that the Stud had joined forces with Dermot Farrington Bloodstock to buy a 50 per cent stake in stakes winner, Amadeus Wolf. He was just two years old. The other half of the colt was kept by John Duddy and Brendan McDonald.

It was an early wager for the Stud and Farrington's clients. The horse had not been put to the supreme test, but Mr Clarke said he was attracted by his good looks and "impeccable bloodlines". The Stud had also had a good record of picking out racers in their second year when they had scant success to their name. These winning horses did not always prove as profitable when they became sires.

The top sprinter, Desert Prince, was a case in point. A scrum of breeders arrived into the Stud after his racing success. But, when nothing much happened afterwards, interest dissipated, his fee dwindled and he was sheepishly moved to Germany.

Amadeus Wolf's co-owner, Mr McDonald, had hoped the colt would win the 2,000 Guineas at Newmarket, if the Coolmore army stayed away. However, this and other victories eluded him that summer. A runners-up spot and two third place finishes in his third year left his owners dissatisfied. He was sent out again as a four-year-old to boost his branding and he won the Group Two Duke of York Stakes. With his record retrieved, Amadeus Wolf was retired to the Stud. The process of bringing in other investors left the Stud owning 33 per cent of the stallion.

In another deal, the Stud worked out a lease agreement to bring the winner of the 2003 Irish Derby, Alshamar, to Ireland. The Japan Racing Association had bought him off the Aga Khan after his winning year and, following two seasons at stud, it decided to let him go.

A few months later, the son of Indian Ridge and the Irish 2,000 Guineas champion, Indian Haven, was sent to live at Tully by his owners, Peter Gleeson and Julian Smith. The Stud took in such tenants in exchange for rent and free nominations.

Such an intense intake of new hooves indicated there was space to fill in the 10 turret-topped stallion boxes and in the broodmare yards around them. Sad exits had always been an inevitable feature of the farm's life. Still, nobody expected the run of departures to be quite so emphatic.

First the much-adored Danoli developed a severe bout of colic in April 2006. He was aged 18. He had won the 1997 Hennessy Gold Cup and endeared himself to millions of punters who backed him during his career. Hundreds of thousands of tourists had got up close to him since he was retired to live alongside Vintage Crop.

"They tried everything but they had no choice but to put him down," said his former trainer, Tom Foley. "He was a great horse and we will always have fond memories."

Ten weeks later, Seskin Bridge, who was owned by the Stud and raced for President Paddy Hillery throughout the 1980s, followed. She was 10 years older than Danoli and suffered the effects of old age. It was 21 years after her glory season of 1985, when she won the Leopardstown International Chase. Nostalgic reasons endeared these two horses to the Stud. Pragmatic ones had kept it sweet on 2006's next fatality.

Less than four months after Seskin Bridge's death, Indian Ridge, the backbone of the business during very bad times, suffered a heart attack. The sensational stallion was gushed about in company report after company report. Ordinarily, his fee was at least six times what the bulk of the rest of the roster justified. In 2003, as an 18-year-old, he generated €75,000 from each mare he covered. The other five stallions took in a combined €70,000 for seeing to one mare each. The average age of these five stallions was eight.

Indian Ridge's workload had been halved in recent years, to spare his health. But three years earlier, Mr Clarke still predicted he could have another eight seasons left in him. He covered 70 mares from February to July in 2006. He had been declared a Chef-de-race on account of his importance to the breed. At that stage, he had eight Group One winners among his progeny. In 14 years, only one of his two-year-old crops failed to have a stakes winner. He was the epitome of the type of prestigious anchor stallion the cavalier critics of the Stud had craved throughout its history.

"Indian Ridge has left behind a wonderful legacy. He was one of our greatest stallions and he was a real old friend of everyone here," Mr Clarke said the day after the horse passed away.

The loss of a racer, a champion and a superb sire in the space of six months could have been devastating. As it turned out, the Stud dusted itself down and returned to the clouded crystal ball of standing sires, searching for the next hero.

The reason behind every syndicate investment varies. For the likes of Verglas, it can be the fact it is easier to replicate successful breeding patterns if they worked well with a particular father and certain families of mares. Others may require a stallion that made an impact at a set distance. Some speculators might just follow the crowd, in the hope of promise and a quick tax-free buck.

Dermot O'Rourke, a former director of the Stud, who bought the Plantation Stud in England early in 2005, said his purchase of shares in stallions such as Motivator helped to widen the pool of genes available to him. This was to lower his exposure to duplication and triplication in bloodlines. He used the same logic to guide his investment in the new stallion of the hour – the Irish National Stud's own Invincible Spirit.

Invincible Spirit was the son of the super sire, Green Desert. This English-based stallion had proven his ability to not only create good racers, but also to create sons that followed him to become cracking stallions. The Maktoum-owned Green Desert had sired many speedy offspring before Nawara Stud Co. Ltd bred Invincible Spirit. The foal was born in 1997. He raced under the maroon colours of Prince A.A. Faisal and earned €379,275 along the way.

He sprinted well as a two-year-old. His three-year-old campaign was packed with promise. Then injury scuppered his shot. These vital few fashionable months were lost. For almost two years, Invincible Spirit was forced to sit on his potential and sensational speed. Brian Grassick, the former director at the Stud who developed links between the key owners and Tully, knew about him. He tipped off the Board.

When Invincible Spirit returned to the track as a five-year–old, the Stud kept a watching brief. He was not racing at a particularly high standard. But the Stud could see his speed. He broke the record at the Curragh for six furlongs. Contact was made with Invincible Spirit's owner, Prince A.A. Faisal, and he was told the horse had what the Stud was looking for.

On September 7th, 2002, the five-year-old lined out at Haydock for the Sprint Cup over 1,200 metres. He let loose. And he won. The following Monday, a cheque for close to £2m was signed on the Stud's behalf.

"As a Group One winning six-furlong sprinter with an international pedigree and a lovely individual, he will make a great addition to our roster of stallions," Lady O'Reilly said to announce the news.

There was a plan for him to make one final run on October 26th at Arlington in America. But he never made the journey across the Atlantic and retired with Haydock as his final and crowning glory.

The syndication, and the gathering together of shareholders, was handled by Mr Grassick's agency. He pitched a stake in a beautiful, well-built and pleasant horse without a career to confirm his promise.

Invincible Spirit's first foals were just as good-looking as their father. They sold for an average of 10 times what it cost their breeders to mate with the freshman sire.

This was the type of lotto ticket that sustained interest in syndicates. All the risks and uncertainties gnawing at investors when money is first transferred can be spirited away when two-year-olds start galloping past the winning lines.

Doubts should have been even more pronounced in the case of Invincible Spirit. His foals were born under a cloud of concern in the bloodstock market. Jitters were caused by stagnant sales and oversupply. However, the standard of Invincible Spirit's offspring was such that they rode the turbulence.

In December, when nine of his first babies went to market at the Tattersall's foal sale, they were sold for an average of €35,000. That was a quick 350 per cent return on those who paid the initial nomination fee. By the time the Deauville sales in France rolled around the following August, all of his sons and daughters in the catalogue were hot property.

Lady O'Reilly put her Invincible Spirit yearling, Lawman, up for grabs. He shared a mother with the winner of the 2004 French Oaks, Latice. The Stud's chairman sold Lawman for €75,000 – a notional 750 per cent profit on the value of a nomination.

At that stage there were more than 200 of his sons and daughters stretching their legs and preparing for a make-or-break winter training regime. Once the evenings began to lengthen the following spring, these juveniles were to be tested for the first time against their peers. Once those springtime gates opened, the task did not prove as testing as their trainers might have thought.

Invincible Spirit's squadron of colts and fillies swooped down onto tracks around Europe. In 35 races, one of his two-year-old offspring was the winner, tying with an eight-year-old world record. The freshman took out the challenge of all other stallions during his scorching season. He had produced a greater amount of individual winners, number of wins, tally of prize money and total of high-value stakes victories. It turned a so-called "solid but not spectacular first season" into a sublime one.

The transformation in the respect he commanded was incredible. In December 2005, a foal of his, later to be called Legal Eagle, was sold by the Stud for €38,000 to Rathbarry Stud. At the Goff's yearling sale 10 months later, Sheikh Mohammed bought the same colt for €300,000. Two days later, Lady O'Reilly took an Invincible Spirit filly from the Irish National Stud for €100,000. With figures like this showing at the end of September 2006, the sire's nomination fee rose from €10,000 to €35,000.

Invincible Spirit was still a worker. This meant he was not even in an area to enjoy the plaudits. He was spending the second part of 2006 in the Chatswood Stud in Victoria, Australia. It had been his winter home since 2003, where an originally slow uptake by just 38 breeders quickened into a foot-rush for his foals.

The demand on both sides of the equator was taking its toll. He looked great and had no problem performing but, after four years commuting to consummate, he was rested. At the time, syndicates were starting to shy away from subjecting stallions to such a gruelling year-round agenda. In 2007, he only had to endure six months' work.

"Chatswood and the Irish National Stud collectively believe that it is in the horse's best interest to be rested.

"It is pleasing in a money-driven industry, Invincible Spirit's welfare and longevity at stud were our main priorities," Greg Willis, of the Chatswood Stud, said at the time. The break spared him a brush with disaster.

Equine flu was discovered in Australia during the summer of 2007. Panic spread quickly among owners. The finger of suspicion originally moved towards the Coolmore contingent, which was anchored by the mighty Rock of Gibraltar. Later, this was rubbished by an official inquiry which found that a horse from Japan had been carrying the infection.

Fifteen Irish horses were among 80 quarantined. This included one Tully-based tourist, Rakti, who was grounded for weeks in Sydney. It cost his syndicate €20,000 to ship him south for the season without him generating an income.

But, right when Invincible Spirit was spared an uncertain spell in Australia, his entire future was put in serious doubt. His record-breaking two-year-olds matured into terrific three-year-olds. Fleeting Spirit had three stakes' wins. Campfire Glow had two. The Lady O'Reilly-bred Lawman had landed the French Derby to crown £770,000 worth of career winnings. This meant the more powerful stud farms did not just want to breed with the sire. They wanted to control him. A number of substantial offers were made. A hostile takeover was on the cards.

The Stud gripped its hand tightly around the dark-coloured treasure. In a frantic summer, it scrambled for the support among those who owned, and fraternised with, Invincible Spirit. Help was desperately needed to keep the new heartbeat of Tully around to pump profits.

8

High Stakes and Incredible Profits

In February 2003, Invincible Spirit lost his virginity in the hexagonal covering shed at the back of the stallion boxes in the Irish National Stud. He got to repeat the experience 131 more times before the breeding window was closed in July. He became a father the following January. By the summer of 2004, he had 44 sons and 38 daughters to his name.

The owners of these were an interesting posse pulled from across the Irish industry and from the pages of the Stud's own history. Charles J. Haughey and his daughter, Eimear Mulhern, sent their mare Adjisa. Indian Ridge's former owner, Sean Coughlan, had his Aguilsa covered. The man Invincible Spirit raced for, Prince A. A. Faisal, used two nominations. On top of that, a couple of the resident Tully band paid a flying visit to their new neighbour. Nearly the entire boardroom of the Stud got in on the action. Directors Sean Twomey, Tony Smurfit, John Osborne and Lady O'Reilly, and company secretary, John McStay, were each involved in some way, shape or form. A future director, Trevor Stewart, was too. All were either shareowners or had been among those who bought nominations at the bargain opening offer of €10,000.

Mr Coughlan's Aguilsa was among the first of these to foal in late January. The Stud's own mare followed three weeks later. Five-year-old Sheba, who was owned by Clodagh McStay, the wife of the company secretary, gave birth earlier that week. Still, more than a quarter of Invincible Spirit's first coverings were not successful. Sixteen mares were barren and five pregnancies were aborted.

The striking looks of the first 86 foals were enough to attract interest. It was not their fault that their father's business slumped slightly for a season. In 2004, cash was tighter across the entire market and people did not have easy money to invest.

The second-year stallion still got to mate with 113 mares. Some customers from his debut season, such as the McStays and Trevor Stewart, shied away in 2004. Others, like Lady O'Reilly, increased their interest. Instead of sending two of her prized mares, Laramie and Landlocked, she sent four. Director Pat O'Kelly joined the party with Hi Bettina.

The result was Bett's Spirit, who went on to earn almost €30,000 on the track. This was amassed during the nine outings she took part in until the night she won €625 for fourth place at the Fianna Fáil benefit event in Dundalk in November 2008. Then she retired.

While the wait was on to see if the likes of Bett's Spirit would spring forth, syndicate members were faced with an eternal dilemma. What was the best breeding strategy? Sell slots or send mares?

The worth of a sire cannot be properly measured until five years after his first covering. This is when his first crop campaigns. To attract investors early in any stallion's career a number of perks are thrown in for these riskier blind bets. If you buy two shares, you automatically get two nominations. A third one can be added on for free. Such sweeteners are offered because people would otherwise be reluctant to expose themselves too soon.

Another trick to entice early investment is the right of first refusal. This means that if one syndicate member wants to opt out, or lessen his or her holding, the share is offered to the rest of the club before being released to the wider market.

When Invincible Spirit first arrived at the Stud, the price of each share meant that to get involved ultimately amounted to a €40,000 gamble. Once his first crop had reached the age of two, and had produced 35 winners, the value of each person's stake rose significantly. So did the amount they stood to lose if the horse subsequently came a cropper. At the end of each successful season, some shareholders sold in order to bank the safe money. Others, who were more optimistic about his future, were anxious to buy up every stake on offer.

John McStay was one of those with the chequebook out. His and Mrs McStay's investment vehicle, Mabaki, made a pitch for any loose share from the syndicate. Through the years, he had proven himself a shrewd businessman and, in the lead-up to this, he had shown a wonderful appreciation for value and timing.

Mr McStay had been chairman of the *Leinster Leader* newspaper group, in which he held a 6 per cent stake. When the group sold in September 2005, the price it achieved floored the industry. The Scottish-based *Johnston Press* paid €138.6m for a dispersed basket of Irish regional newspaper titles that printed approximately 130,000 newspapers each week. The group included the *Limerick Leader*, the *Leinster Leader* and the *Dundalk Democrat*. In a day of high-drama, the outgoing 'Leader' Board sealed the €5m deal for the *Echo Newspaper* group in Tallaght only to sell it on to the Scottish group, along with the rest, in the afternoon.

It was a whirlwind deal which exploited *Johnston Press's* reckless regional investment policy at the perfect moment. Mr McStay made €8.3m for his 6 per cent, and the shareholders even got to keep some valuable property.

It could not have been timed better. The collapse in newspaper revenues and the hemorrhaging of sales over the coming years rendered *Johnston Press's* portfolio near to worthless, given the debt latched on to it. Individual papers in the old *Leinster Leader* group were sold back for fractions of what Mr McStay and his cohorts had earned for them.

The rise and demise of *Johnston Press* was symptomatic. Be it in newspapers, property or stallions, international investors, like the Scottish group, saw the Irish market as a place to make a buck. Prices were spiralling so fast that speculators could borrow heavily to get hold of assets and use the immediate equity to expand their empire.

It was no surprise that a juicy tax exemption, coupled with the race results of his offspring, set up a stratospheric spike in Invincible Spirit's value. It was the syndicate's opportunity to name its price. Unlike the shareholders in the *Leinster Leader*, the Stud did not want to sell. It had seen Tulyar, Royal Charger and Ahonoora all leave at various times because of money. Holding onto the reinvented speed merchant was a chance to prove how its grip had been strengthened. It knew it had a fight on its hands. So it got to work early to try and hang on. A courtship began with the manager of Queen Elizabeth II's stud, John Warren.

The tactic was that, by selling a stake to the Queen, it would give muscle and mares to the whole syndicate. The Queen's involvement would have helped create the type of stable situation Mr Warren orchestrated when the £6m Motivator was going to stud.

Breeders had a more natural motivation for keeping hold of the likes of Invincible Spirit. Ultimately, he could add long-term value to each band of broodmares, rather than the more loosely connected speculators tempted by a profitable takeover.

Mr McStay was not just a highly successful business man. He and Mrs McStay ran the Oaklawn Stud and campaigned their own horses. The nominations were as valuable to him as they were to anybody else. Although he had a right of first refusal over outsiders, he had no greater sway among the other members of the syndicate when shares came up for sale.

On at least four occasions, Mr McStay submitted a bid to buy extra shares. He went through a lottery process against the other owners of Invincible Spirit. Each time fortune knocked him back. Then his moment came. He won the chance to buy a coveted extra share. He took it.

Noel O'Callaghan had put the stake up for grabs. His Alexander Elegance had had one of the first foals produced by the stallion. This colt went to Tattersalls in October 2005, but was withdrawn from the sale. At Halloween in 2006, Mr O'Callaghan parted with one share. It went the way of Mr McStay. This automatically meant the company secretary had more clout when other options came knocking.

At the time, it was rumoured they were selling for approximately €200,000 each. And it was trading season. Within two weeks, another share came on the market. Mr McStay's Mabaki had the wallet out. This time the offer was put up by Dermot Cantillon.

Mr Cantillon was the stud manager for the Smurfit's Forenaughts Stud, son-in-law to the Irish National Stud's former manager, Michael Osborne, and brother-in-law to the then director, John Osborne. In either his own or Forenaughts' name, Mr Cantillon had sent two mares to Invincible Spirit in his first season. One, Cheviot Amble, was among the 16 that turned out to be barren. The other, Kentucky Fall, lost her foal.

The next year just one Invincible Spirit foal was delivered to Forenaughts, through Tasha's Dream. The gelding helped make up lost ground when he was bought by Dermot Weld at Goff's 2006 October Millions Sale for €160,000.

The same autumn, Mr Cantillon and Mr Smurfit released another share. Mr McStay had his option to buy. So he did. It left the Company Secretary with a powerful four shares in the stallion and increased influence over his future. The downside for this, and other internal share swaps in the syndicate, was that the personality of the pool was not broadened to include new breeders.

At an Oireachtas committee three years later, these deals were questioned and the Stud was asked how it had allowed the internal sales to hold back outside investment. The Stud said its Company Secretary's appetite for extra shares coincided with a time in his career when it suited him to make these types of investments. Mr McStay was no different to thousands of other people in the midst of Ireland's property and investment boom.

Plus, whether it was a consideration or not, buying shares in stallions ensured all profits and whatever windfalls could be harvested tax-free until July 31st, 2008. The window for exploiting the exemption was closing, because of European Commission demands. While it existed, the tax break made the scores of customers sending hundreds of mares to Tully an interesting case study on who was making money from the then Finance Minister, Charlie Haughey's, policy brainchild.

Along with a plethora of personalities in some way connected to the Stud, there were also players adept at fashioning quick money in major deals. Dermot O'Rourke was a regular. In 2006, he and his business partner, Jerry Conlon, sold a spread of land on the outskirts of Naas for a tidy €320m. The property was to become the new and largely disused Millennium Park. When the hysterics died down four years later, it made its way onto the books of the body responsible for rescuing Ireland's toxic property debts – the National Assets Management Agency.

Before he cashed in on the Millennium Park, Mr O'Rourke, a former director at Tully, had bought the Plantation Stud in England and was an enthusiastic entrant into a number of high-profile syndications.

Another repeat customer of the Stud's was Joe O'Reilly, who pumped €200m into Killen Castle and had a vision to transform Dublin's O'Connell Street before his assets ended up with NAMA. Yet, Invincible Spirit's single biggest client for the 2007 season came from a more traditional background.

It was the chairman of the Stud, Lady O'Reilly. She was involved in the ownership of at least 10 of the mares covered by the stallion between February and July that year. This was in keeping with her desire to breed with good stock where possible. For her investment, equivalent to €350,000 at the full market price, she got a nice return. Nine foals were delivered the following year. She was already realising how good the DNA of Invincible Spirit could be. At the end of 2007, she was declared French breeder of the year for weaving his genes in with that of her own mare Laramie. Their colt, Lawman, won the French Derby and the Prix Jean Prat just three years after the pair met in the same hexagonal covering shed where the sire momentarily met all his partners.

The brevity of the breeding process set a tone for the speed at which some gambles could mature. By the end of his French Derby-winning summer, Lawman was retiring to a life at stud himself. He went to the Ballylinch farm in Co. Kilkenny at a cost of €25,000 per nomination.

Behind Lady O'Reilly's gaggle, the Stud sent five of its broodmare band to Invincible Spirit in 2007. The company sold the rest of the opportunities, which its majority shareholding entitled it to. If it got the maximum amount for all of these, its flagship sire could have contributed €1.2m of the company's €7m total turnover that year. The Stud does not break down its accounts in that level of detail.

Another man to bring multiple mares during those months was Dubai's ruler, Sheikh Mohammed. His Darley group took a passing interest and arranged for Amusing Time and Rawabi to scope out the horse's true potential. The arrival of the property-driven mega-wealth of Sheikh Mohammed reflected a bolder and more international ambition for the horse.

In his first year, Invincible Spirit largely served Irish registered mares, apart from a smattering from Italy, Germany, France and America. Just four of his first family of foals were living abroad at the end of that season. As his progeny's reputation grew, more overseas visitors started to circle.

But just because a mare stayed local long enough to give birth and ensure a foal carried the IRE suffix, it did not mean it stuck around to train in the country. Eleven animals from Invincible Spirit's 2006 crop were sent out of Ireland early. Lady O'Reilly exported the foals from her mares Mirania and Paix Royale to Europe.

Yet it was not the international investment community that gained most in the shifting sands of 2006. The McStays were the main movers and had four shares active from January 1st 2007. These were not used for breeding, according to Weatherby's annual Return of Mares record. Selling that amount of nominations privately would have been worth up to €280,000 tax-free.

Where Invincible Spirit was concerned, the McStays generally had taken the selling option. However, they dabbled with a breeding strategy. The couple had one filly born to Invincible Spirit in his first crop. Bronze Queen, as she became known, was not one of the sire's finest.

Trained by John Oxx for three races, a 12th place, out of 13 horses, in Tramore was the best she managed as a four-year-old. She started out in the colours of Clodagh McStay, but a few months after her first outing she was sold on at the Goffs' November sales for €2,200 to the prolific English buyer and owner Martyn McEnery. As Bronze Queen was preparing for her track debut at the Curragh on August 25th 2007, something far more significant was about to happen to her father and her owners. This was to eclipse anything she could have achieved over the eight furlongs in front of her.

Quite simply, there was consternation rumbling around the world of Invincible Spirit. In August, many studs were experiencing difficulty attracting investment because the cost had become so outrageous. Invincible Spirit had the opposite problem and the Stud was trying to swat away suitors. A number of groups made an offer for the stallion, but were rebuffed. Then, an American-based buyer decided it wanted the record-breaking sire and money was not an obstacle.

Recollections of that time have it that the phone in Tully rang every day. Each time, another few million would be offered to prise him from Ireland. This went on for more than a week. The Americans were told he was not for sale. Still they came back. Again they were told to back off. The Stud was desperate to keep the stallion.

The independent shareholders had a more textured attitude. The syndicate included Lady O'Reilly, new director Trevor Stewart and the most involved of all, John McStay. Overall, between the company and those connected to it, they controlled more than two-thirds of the stallion. The remaining shares were held by a handful of powerful individual customers. It would have been bad business to cheese them off.

Each additional million offered by the Americans lumped extra pressure on fault-lines emerging within the team. The Stud hunkered down and stood firm. The American group wanted to buy him outright. So the syndicate had to make a unanimous decision. Shareholders got more and more restless. The seasonal window to make such calls was starting to run out. As ever, there were distractions and problems brought on by the Stud's own internal failures. While the horse trading heated up, the company was needlessly fighting fires within its own yard.

A young gardener, Andrew Lacey, had felt that, like Pat Mullarkey, he could no longer work at the Stud. This was because of a fresh and unconnected allegation of bullying and maltreatment. He fought for his rights and, in May 2005, he placed his case at the mercy of the High Court.

The Stud feared that the sums involved in the Mullarkey case had opened the floodgates and it could not be seen to hand over compensation at each time of asking. John Clarke was not directly involved, so he represented the Stud this time.

First, the Stud opted to contest the case. The process took a long time to sort out. In April 2007, a trial date was set. Mr Clarke filed the company's affidavit on September 19th, 2007.

In autumn 2007, while it was trying to weave a scenario which allowed it to keep ownership of Invincible Spirit, it was paying the six-figure bills associated with appearances before a High Court Judge. Between legal fees, High Court costs and a €120,000 confidential settlement to Mr Lacey, it spent €216,265 on this issue before the end of 2008.

This staff compensation claim, on top of the Mullarkey case, was hugely disproportionate to the small size of the company. It would dwarf the exposure expected of a firm with just three dozen full-time workers. But, alongside the offers for Invincible Spirit, the sum looked more manageable.

Eight-digit amounts were still being called down the phone from the aggressive American group. These were unsettling the Invincible Spirit syndicate. According to the company, the stallion's shareholders began to feel Tully's tactics were making prisoners of their potential profits.

"While we were saying 'no', the individual shareholders were feeling cheated on their investment.

"They were like the guy with the $1m cheque. They were worth a great deal of money but they could not cash it in. To an extent, that was unfair on them," its new chief executive, John Osborne, said in 2010.

There had to be a Rubicon when it came to the ransom. This turned out to be €40m. When the bid hit this, the Stud felt it had to respond. The long-held veto buckled and broke.

Crucially, it did not manage the stallion. A three-person committee, chaired by Lady O'Reilly, did. The Stud was represented by John Clarke. Still, up to that point, the Stud and its connected parties had between them, a strong majority interest in the stallion.

Then Darley rode onto the horizon. Sheikh Mohammed was building up to a summer spending-spree. Breeding rights for the three-time Group One winning Manduro were negotiated to go along with the Sheikh's three new American-based prospects. He now wanted a bit of Invincible Spirit in his shopping basket. It was a quick bid, a straight bid and he needed an answer.

The Sheikh did not usually get involved in these syndicates. He had the money to buy such horses outright and monopolise any benefits. But Invincible Spirit was no ordinary prospect. He was the son of the Maktoums's wonder-stallion Green Desert and he was one of the few high-demand sires who was not owned by its enemies in the industry, Coolmore.

Earlier that year Darley had sent three mares to Invincible Spirit. Shadwell Estates, which belongs to Sheikh Mohammed's brother, sent one. Now Darley wanted 25 per cent of the horse. It valued him at $60m (€42m). The 45-share split would become a 90-share syndicate to allow room for everybody to manoeuvre.

Each shareholder was given three options. They could hold onto both shares and use the nominations that came with them. They could sell half their interest for €666,000. Or they could sell both new shares for more than €1.3m.

Darley gave the syndicate one chance: a simple "yes" or a final "no". The Stud said it had not been a willing seller, but recognised that the deal offered a significant return for its fellow shareholders.

The arrangements took a mere three weeks to tie together. Invincible Spirit could relax. He was staying put for the winter. He would continue his daily trots around the paddock where he had worn a five-foot-wide path in an L-shape along two sides of his five-acre personal space.

"It was a dream result from the Irish National Stud's perspective, as we did not have to share any of our shares and we stayed roughly around where we had been.

"It introduced capital that the cash-hungry shareholders needed and a number of them took the option of selling out completely.

"Others took the medium option of taking some money off the table but staying in for the income stream that shareholding presents. Others stayed with us all the way. We had a new stronger partner and the horse was retained for the Irish National Stud," Mr Osborne explained three years later.

In an explanation statement published in 2010, the Stud said that, as syndicate manager, it canvassed the views of all Invincible Spirit's shareholders. Because some held onto their stake, the Stud sold 2.5 of its shares to Darley. This ensured the new partner got to the 25 per cent threshold. The Stud entered the deal owning 21 out of 45 shares in the syndicate (47 per cent).

After the Darley deal, it had 33 out of 90 (36 per cent). An explanation note sent to Agriculture Minister, Mary Coughlan, on September 28th, 2007 was a bit more explicit. It said the Stud sold 2.5 of its 21 shares and earned $3.3m for them. This meant the remaining portion of its stake was worth $24.66m or €17.6m, based on exchange rates for that month.

The sum involved was enormous for a minority stake in an older horse. Such a share shuffle had not been done before. The syndicate felt it needed speed and sensitivity to bring it home. It turned to the Stud's company secretary, John McStay, to provide the necessary accountancy expertise.

This role meant Mr McStay had multiple roles to play in the deal. He was one of the largest individual shareholders. He was the pre-eminent financial advisor to the majority stakeholder. Now, he was the accountant charged with getting the deal over the line. The arrangement which was thrashed out involved the Stud being the ultimate middleman.

"For simplicity, the transaction was essentially structured as one where the INS entered into a single transaction with Darley and acquired the shares from each of the third-party shareholders including (Lady O'Reilly, Mr Stewart and Mr McStay).

"The transaction with the outside shareholders was at no profit/loss to the company. And the legal and other costs associated with the transaction were born proportionately by the vendors and share-holders," it said.

Following the syndication shift and the shuffling of shares, there was a big change in Invincible Spirit's business and the identity of the mares visiting him. In 2008, Mrs McStay, Mr Weld, Ms O'Kelly, Mr Stewart and the Ski Lodge Partnership each sent a mare. The Stud itself booked in five. Lady O'Reilly pared her interest back to seven. Between Darley (9 mares) and Shadwell (3 mares), the Maktoums were responsible for a dozen bookings. Significantly, the Queen remained involved after dipping her toe in the previous year. The Stud and the shareholders also saw a welcome injection into their bank balances. This expanded the range of choices they could justify for that season.

The Stud has said in all its annual accounts that it actively encouraged its directors to trade with the company where possible. This occurred when they bought and boarded mares, used stallions or purchased yearlings. In the case of Dermot Weld, he also trained the President's horses.

Under the memorandum of association, which rules the company, there has been a certain code of practice spelled out.

This has it that a director should be disqualified from the Board if he participates directly or indirectly in its profits or benefits from any activity, scheme or undertaking of the company.

However, this specifically says nobody will be asked to leave simply because they own, or part-own, a mare that visits one of the Stud's stallions. Figures finally published in 2010 showed that during two years [2008 and 2009] the Stud, some of its directors and Mr McStay shared €5m in income from various syndicates they were jointly members of. The Stud would have reaped the vast bulk of this because it held the largest stake in each stallion. The company said that at no stage did any of the directors, or the company secretary, have more than 15 per cent of the shares in the relevant syndicates.

The only rule governing joint investments, between the Board and the company, is that if these individuals want a nomination they have to absent themselves from votes on the issue.

The memorandum of association also said that directors are allowed to trade with the company using businesses of their own, provided they are not involved in the decision to pay for such services. Separate to that, directors and key personnel are bound by the code of ethics covering all appointees in the public sector. This means that people cannot get directly involved where they are compromised by their own business interests. In addition directors must make declarations to that effect.

There are also rules which stipulate that all deals above €5,000, paid for by public sector bodies, must be advertised in the open for all prospective service providers to see. State companies must get quotes from various competitors before signing contracts. If the sum is more than €50,000 a full tender process has to be carried out.

The Stud did not put a lot of its business out to tender. Mr McStay's company was retained for years without going to competition. The information relating to these payments was not generally published. It emerged in a Freedom of Information request the Stud responded to in May 2010. The company was not obliged to declare its annual dealings with Mr McStay under any law. Moreover, it said, the lump sum he earned in the Invincible Spirit transaction was paid for by the syndicate it controlled, rather than the Stud alone.

The company also used Mr Weld's training without going through a tender regime. The Stud's reason for this was because it wanted to match each racehorse up with the right trainer.

Separate questions were also raised about how it interpreted the rules laid down in the memorandum and the more general code of ethics. Lady O'Reilly was chair of the Stud and led Invincible Spirit's stallion's syndicate, despite also being a shareholder and repeat customer. However, there was nothing stopping her, or the other connected parties, from profiting in his re-syndication.

This meant that, in September 2007, two Board members, Lady O'Reilly and Mr Stewart, and Mr McStay reaped €2.9m between them. This was the equivalent of selling one full syndicate share each, or six of the new split shares.

The Stud said it published these details in full in its annual accounts. In a statement, it said the nature and terms of the re-syndication were widely known in the industry at the time.

A note on page 22 of its annual accounts for 2007 did address the topic. It said:

> "During the course of the year the company and other participants in the Invincible Spirit stallion syndication disposed of shares (fractional interests) in the stallion to a third party.
>
> "The members of the syndicate included Lady O'Reilly, Mr Stewart (both directors of the company) and Mr McStay (the company secretary) or entities connected with them.
>
> "For commercial reasons the structure of the transaction involved the sale by the company to the third party of a number of shares in the stallion and the purchase by the company of a smaller number of shares from the members of the syndicate.
>
> "The officers of the company participated, on a pari-passu basis with the syndicate members in the underlying transactions.

"The terms of the transaction as it related to the officers of the company and those connected them were the same as to those other syndicate members.

"In the course of the transaction, which was conducted in US$, the company purchased shares to an approximate net value of €2.9m from the connected parties."

However, when the nature of the deal was aired to a wider audience, it did not win the Stud any friends. In an Oireachtas committee, Fine Gael's Michael Creed took specific exception to Mr McStay's role and the multiple parts he played in the deal. The Cork Northwest deputy said that the Stud had a case to answer because the shares bought by its company secretary in 2006 potentially blocked the Queen's outside investment. This was at a time when the Stud felt it needed her involvement to stymie a hostile takeover.

"In respect of the role of the directors of the Irish National Stud, there was a clear conflict of interest because they stood to gain by increasing the shareholding in the premium sire in the National Stud.

"By increasing their own shareholding they were locking out business which could have been brought to the Stud," he said.

Mr Creed also felt that the directors and Mr McStay had enjoyed a privileged place and a dominant position, which had earned them €2.9m, tax free.

"It is in conflict with the primary responsibility as directors... If blue-chip clients had put down bids and were interested but could not get involved because of the activities of the company secretary, is it a problem for the Irish National Stud?" he asked of the new chief executive Mr Osborne.

Throughout that meeting, and before, the Stud refused to accept that anything untoward had gone on. Instead, it maintained that the deal was one of the company's finest hours.

"The Invincible Spirit re-syndication was one of the most important moments in the history of the Stud.

"A hostile bid from a farm in the USA was resisted by introducing a strong new partner to the syndicate and retaining the investment of the loyal shareholders," it said.

It was not the first time that concerns about the involvement of Board members had been aired. At one stage, French syndicate members grumbled because they felt the directors were getting preferential treatment in Verglas's first few seasons at Tully. In response, Jim Beecher had ordered a mini inquiry and produced a report. The Stud said that this found that directors were in fact treated worse than ordinary customers when dealing with the company they oversaw. Mr Osborne endeavoured to make this report public, but as yet has not been able to find the hard copy.

The Oireachtas committee was not the only occasion when clarity was sought on the Board's understanding of the rules governing each director's responsibilities. In April 2008, after the Invincible Spirit re-syndication, the Department of Agriculture wrote to the Stud and sent it a copy of the Code of Practice for the Governance of State Bodies. An e-mail to Mr Clarke said that, having reviewed the information supplied by the Stud, the Department felt there were gaps which needed to be addressed. It told the Stud it could not ignore provisions in the Code unless the Minister of the day agreed to leniency. A Departmental official sent Mr Clarke a check-list of perceived shortcomings. He was asked to describe how they were going to be addressed.

The first item on the list was a need for confirmation that the chairman and directors were aware of, and in compliance with, the 2001 law dictating the standards expected from those in public office. The same was asked of employees, to ensure that there were no conflicts of interest and that all gifts were accepted honestly. It asked for reassurance that competitive tendering was followed and assets were sold in line with proper rules. This check-list said the Stud regularly failed to meet its deadline to submit unaudited six-monthly accounts to the Minister with a twice-annual report on significant developments.

Mr Clarke responded. He said Mr McStay would put additional details into the annual report. He assured the Department "competitive tendering is the normal procedure except in the case of stallions, where it would be totally inappropriate".

This, and a follow-up letter from Lady O'Reilly, did not satisfy the Department. It wanted a clear confirmation of a level of knowledge and compliance with the various rules.

On May 2nd, 2008 the Board met in Tully and was handed a copy of the Code of Practice to bring it up to speed. A month afterwards, the new Agriculture Minister, Brendan Smith, came to the boardroom to address the directors.

"I would like to draw your attention to a number of 'housekeeping issues' which may appear mundane but are nevertheless important to the ongoing successful functioning and public reputation of the Stud.

"These issues are encapsulated under the term Corporate Governance. I know that the Board is very conscious of the relevant guidelines and I would urge you to continue to pay attention to the application of the Guidelines for the Corporate Governance of State Bodies," Mr Smith said.

Two years after this, the Stud remained confident that all activities involved in the Invincible Spirit deal were kosher. In particular, it said, Mr McStay's roles were in keeping with its requirements. The Stud said he was an integral and valuable ally in the successful bid to keep Invincible Spirit in Ireland.

"The INS gained enormously and the Irish industry needs to be able to retain the availability of the elite stallions.

"The alternative is to surrender the advantages we have to competitor countries and Ireland Inc is the loser. The deal was praised widely within the breeding community worldwide. Mr McStay's input was central to the success of the transaction," it said in a statement.

This message was consistent with the views adopted by the Stud since the ink first dried on the Darley deal. They heaped praise on each other and the supportive shareholders, despite almost half of them having more than a passing involvement in the company. In her report for 2007, Lady O'Reilly singled out its chief executive.

"John Clarke deserves special thanks for his key role in enabling the Irish National Stud to retain Invincible Spirit.

"He and his staff deserve great praise for the way in which they continue to market our stallions and present the Irish National Stud as a major component of the Irish and international breeding industry. Thanks are also due to our company secretary John McStay for his wisdom and support," she said.

The Irish National Stud has been resolute and unwavering in its belief that the crucial result was the fact that Invincible Spirit's brass identification plate remained fixed to the bottom half of the split wooden door of his stallion enclosure. The sire was retained to peek his head out of his box every day and keep an eye on the knee-high row of yellow bushes across the broad black pavement below.

Invincible Spirit's presence meant the company could still profit from more than 150 visits by mares to his stomping ground in the hexagonal covering shed. All involved in the deal had profited. The Stud felt vindicated.

Meanwhile, nobody in the boardroom had any inkling that the work to find mares to mate with the €42m stallion, in the month of the Darley deal, would sow the seeds for one of the most destructive turns in Tully's troubled history.

CHAPTER

9

Love and Losses

Indian Ridge could not have picked a better moment to pass his mantle on to Invincible Spirit. He never inspired headlines as a racer. Then, as a father, he quietly and professionally packed his offspring with so much talent that they trundled off to achieve all the glory instead. Dutifully, he saw to all available mares for 12 years until his workload was cut in half to accommodate the effects of his advancing years.

Finally, in 2006, when Invincible Spirit's record-breaking crop was just wrapping up its stand-out season and promoting its sire as the star of the Stud, Indian Ridge slipped off the stage. There was never a better time for Tully to suffer such a sad loss.

It had a new prestigious pedigree to promote and it had the wherewithal to build a lasting financial foundation. The Stud also had a new person responsible for managing the breeding careers of its stallion roster. This fostered a fresh, and very different, dynamic in the office building in Tully.

Julie Lynch was a bright and determined recruit. She was 27 years' old with an innate aptitude for her job. Her chance to work at the Irish National Stud arrived in late 2005, while she was employed at the John Magnier–Vincent O'Brien Coolmore operation.

The move from Tipperary to Kildare happened pretty quickly. There was a job interview in early December 2005. An offer of a management assistant's post arrived on December 18th and a contract came with it. She gave Coolmore her notice. Then she started working in Tully on January 30th, 2006.

Ms Lynch's nature was to work hard and she impressed her new employers.

"I was delighted with my appointment and extremely enthusiastic," she said.

Two months later, there was another opening. The manager overseeing breeding bookings left the company. Ms Lynch was promoted. After a six-month trial, she was established as the stallion nominations manager on a permanent basis. It was September 2006, a hectic time of year for this line of work.

At Tully it was made worse because its €60m stallion roster was in the midst of one of the most upending transformations in its history. Indian Ridge had died. The same month, Huma Park Stud in Meath was sold. Two of its stallion attractions, Rakti and Elusive City, became tenants of Tully instead.

Meanwhile, the real frenzy to get a spot with Invincible Spirit began. His fee was more than doubled to €35,000. That September his yearlings broke the €300,000 mark at the sales. This was always a delicate decision to manage the demands of the eager syndicate members with the willingness of breeders to pay up. Despite the death of three much-loved animals – Indian Ridge, Danoli and Seskin Bridge – there was a bobbing buoyancy around the yard.

A racehorse called the Last Laugh landed the nursery at Navan at odds of 13-2. Trained by Michael Grassick, the horse was leased by the Lads Only Syndicate, which was made up of a group of staff at the Stud.

Then, in the last week of September, the company accounts enjoyed the benefit of a bumper yearlings' sale at Goffs, when trading was up 14 per cent on the previous year.

Tully had brought a mixed bag to the Kill arena. Yet it strutted back down the N7 motorway with a fistful. Sheikh Mohammed paid €425,000 for a colt from the Stud's mare, Nebraas. The broodmare had been bought in December 2004 for Stg£170,000 while she was carrying the same son. Director Dermot Weld bid for two of the Stud's yearlings and took them home for €195,000. Lady O'Reilly had her eye on the company's Invincible Spirit filly, which she grabbed at auction for €100,000. Capping the day, the ever-glorious doyenne of the Stud, Sabaah, saw her one-year-old offspring leave the yard for €240,000.

Meanwhile, the suggestion of an even more substantial return was starting to circulate. This was because of a show of benevolence from the Department of Agriculture and the Government. Their legislative changes freed the company to cash in on the Celtic Tiger's property bubble and reap the resulting demographic shift, which saw young workers migrating from Dublin to more affordable homes in towns like Kildare.

Minister Joe Walsh's willingness to alter the law came into effect when he signed, on September 28th, 2004, the order vesting four land folios, made up of 332 hectares, in the name of the Stud rather than the State. This was one of Mr Walsh's last acts in the Department after a combined nine years as Minister for Agriculture. He resigned from office as part of the Cabinet reshuffle the next day. The land asset he signed over was immediately earmarked to remove the pall of debt which had been hanging over the Kildare farm for the previous two years.

The Stud had 10.55 acres it decided it could not use to keep horses anymore. The Grey Abbey tract had been cut from the main campus by the Kildare by-pass and had been re-zoned for houses to cater for the commuting community. In 2005, the Stud had asked the new Minister, Mary Coughlan, to allow it to sell up. It outlined three options. The first was to keep 12 cattle on it from April to October and earn €1,200. The second was to sow barley, but it feared this would be hampered by "considerable damage carried out by local children". The third was to hand it to an estate agent for auction.

Fortune arrived by way of a seemingly frustrating delay. A deputation from Kildare met with Minister Coughlan and the Stud was subsequently asked not to go ahead with the sale. The 12-month stop spanned a period when land prices rocketed up 12 per cent.

On September 18th, 2006 the Board met and finally decided to let the site go. Jordon Auctioneers won the tender with an offer to charge 0.5 per cent commission. Sales in the area were feeding expectations that the Stud would earn €750,000 per acre, a potential bonanza of €7.9m. The company sat and waited. On December 8th the Board gathered to inspect the offers. The directors were not disappointed. Like many land deals at the time, the size of the purchaser's pockets exceeded what went before. The auctioneers recommended a bid of €9.1m. The Board agreed. It was 15 per cent more than local trends would have suggested.

Three days later, chief executive John Clarke wrote to the Department of Agriculture for quick ministerial approval.

"As it is important that the Irish National Stud receive the ministerial permission quickly I would be grateful for an early and positive answer," he said. Minister Mary Coughlan said "yes". She confirmed the company's right to sell the 10.55 acres. The trade went ahead.

Two years earlier, this seven-digit windfall would have gone back to the Government to spend on services across the whole economy. As a result of the changes contained in Mr Walsh's Statutory Instrument of September 2004, the Stud got to keep the money for itself.

The sum was directed to temporarily clear €3.5m off its overdraft. It was not used to address the shortfall in the workers' pension scheme, which grew 11 per cent to €788,000 in the year the sale was finalised. A decision was made to buy another seven acres of cheaper grazing land on the far side of the farm. This cost €1.2m and was snapped up because the plot was considered to be of "strategic and vital importance". Four new stallion paddocks were developed on it.

The transaction took place when property prices were at their very peak. This was lumped on top of the €5.6m it earned from selling shares in Invincible Spirit and off-loading its crop of sought-after young animals at the bumper sales' event. All together, the deals provided a profit which was almost twice the company's expected annual turnover. This meant it could have closed its doors to all its customers for two years and still sustained its normal level of business entirely from its own coffers. As it transpired, the fund lasted nowhere near that long. At least for a while, money was not an urgent concern. Living was easier.

The same could not be said of the Stud's half-sister across the Irish Sea. The British National Stud had to turn to one of Ms Lynch's predecessors to get it through an exceedingly difficult moment.

The *Racing Post* had broken a story that an internal investigation was set up by the directors after a former employee made allegations of sexual harassment and bullying. Reid Coulter, the erstwhile general manager, went on temporary leave and soon afterwards left the company by mutual consent. David Somers was hired to fill the vacant general manager's position.

Before moving to the Newmarket farm, Mr Somers spent 10 years at the Irish National Stud working his way up from student to yard manager and stud groom. He left for a while to work in Australia. Initially, he came back to Tully and preceded Ms Lynch as the stallion nominations manager. He switched hemispheres once more before he was lured back to the heartland of England's thoroughbred industry. The geography turned out to be far more idyllic than the task at hand.

Britain's Stud was losing money fast. Its main stallion, Bahamian Bounty, was good for the middle-value market, but he was more than 10 years' old and could not bankroll the operation on his own. The Stud needed a loan from the British Government to survive. The number of mares it owned dropped by 50, to 80. Westminster decided to orchestrate a takeover by the Jockey Club to secure its future.

Over the course of the next three years a strategy was adopted to cut costs, slim down the enterprise and focus on restoring its core breeding business. Mr Somers, his successor Brian O'Rourke and the Jockey Club managed to stop the rot. How much easier that work would have been if they had happened across a sensation such as Invincible Spirit?

Adverts in English owners' magazines and pamphlets were showing just how good the Irish National Stud had it. These carried cut-out

132

images of the league table of European sires, beside a roll call of wins from Invincible Spirit's progeny. Tully was out to ensure that nobody was ignorant of the value of its asset. Yet, although the Irish National Stud could boast control of Europe's best young sire, there was no guarantee of future custom.

Each autumn the company had to get out into the market and aggressively sell his pedigree and his promise. Every pitch had to be sensitive to the family background of the mares. It also involved appreciating the individual requirements for stallions more inclined to produce sprinters or stayers. Targeted adverts, like the one run in Britain, needed to be placed for all the stallions. Former customers had to be coaxed to come back and the right price needed to be struck. Fees always had to be tweaked to ensure a stallion hit the balance between supply and demand.

Before the Stud released its pricelist for the 2007 season, Verglas had his fee increased by 50 per cent, to €15,000. The price for Alshamar, who came to Ireland after starting stud work in Japan, was cut to €5,000. Desert Prince, the Stud's great hope of the new Millennium, had his fee slashed from €12,000 to €5,000. Three years earlier, it had cost seven times more for owners to nominate a mare to visit him.

Once the prices were set, it was up to the Stud to get into the market, find suitable breeders and flog the nominations. Responsibility for selling these spots fell on two people: Ms Lynch and chief executive John Clarke. Generally, the stallion nominations manager had to constantly gauge appetite among breeders. The manager would suggest a figure. This would include an advertised fee and the scope for discounts through haggling with bulk buyers and good customers. This allowed wriggle room of anything up to 50 per cent on the published price, depending on the stallion and the difficulty there was getting business for him. Each sire's strategy was discussed between the chief executive and his stallion nominations manager. Together they brought a recommendation to the Board. In Tully this was done at a meeting towards the end of each flat racing season.

John Clarke and Julie Lynch's first autumn working together was an extraordinary success for the stallions. Turnover for the stud farm jumped from a steady €4.4m to €5.7m. Impressively, this was without the keystone which had held the place together for more than 10 years – Indian Ridge.

The new charge was led by his successor and the continent's new leading first season stallion, Invincible Spirit. But striking the right price range in any stallion roster, especially one with a mix of pedigree and age profiles, was a bit like getting a pin to stand on its head. Buyers are normally reluctant to get involved in certain years of a sire's career, particularly when his first crop are about to start racing. This can change the product from year to year and horse to horse. In the case of Invincible Spirit, he was delivering a 10-fold increase for investors, which made for easier sales.

Interest also perked up in Verglas, even with his higher fee. The pale grey stallion was trying to restart his career in Ireland. But breeders were faced with uncertainty, while they waited to see what would emerge from his first season with predominantly Irish-based mares. He still covered 159 mares in 2007. Indian Haven, the son of Indian Ridge, who was owned by Waterford Hall Stud, had 99 mares visit him at a cost of €6,000 each. Invincible Spirit saw to 185 mares at almost six times that fee.

To get all this together involved a close partnership between the stallion nominations manager and the chief executive. They deployed all the trade tricks to pair fathers with mothers for fine foals and future racers. Yet this was all about to take a back seat. Their work soon became complicated by other factors.

In September, Ms Lynch had just accepted the permanent position of stallion nominations manager. It was then she and Mr Clarke began having an affair.

Mr Clarke was living on the grounds of the Stud with his wife, Monica, and their family. Ms Lynch was also living in one of the Stud's houses. This was on a different part of the campus. The romance between the co-workers continued throughout the 2007 breeding season. It incorporated the calendar of race meetings, sales events and the annual networking extravaganza at Royal Ascot. Colleagues, who did not know what was going on, have said Ms Lynch and Mr Clarke worked exceptionally well together and the company's business benefitted from their partnership. Much later, an internal report into the period said Mr Clarke had also ensured his lover was well looked after while the affair was going on.

"There is no doubt Mr Clarke treated her in an exceptional manner during the period of the affair, authorising and including her in extensive foreign travel and social events connected to the INS," it said.

The Stud's heady year of 2007 was building to its crescendo with the autumnal acrobatics to re-syndicate Invincible Spirit. Then, in the seasonal lull before the transactions really took off, Mr Clarke took a holiday with his wife. When he came back, his personal circumstances changed. It was August, and his relationship with Ms Lynch started to cool.

Around the Stud, the sleeves were rolled up to build for what would be a sustained effort to defy the industry's critics and keep the good times rolling into 2008. In the office at Tully, Ms Lynch was preparing her work for that year's nominations fees. The new syndicate for Invincible Spirit decided his emphatic results justified a jump in his fee from €35,000 to €75,000. This was just below the amount commanded by Indian Ridge at his height. It narrowed the pool of customers who could afford to bring their mares to him.

The Stud was also getting ready to add to its roster. A $6m fee was agreed for an English-based stallion called Jeremy. At that stage, he had earned $462,150 and was about to make a final, and ultimately unsuccessful, bid to end his racing career with a win at the Breeders Cup Mile. As with every autumn, one eye was already on the bookings for its roster the next year. The other was on the outcome of the upcoming sales. The single most significant weather vane for the Stud was Goffs' Orby Sale on October 5th.

In the weeks leading up to it, there were growing fears that the market was about to wobble. It did. The Stud and others witnessed a massive drop in demand for stock at the lower end of the market. But, importantly, the headline figures and the optics remained upbeat. The main reason for this was the podium prices secured by Coolmore and the puffed-up Irish National Stud. Of Coolmore's 191 sales at Goffs, it got an average of €139,005.

The Stud sold 40 lots and got an average of €128,250. There was no doubting what were the main props keeping the market from caving in. A colt from the now deceased, long-time-saviour of the Stud, Indian Ridge, was bought by Charlie Gordon-Watson for €600,000. His chestnut-coloured successor, Invincible Spirit, proved just as bountiful. Of 14 yearlings from the sire, the average price paid was €173,143.

Back at Tully, the rumblings at the lower end of the market were not dwelled on. In a report to the Department, Mr Clarke recognised the danger caused by the overproduction of foals, but said the Stud's higher quality stallions were sounder investments. The wisdom of that policy was disputable. So was the status of his affair with Ms Lynch.

Mr Clarke told an investigator that the relationship was not going on during this period and that he had no recollection of anything happening after he and his wife's holiday in August 2007.

Ms Lynch said differently. She swore an affidavit before Ms Justice Mary Laffoy that said the affair, as it had been going on, did not finish until much later.

"The relationship ended in April 2008 at my instigation when I asked Mr Clarke by text not to contact me anymore at night or at any other time," she said.

That April was settled and sunny; it had been a pleasant spring so far and the Stud was in good spirits.

The first Monday in April brought good news. The debut crop of Elusive City had its first winner in the northern hemisphere. Man River saw off the favourite in France's Prix Morny. This was to add greatly to the value of a stallion that was increasingly becoming a rival to

Invincible Spirit's vaunted status. At no stage did the Stud benefit much from Elusive City's success, because he was only ever a boarder for another firm. But, just as gallops on grass tracks in France could influence Tully's moods, the frantic activity in other fields would begin to impact on its future. This run of events was soon to have terrible ramifications.

That March, international investors rounded on Ireland's richest man, Sean Quinn, in a stock market move which became known as the St Patrick's Day Massacre. For the first time, fund managers around the world not only began to doubt the strength of the Irish banking sector, they began to bet against its survival. Anglo Irish Bank, the go-to lender for the country's developers and property speculators, lost 15 per cent of its value. Although the public did not yet know, the main reason why this happened was because of a substantial stake Mr Quinn had in the bank. He had kept this under the radar. Now it was under attack.

The Stud already had its own exposure to these boom-based sectors. Some of its most reliable customers in the money-spinning years were builders or share dealers. Three days before the stock market massacre, Mr Clarke took two developers to dinner at the Guinea Pig Restaurant in Dalkey to discuss their interest in acquiring shares in one of the company's stallions.

The sinister stock market attack on St Patrick's Day was part of preparations for an all-out investment exodus from the Irish banking sector five months later.

As this desertion developed, Ms Lynch claimed she was also the victim of an equally vindictive turn. This was at the hands of Mr Clarke. Moreover, she said it had begun seven months before the text message she sent in April.

"From September 2007 onwards Mr Clarke began a campaign of victimisation, bullying harassment and humiliation," she said.

In an internal report written by the investigator and former chairman of the Labour Court, Finbarr Flood, she said her treatment at her chief executive's hands was abominable. Mr Clarke denied this. In the same report, he said his former lover was argumentative and unstable. However, his accusation was not aired until a second interview with Mr Flood. Even after the affair ended, the chief executive told the investigator he was totally supportive of her work record.

"He felt she had performed at a level in excess of what the Board had acknowledged and rewarded her for," Mr Flood said.

Soon Ms Lynch would be less concerned about getting a reward from the Board. Instead, she was crying out for its protection from what was happening around her. Despite the texted request Ms Lynch made in April 2008, she still had to work with Mr Clarke. On top of that, they had to travel together.

In March they both went to the Deauville sales in Normandy, staying in the four-star Hotel Royal for four nights at a cost of €2,500 each. Mr Clarke spent €1,450 on a meal at the SHCD restaurant to entertain clients. In May they were at the Irish Thoroughbred Breeders Association dinner at the Keadeen Hotel, where Mr Clarke accepted an award for the success of Invincible Spirit. By then, the racing season had begun in earnest.

Ms Lynch and Mr Clarke went, along with director Pat O'Kelly, to Royal Ascot in June. Again they stayed at the luxurious Pennyhill Park Hotel where five nights of bed, breakfast and individual chauffeur-driven travel cost more than €8,500. It was at this week-long event that Ms Lynch said the affair, which had been dormant for two months, reignited briefly. Then it stopped. But Ms Lynch told Ms Justice Laffoy this did not mean there was a clean break from what had gone on before.

"From August 2008 to December 2008, Mr Clarke sexually assaulted me in the office on numerous occasions and engaged in sexual and other forms of harassment," she told the Court.

A similar allegation had been made to Mr Flood. He was told Mr Clarke had exposed himself in her office. The chief executive denied it and Mr Flood said he did not have enough evidence to decide on what had actually happened.

Another major concern for Ms Lynch at the time was her fear that the bullying tactics were designed to undermine her future career. This included Mr Clarke getting her assistant, Sinead Hyland, to do her work.

"He would withhold information critical to the performance of my duties with the deliberate intent of making [me] look inefficient, particularly with customers and clients of the Irish National Stud.

"This was part of a protracted campaign to discredit [me] and damage my reputation within the industry," she said.

Before Ms Justice Mary Laffoy, company secretary, John McStay, swore that the company had never been made aware of the worst of her claims – that she had been sexually assaulted.

"I say that this is a serious allegation and was never... previously reported to the [us] or put to Mr Clarke," he said.

Mr McStay said the full nature of Ms Lynch's complaints did not come to light until an e-mail was sent by her to the Minister for Agriculture, Brendan Smith, at the end of 2009. Long before that Ms Lynch said that, as a direct result of victimisation, she began to suffer from significant stress and anxiety.

On Monday, August 25th, 2008, she visited Dr Ancilla McGoldrick at the Kildare Medical Centre and was put on a course of anti-depressants. She was also advised to attend counselling. This was the first time in Ms Lynch's life that she had to contemplate such treatment. There was no family history.

On Thursday she returned to work hoping for a reprieve. At this time of year, breeding had stopped. It was time to look at the start of a new sales season. This was a chance for the entire company to look to the next year instead of getting mired in the problems of the past.

If Ms Lynch was hoping that this year would be different, and that her trip to the doctor would be her last, her dreams would not last long. She has testified that on the day she returned to her office, Mr Clarke came in. She said her former lover assaulted and harassed her. Soon even the doctor's help would not be enough.

CHAPTER

10

Everything Goes Wrong

On June 3rd, 2008, key directors of the Irish National Stud gathered at Tully to reflect on the most successful year in its history. They poured over the origins of a profit which was enormous for a company of its size. The text of Lady O'Reilly's report, explaining how the extraordinary year came to pass, was accepted. Her Board also signed off on the language deemed appropriate to inform the public about the multi-million euro profit three people at the table had reaped as part of the Invincible Spirit syndicate.

None of the directors were to know, but the same month would see the final fling in an affair between their chief executive, John Clarke, and their stallion nominations manager, Julie Lynch. On the basis of Chairman Lady O'Reilly's report, they were equally unaware of the scale of the financial firestorm that was now just weeks away.

"The underlying commercial trend in 2007 reflected the years which preceded it.

"Demand at the yearling sales was best described as patchy. Buyers were extremely selective and only those animals who met exacting standards provided a worthwhile commercial return.

"In many ways this is as it should be, as there is undoubtedly still a level of overproduction which, given the current overall economic situation, may lead to further difficulties for breeders in a potentially softening market later this year," Lady O'Reilly said.

Her assessment could have been lifted and easily transplanted into the arguments of many leading economists on the likelihood of a gentle landing in the Irish property market. Those analysts were all wrong. So were Lady O'Reilly and her Board. The market did not just soften. It went into seizure.

When Minister Brendan Smith arrived for the Annual General Meeting three weeks later, he told the company not to be too self-satisfied. He warned it against using large, once-off profits to project big shadows on the wall, when the accounts actually held little to justify long-term optimism.

"I am pleased that the company returned a significant profit before taxation on its 2007 activities. I note, however, that when the profits from once-off activities are stripped out, an operating loss for the year of over €300,000 was incurred.

"I am well aware that trading in shares in mares and stallions is a normal part of the business of any public stud. In this context the fortunes of studs can fluctuate wildly from year to year," he said.

The company knew the heat was coming, but felt it had the wherewithal to endure it. In an e-mail to the Department of Agriculture earlier that month, Mr Clarke expressed a form of upbeat anxiety.

"I would emphasise that in the bloodstock field it is virtually impossible to predict future earnings and profitability as there are so many imponderables.

"The trend is that earnings from fees will increase as the success of Invincible Spirit brings us additional opportunities," he said.

The Stud benefited from the experiences and insight of many of its directors who had a personal interest in ensuring they read the market right. Company secretary, John McStay, was among these and had been the Stud's chief financial advisor for 15 years. His company, McStay Luby, had also handled the firm's accounts. But the industry had become more financially intricate. Mr McStay felt the Stud would benefit from more full-time, in-house expertise.

Just before the AGM, the Board started the quest to recruit a financial controller. This had a direct effect on Mr McStay.

Mr McStay's firm had earned €464,000 from its work for the Stud in the eight years leading up to that advert. It billed for another €24,250 in the six months before the position was filled. This was mostly accounted for by regular annual bills that rose from €23,045 a year in 2000 to €48,450 in 2008. The total sum also included €48,400 for the work Mr McStay had done in the Mullarkey case and €59,895 which he charged to the Invincible Spirit syndicate for helping to manage the Darley investment. He and the company had enjoyed a huge profit on this particular deal. But Mr McStay and the Board knew there would be no such windfalls in 2008.

Lady O'Reilly's report said there was nervousness in international markets. She argued that the company's foundation was still strong. It had the capacity to cover more than 1,000 mares a year. She hoped that the Government would provide more of taxpayers' money to pay for continued investment in stallions. There was still €17m in unused equity that the Finance Minister could buy up at any stage.

The Board also wanted to increase the population around the rest of the yard.

The Stud had 22 broodmares, but a band of 25 had been its target for a number of years. To increase its family, it decided it could use the name and status of the Stud, along with the expertise of Mr Clarke and the Board, to coax additional money directly from the public.

Lady O'Reilly promised to announce an "exciting and innovative" proposal in late 2008. The scheme was akin to the ownership club operated for a time by the British National Stud.

For eight years, the Stud had the ability to set up subsidiary companies but had never seen the need to. A new "Breeders' Club" was to be its first offshoot, and the details were spelled out in a plan sent to the Department three weeks before Mr Smith addressed the June AGM. The Stud said it had been approached on many occasions to set up an investment vehicle to allow enthusiastic novices, small breeders and racing followers to mix their money with the international elite. At last, the company said, it could make its move.

"The Stud has decided with an Irish-based brokerage house to speak to and establish a breeding syndicate to purchase a number of high quality broodmares and fillies, to breed from them and to sell the resulting offspring.

"A syndicate of this nature would serve to raise the profile of the Stud and will give investors the opportunity to participate at the highest level of the breeding industry. The Stud would also be an investor in the syndicate which could potentially be profitable for the Stud," an internal company plan said. The breeders' club would have involved high up-front costs to purchase mares. These would have carried significant risks.

"It would not be an investment for those seeking instant returns but rather for those aware of the high costs of entry at the top level of the industry, seeking to minimise and spread their risk, and benefit from the Irish National Stud's reputation for integrity and expertise," it said.

The plan accepted that the timing of the club's launch would be crucial. The financial climate would need to be favourable. The pace at which disaster bore down on the Stud in the weeks after the AGM ensured that the Breeders' Club idea was stillborn. This, at least, avoided further exposure to a problem the company was already unable to afford.

For a time, investing in stallions was attractive on so many levels. It was tax free. The money spent on these horses could be written off and so could earnings from syndicates. A developer could walk in with a €10m lump sum. He could buy into a proven stallion and sell the nominations his shareholding entitled him to for thousands each – tax free. If it suited, he could sell the shareholding again – tax free. Then, should this man have a mare, he could add greatly to this with the price his yearling could make in the sales' ring – tax free.

The industry became a stomping ground for money men. By 2006 the Goffs' Million Sale, pioneered by Charlie Haughey two decades earlier, was generating gross revenues of almost €60m, a jump of 15 per cent in 12 months. The same year, the total value of thoroughbreds sold in Ireland hit €191m. Like property and banking, Ireland was responsible for a far greater share of an over-stocked market than its size would suggest.

The country was producing 42 per cent of all thoroughbred foals in Europe and had seven out of 10 of the world's top stallions. In early 2004, a complaint was made to the European Commission that the lucrative tax exemption for stud fees and profits, introduced by Mr Haughey in 1969, was anti-competitive. There was a lot of posturing between Dublin and Brussels. A year later, the Commission made the decisive move and ruled that the exemption constituted illegal State-aid. It put the pressure on. Ireland had to back down.

There was no definitive data on the value of the measure. Figures from the Revenue Commissioners in 2006 suggested that at least €90m worth of profits fell into this category, which translated into an effective subsidy from the public to those trading in thoroughbreds. It was worth in excess of €20m in foregone taxes.

On December 7th, 2005, Finance Minister, Brian Cowen, said the bloodstock-boosting exemption would be abolished. But he allowed a sunset period, which meant it stayed in place for three more breeding seasons. The light eventually went out on August 1st, 2008. But if the horse racing industry thought that the loss of its competitive edge was the worst thing that would happen to it that autumn, it was very, very wrong.

Traditionally, there had been a slight lag between property crashes and downfalls in the stallion markets. The summer of 2008 saw the bloodstock business match its speculative sister stride for stride. Throughout August, bankers and consultants were passing each other in the Department of Finance to try to figure out a way to solve the impending banking crisis. Money was leaving Anglo Irish Bank so fast it had only a matter of weeks before it ran out. At any point, Irish Nationwide Building Society was just days from demise.

Then, attempts to keep the ship steady were sunk by a tsunami originating on the other side of the Atlantic Ocean.

It was September 15th when the American banking giant, Lehman Brothers, went bankrupt. Money markets around the world went into convulsions. The American presidential election campaign was put on hold to allow all sides to deal with the crisis. Less than two weeks later, already exposed buyers were asked to dip into their pockets at the most important event on the Irish National Stud's calendar – the Goffs' Orby sale.

This was the premier trading event in Ireland for top-class yearlings and it had traditionally been Tully's preferred market. The Stud had already got into a spot of bother. Legally, it could borrow up to €30m, but could only increase its lines of credit if it had the express approval of the Minister for Agriculture. In August and September, it had gone it alone and borrowed more; the Department was not happy. In a letter to Mr Clarke, which outlined seven areas where officials felt the Stud did not comply with its corporate governance rules, the Department also criticised the failure to get permission before it extended its short-term loans.

"From the returns submitted by McStay Luby last week, the Irish National Stud exceeded its authorized level of bank overdraft in August and September 2008, albeit in a time of extraordinary turbulence.

"The Irish National Stud must put in place measures to ensure it has the requisite borrowing approval in place before proceeding to borrow; the Company must adhere to the provisions set down in legislation," it said.

During those months of August and September, the company would, ordinarily, have been certain that its biggest pay day of the year, the yearlings' sale, would cancel out any short-term overdrafts.

On September 29th, trading at Goffs began. The Board felt it had prepared its best package yet. Unfortunately, the second day of the event just happened to be one of the most important in Irish economic history. After weeks teasing out possibilities, the sands were running out at the Department of Finance. During the day, the share price at Anglo fell 50 per cent. That evening, the Government made the dramatic and irreversible decision to guarantee the entire Irish banking system with a promise to cover €440 billion worth of liabilities. With Fine Gael support, Fianna Fáil and the Green Party went into the Dáil the next day and worked through a measure that allowed the most emphatic possible intervention into the country's financial sector.

Back at Goffs, the Stud was stuck trying to get the best prices for its selection of young well-bred yearlings from undoubtedly proven mares. The company felt it was an "outstanding crop" falling victim to forces outside of its control. A year earlier, the till receipts would have been rolling. This time, the Stud only got half the money it had budgeted for. At the Sportsman-Sale that finished off the week at Goffs, there were fewer horses offered and lower prices paid and turnover for the day was down more than 50 per cent on 2007. Goffs' chief executive, Henry Beeby, had a frank reflection for the *Racing Post*.

"Overall it has been a tough week that coincided with the world financial crisis. The current recession in the Irish property market undoubtedly had a negative influence, with many Irish property developers, who've been such active purchasers in recent years, notably missing from the list of buyers this week.

"This is a problem unique to Ireland. While we've enjoyed their patronage in recent years, we've certainly felt their absence very keenly this week," he said.

There was some activity. This was led by Dermot Weld who bought the last of Indian Ridge's yearlings to come to Goffs. He took this off the Irish National Stud for €75,000. That trade was six times the day's average. It was not nearly enough to stop the shuddering sales week from scaring many people. Publicly, John Clarke was not among them.

"The stud fees are dictated by supply and demand and those stallions who are doing well will stay the same or go up, and those who aren't will have to come down.

"I believe the current situation is just a hiccup and I foresee no major changes. If a breeder has a reasonable mare, they have got to breed from her and by the time they come to offer the progeny in a couple of years hopefully things will be different.

"It was very hard for a sale (Goffs) to buck financial catastrophes outside the industry. Most of the right people were here, but they had less to spend," he said in a contribution to a media analysis of the dismal figures. He was not the only person to hold this opinion. Prominent businessmen, the country's leaders, senior bankers and the money-men who built the boom all appeared to be of the belief it was just a scare. Anglo Irish Bank was so confident of recovery it arranged with Irish Life and Permanent for an overnight transfer of €7.5 billion to massage its accounts to appear healthy enough to ride out the storm. The controversial transaction did nothing to prevent the bank going to the wall three months later. Neither did the proud posturing after the Goffs' sale manage to restore confidence among buyers.

Just seven weeks after the Orby Sale, the bloodstock figures got much worse. At Goffs' November foals' event, turnover was a third of what it had been a year earlier and the average sale price was halved. A colt from Invincible Spirit, sent to the ring by Tully, salvaged some smiles with a nice price in one of the final trades of the event.

There was an underlying worry grating at the bloodstock business. It relied on a small number of key players. These people knew there was a greater chance of the sector falling foul of a collapse in building and banking. Construction income had underpinned the industry for more than a decade. Large investments were secured on the basis of hefty rolling debts. Even people who were not immersed in those exposed areas were still tangled up in other vulnerable pursuits.

Lady O'Reilly, her husband and her family had been behind a €100m rescue attempt for Waterford Wedgewood. But its position was getting precarious. Worst of all, the squeeze was starting to come on the most powerful force in the industry.

In Dubai the lenders behind its architectural playground of imaginative skyscrapers and concept cities were starting to call in their debts. Construction on the world's tallest building, the imitation archipelago of islands fashioned in the shape of the planet, and a host of other standout sites around Dubai came to a stand-still. The principality had a €59 billion debt to rearrange quickly and economic commentators were pessimistic about the prospects for the rest of its liabilities. The saving grace for Dubai was that the oil wealth of Abu Dhabi provided a subtle guarantee to its property price-dependent neighbour.

But the second Dubai got into trouble, a sobering realisation struck – Abu Dhabi's support would have to come at a price. Speculation was that this could lead to a curtailment of Dubai's exuberance in horseracing. Sheikh Mohammed was the ruler of Dubai, the heir behind its innovation and the owner of the Godolphin and Darley breeding enterprises. The wealth he and his brothers in the Maktoum family brought to breeding was the support pole on which the market was pegged.

Since the early 1980s, the Maktoum's outlandish spending had provided a constant injection into the industry at almost every big sales event. Sheikh Mohammed was the single biggest buyer in the thoroughbred market and the most prolific actor in the history of the business. Even the family's protracted dispute with Coolmore served to drive prices up as opposed to down.

When questions started surfacing, Sheikh Mohammed's racing team stressed to whoever asked that horses were a personal indulgence. They were not directly connected to the fortunes of Dubai, in either good times or bad. Even if this was the case, the reassurances could not stop the second-guessing on whether the Maktoum's cheque book would be closed. It was a period when any optimistic financial outlook could not be taken at face value.

An acceptance soon set in that a harsh depression was looming. Within 12 months of the seminal Goffs' sale, the final Million yearlings' event it could afford, even the Stud had begun to sober up.

"A huge amount of our clients would have been people who got in on the Celtic Tiger boom. People in IT and property developers were among the buyers," stallion nominations manager Ms Lynch told Bloomberg. Indeed, the realisation by the wider industry of the trouble it was in happened well before that.

Towards the end of 2008 there was panic among all breeders and studs. There was a dash to cut prices and still try to secure bookings for 2009. A month after it published its 2009 price list, the Irish National Stud released a more attractive redraft. Invincible Spirit's fee was lowered to €50,000, down €10,000 from what the Stud originally thought it would get for him in 2009. It was two-thirds of what he had been valued at the previous year. This cut more than €1m worth of earning potential off him.

His neighbours in the sunlit stallion boxes were also devalued. Celtic Swing had his price cut by 33 per cent to just €4,000 for his final season before he was shipped to Italy. Verglas came down by €2,500. More recent arrivals, Amadeus Wolf and Jeremy, dropped to €8,000.

Once the syndicates and the Board set the prices, it had always been back to Mr Clarke and Ms Lynch to sell the nominations. Invincible Spirit worked out fine at a reduced fee. The new boy, Amadeus Wolf, was not so popular.

It was always desirable to have the books for each stallion finalised by Christmas. So it was typically a frantic few months leading up to the December break. Still, the Stud's efforts to shore up its stallion roster for 2009 just about worked. Between all the stallions, the team managed to ensure there were more than 900 mares booked in to be covered at Tully for 2009. Most of the interest centred around the cheaper sires and Elusive City. This stallion was living at Tully since the demise of the Huma Park Stud. But the semi-State company did not own any part of him.

Lady O'Reilly, her husband Sir Anthony and her brother, Peter Goulandris, were not as successful at keeping the furnaces at Waterford Wedgewood firing through the winter months. In December, it accounted for pre-tax losses of €63m. On January 5th, it blamed the volatile international markets and suspended trading of its shares on the stock exchange. More than 800 workers in Ireland were to be let go.

Similarly, the Government's strategy to keep the banking sector intact through the tempest had become submerged by an onslaught from overseas. Sean Quinn's stake in Anglo and the bank's chronic accounts had failed to convince investors that even a guarantee from the Irish people was enough. The Government admitted its efforts to paper over the cracks had failed.

On January 15th Anglo Irish was sensationally nationalised. The run on the sector had already meant that it brought large portions of Bank of Ireland and AIB with it. On the Thursday the toxic Anglo Irish Bank was nationalised, the poisonous atmosphere in the office at the National Stud also got too much for Julie Lynch. Anxiety forced her to go home from work. After a weekend's reflection she came back to work and decided she could no longer remain quiet. She made her first formal complaint about the chief executive's behaviour to the human resources manager. Two days later, she approached one of the directors, Trevor Stewart. She opened up about the affair and asked for something to be done to stop Mr Clarke's alleged bullying behaviour from repeating itself.

Mr Stewart had been the most recent addition to the Board of Tully. He was an investor in bloodstock and was involved in the Invincible Spirit syndicate. Mr Stewart duly took a note of the conversation and passed it on to the Board. Ms Lynch said that, after this, Lady O'Reilly agreed to meet her. She also claimed the chairman changed her mind and had her chauffeur hand-deliver a letter on January 28th. This explained how the Board wanted to deal with the situation.

The matter was recognised as serious. Concerned by Ms Lynch's admission of an affair with Mr Clarke, the directors had decided to appoint the former chairman of the Labour Court, Finbarr Flood, to mediate between the two senior staff members.

The clean-cut Mr Flood began work as a messenger boy in the Guinness brewery at the age of 14. He climbed the ladder to become the managing director of the St James's Gate facility. The lanky, inner-city Dubliner was a professional footballer in the days before the game got glamorous. In 1998 he was made chairman of the Labour Court and held the post until the end of 2003, during which time he was responsible for restructuring and reforming how it operated. Afterwards, he was made chairman of Shelbourne Football Club at a time when it rose to become league champion and, subsequently, crashed into collapse within the space of a few months.

So, Mr Flood knew all about difficulties and disasters. The Board looked for the benefit of his insight. The former Labour Court chairman sat down with both parties. He had spelled out a full list of the allegations and gave the chief executive a chance to respond. These accusations had suggested Mr Clarke was very difficult to work with, had left Ms Lynch out of essential meetings and did not treat her with respect. They also said his behaviour towards her was not acceptable during 2008 when they travelled to the Milan sales, the Keenland sales, the major Tattersalls' event in Newmarket, the outing in Deauville and when they recommenced their affair at Royal Ascot. At some of these events the travelling party had included Mr Clarke's wife, Monica. It was deemed to be all too much.

"[Ms Lynch] stated she could not take any more of this pressure and that something had to give. She mentioned that she considered resignation and would have to if the situation continued," Mr Flood said. In fact Ms Lynch had already attempted to resign.

"At one point, on or about the 19th of March 2009, I became so stressed that I handed Mr Clarke a letter of resignation.

"I subsequently withdrew this. Mr Clarke exploited this situation by utilising it to accuse me of being mentally unstable.

"He reiterated this accusation on numerous occasions, both to employees, members of the Board, customers and clients of the Irish National Stud," she later told the High Court.

John McStay wrote to the stallion nominations manager as soon as the Board heard of her resignation letter. He told her Mr Flood was investigating the debacle and it was being addressed urgently. This letter also referred to another complaint that Ms Lynch had made. This was against another staff member – the Stud manager, Annette Boland. This was also passed on to Mr Flood for a separate inquiry.

On March 26th Ms Lynch texted Mr McStay and said she was suffering from panic attacks. He asked her to attend the company doctor. Mr McStay said he was concerned because counselling had been offered by Stud but was not taken up. The offer of paid leave was put on the table.

On April 1st Ms Lynch withdrew her resignation and the next day she went back to Dr McGoldrick who certified her fit to return to work. She was also advised to submit a written account of her relationship with Mr Clarke to Mr Flood. This covered her entire time at the company. Separately, Mr Clarke recounted his version of events in writing, but this only spanned the era after the affair ended.

After getting her timeline of trauma to Mr Flood, Ms Lynch began to feel the investigation was going on too long. She said that Mr Clarke had continued to harass her even though their relationship was under scrutiny.

"Despite the Board being aware of this conduct, members such as John McStay and Orla Hennelly of human resources failed to take any action to prevent recurrences.

"I raised the issue with Mr Clarke. I asked for a meeting with the Chairman. Mr Clarke refused my request.

"I further raised the issue with Orla Hennelly to no avail. There was still no indication of when the investigation would conclude, nor was any action proposed to prevent the ongoing bullying or harassment," she testified in Court. Furthermore, she said, Ms Hennelly had put her under pressure to withdraw the accusations she had made against Stud manager, Annette Boland.

Mr McStay said Ms Hennelly was only trying to help and simply passed on a message that Ms Boland wanted to meet and apologise. He also denied that the Board had done little to protect its stallion nominations manager. He said he and other senior personnel were in constant contact with both parties during that time. They had asked Mr Clarke to make sure his behaviour was appropriate, cordial and respectful. But, whatever had been done throughout March and April, in Ms Lynch's mind it was not enough.

The country was in despondent form. That week Finance Minister, Brian Lenihan, had got to his feet for the second time in six months to announce an emergency budget to stop Ireland's own debt crisis becoming terminal. The next day was Ash Wednesday and the public was left to stew over the sad situation it found itself in. Ms Lynch spent the day doing the same.

On Holy Thursday, thirty months after the first signs of romance between Ms Lynch and her boss, she took it upon herself to set the affair on its darkest turn.

"I decided I could take no more," she said, "I had to end the pain."

"I wrote my will and left it in an envelope addressed to my mother under the door of Mr Clarke's office that evening.

"I had to leave it in his office as it was Easter weekend and so that my body would be found and not left undiscovered in my house for a few days."

11

Breaking Point

Julie Lynch recalled swallowing 288 Donormyl sleeping tablets on Holy Thursday, 2009. Beside those were 400 Solpadeine painkillers, which she also planned to take. Fortunately, the Donormyl took hold quickly and she passed out before completing her bid to take her own life. At one stage that night, Ms Lynch roused herself. She tried to call for help. But she was violently ill.

"I was afraid to take the Solpadeine and waited and prayed from then onwards I would live and someone would find me the next day," she said.

She was sick and alone. All around her at Tully her unknowing colleagues had one eye on a race meet in Tipperary. Sualice, running in the President's colours, had been trained by Dermot Weld and was starting her third season after a frustratingly mixed 2008. On saturated ground, the Stud's contender was heavily backed. She started second favourite, under jockey Pat Smullen. Once again, it was not to be Sualice's night. She finished third over a mile and six furlongs.

The next morning was a sunny one across Kildare. It became a bit showery. But there was a mild, spring-time breeze in the air. It was also Good Friday. For many workers it was a down day. In Tully Mr Clarke was in his office. While in there, he mistakenly opened a letter addressed to Julie Lynch's mother. In his hand was Julie Lynch's will. It was lying with other letters on the floor, where she had hoped it would be passed on before the weekend. The chief executive then phoned his long-time friend, John McStay.

Mr McStay said Ms Lynch had been in the office block before Mr Clarke arrived. Still violently ill, she tried to reclaim her will from under the door. After deciding not to take the 400 painkillers, she wanted the letter back. She took another envelope by mistake. The company secretary told the High Court that he and Mr Clarke did everything expected of them that morning to ensure their stallion nominations manager was well.

Ms Lynch testified to the contrary.

"It subsequently transpired that John Clarke had telephoned John McStay, company secretary of the Irish National Stud, early on the morning of April 10th 2009 when he suspected that I had made an attempt to take my life.

"He was informed by John McStay not to call down to my house himself and not to call the emergency services, as it would attract adverse publicity," she said. Instead, Ms Lynch said, an unsuspecting colleague was sent around to check on her.

Mr McStay said this was not done to protect the company. Sending a friend of Ms Lynch's to the house was considered a better way to assess the situation. This woman was asked to try and see Ms Lynch.

"If she did not [get into the house] it was accepted there was a danger [Ms Lynch] had harmed herself and it would be necessary to call the emergency services.

"That friend did visit and reported to Mr Clarke that [Ms Lynch] was 'a bit low, feeling a bit ill' but 'she was going to go to the doctor'. It appears she did not do so until much later in the day," Mr McStay said.

Ms Lynch was due to fly to London on Easter Saturday morning. Because of this, she opted not to go to the doctor. Soon she got worried about her decision and rang Kildare's 24-hour doctor service, KDOC, who told her to go straight to Naas General Hospital. Mr McStay said it was Mr Clarke who sent her the number of KDOC by text message. Ms Lynch said Mr Clarke also tried to call her while she was in hospital. Once Ms Lynch was discharged, she went back to the company GP,

Dr McGoldrick. The doctor said Ms Lynch should take a break from work for two weeks, because of the stress.

Irrespective of the events of Easter weekend, it was a troublesome period for all at Tully. The financial risks it was exposed to became clearer.

Martin Myers' Mountgrange Stud had gone into administration with hefty debts. The semi-State company was owed more than a lot of people on Mr Myers' books – Stg£70,497.

Separately, the Stud had upset one of its best customers. While Ms Lynch was out on sick leave, one of the country's most important breeding operations, Lord Weinstock's Ballymacoll Stud, sent two mares to Tully. The Meath-based Ballymacoll and the Irish National Stud had a close relationship and had been involved in a number of deals together, going back four decades. The business, managed by the well-regarded Peter Reynolds, had intended for one mare, Seeking Kali, to be covered by the expensive and record-breaking Invincible Spirit. Another mare, Mary Stuart, was destined for the less popular, pale grey stallion, Verglas.

En route to the covering shed, there was a €40,000 mix-up. Mary Stuart found herself under Invincible Spirit. Once the stallion had seen to her, there were no more breeding spots available with the star sire. So, his intended target, Seeking Kali, was sent to the lower-grade Verglas. The Stud still charged for the service, although the price commanded by Verglas was five times less than Invincible Spirit's.

After 16 days, Ballymacoll had a pregnancy scan carried out. Mary Stuart did not go into foal with Invincible Spirit. It was left with the outcome of Seeking Kali's quick encounter with Verglas. Fifteen months later, the two studs were still in dispute. Ballymacoll felt aggrieved that, at the very least, a much-reduced option should have been offered for Seeking Kali to visit Invincible Spirit in 2010. The Stud did not think this was necessary.

With all these problems festering, early summer was a time for Lady O'Reilly to begin preparing her yearly chairman's statement. In it, she would have to reflect on a sobering return to losses after the heady profits of 2007. At the end of the accounting year, December 31st, 2008, the company was €2.3m in the hole. There had been a rapid decline in business. The Stud sold all of the yearlings it offered that year. But, in the panicked autumn sales' season, that crop only yielded half the financial harvest the company had been expecting.

At its final board meeting in 2008, the directors had discussed the problems it had encountered collecting cash from breeders hit by the sales slump. Mare owners had been resisting the stallion rates and service fees when Mr Clarke had been out selling for 2009. He was given permission to haggle down the price-list in order to fill the books. Plans were made to take the axe to part of the company's forest stock. Consideration was given to relinquishing the much prized Q Mark for quality, because it was costing too much to achieve. Staff Christmas and work-related bonuses were lowered from 2007 levels. Mr Clarke's own bonus was reviewed by board member, Jim Beecher.

Lady O'Reilly said the calamitous run to the end of 2008 was not the Stud's fault. Her job was to report on the company every 12 months. In addition, like her predecessors in the Tully chair, she was also minded to give an assessment of the prevailing climate right across the bloodstock industry. Lady O'Reilly said the exuberance of the boom would not be corrected quickly.

"As you experience one difficult yearling and foal sales in 2008, two further crops of offspring produced at high cost during better times are already committed to in the production cycle.

"It is equally inevitable that supply will exceed demand for the next two sales seasons," she said. The chairman said the Stud's own stallion business was mixed. There had been a reluctance to breed with Celtic Swing, which amazed her. But there was good news for Elusive City, who was declared Europe's top freshman sire for his first crop of two-year-olds in 2008.

In early 2009, Verglas had a classic winner from his progeny. The runner was called Silver Frost. Lady O'Reilly also reckoned the quality of mares Invincible Spirit covered after his 2006 success, coupled with the improved connections after his re-syndication, would add further fire to his next generation of runners. She guessed it would get even better than his phenomenal first season.

The Stud's patron, Agriculture Minister, Brendan Smith, needed to be convinced. On April 22nd he summoned Lady O'Reilly, John McStay and John Clarke to his Department's headquarters to discuss its potential money troubles. It was 12 days after Julie Lynch had attempted to take an overdose and 251 days before the Minister was to find out about it. The Secretary General of Mr Smith's department, Tom Moran, was also present at that meeting. The company accepted there were already difficulties.

Ireland's commercial courts were swamped by an increasing volume of business people admitting they could not repay loans. The Stud was particularly vulnerable to bad debts. This was because the costs associated with running a stud were front-loaded. Workers had to be paid up front, as did the cost of feed and care.

"The company must await receiving monies owed from asset-rich but cash-poor breeders when they can raise funds.

"It is the view of the company that some of their debtors can't pay at the moment rather than they won't pay," the minutes of the meeting recorded. The Stud said the extent of bad debts would have a "considerable impact" on the 2008 accounts, which were about to be finalised.

"The company is concentrating on collecting as much as possible of all outstanding debt, in some cases this will require allowing additional time for breeders to pay and dealing with each individual breeder on a case-by-case basis," the Minister was told. The delegation from the Stud also conceded that lucrative land sales were no longer an option. This was devastating.

Following the €9.1m sale of 10.55 acres of land at Grey Abbey in 2007, the company had more to offer the market. An additional 18 acres had been nicked off the main farm when the planners plotted the route of the Kildare by-pass. The Stud had lobbied to get this tract re-zoned, to allow houses to be built on it. If a deal could have been arranged before the property crash, the value of the annexed area would have topped €15m. But the opportunity was lost. Instead of the Stud raking in a multi-million euro jackpot, it was looking at seven-figure losses.

By that stage, the Stud knew that its traditional business model was not working. It had been developed on a more prosaic breeding schedule. Mares belonging to customers would live at Tully for anything up to a couple of months, while they were waiting for diary dates with sires. Their owners paid for this lodging.

Very quickly the industry moved to a more conveyor-belt approach. Now, mares were being driven into the yard for coverings and straight back out the gates of Tully afterwards. This denied the Stud extended boarding fees. In 2004, seven out of every ten visiting mares boarded at the Stud. This fell to one in ten in the space of just five years. The Minister was told that the Stud had thought about opening a "stallion station" style of business, to make life easier for mares to use the revolving door. But there were risks about how this would affect international clients.

Lady O'Reilly and Mr McStay had arrived into the boardroom during the miserable cuts and sorry job losses of the early 1990s. John Clarke had been in charge during the same period. Sixteen years later, in conference room 5W of Agriculture House, the trio accepted that staff could again have to suffer for the company's losses.

"[The Stud] has introduced a ban on overtime payments but acknowledged that the Board may have to consider a redundancy programme in order to achieve cost reductions," the minutes said.

That spring was a stormy financial season when claps of thunder could be heard rolling along whatever stretch of the horizon the chairman or her Board were inclined to face. This made them all the more keen to revel in the rousing applause that was starting to surround one of its own sons – Sea the Stars.

Julie Lynch was still on sick leave when the horse shook off the winter cobwebs, and a recent fever, to launch his make-or-break three-year-old campaign. It was May 3rd and John Clarke had travelled to Newmarket in England to do more than witness the horse's first true test. He was at the track to play a prominent role in the day's events.

The Stud's chief executive wore a plain black suit with white shirt and deep red tie. He had gone bald on the top of his head, save for a few light wisps. The tufts along the sides were grey. He still had his dark eyebrows. From the stands, he and tens of thousands of others would have seen Sea the Stars coolly trot into stall number one for the 201st running of the 2,000 Guineas. The horse was left there for two minutes as his fellow competitors were coaxed into spots to his right. The green gates opened.

The bright yellow silks of Sea the Star's jockey, Mick Kinane, stood out from the predominantly bluey hue in the rest of field. At half-way, the tempo lifted. Sea the Stars held his line near the railings. Smoothly, he kept pace along the immaculately manicured track. Two horses, Evasive and Delegator, drifted towards him as he went for the front. It was a distraction. But, with the line approaching, just Delegator was left. He was nose-to-nose with the son of Urban Sea. Mr Kinane nudged his mount. The horse responded. A fistful of dirt was thrown up by his back hooves, as Sea the Stars kicked for the post. Delegator and the rest were left trailing.

Sea the Stars was guided back to the winner's enclosure where the Stud's work nursing and rearing him was rewarded. Mr Clarke was nominated to accept the trophy on behalf of the horse's registered owner, Christopher Tsui.

The colt was to go on to even loftier heights that summer. Mr Clarke and the rest of the Stud watched all the way.

"All connected with the company share the dream of our clients, the Tsui family, that Sea the Stars, who was born and raised at the farm, would prove to be as successful as his illustrious half-brother Galileo.

"The Irish National Stud is proud and privileged to be associated with raising a great champion," said Lady O'Reilly. Lady O'Reilly and her Board could only have imagined what was still to come from Sea the Stars after she wrote those lines. All the while, those directors kept hold of a dream that the Stud would soon benefit because of the titles this horse seemed destined to land.

Ms Lynch was not in the office when Sea the Stars launched his 2009 season. Her sick leave lasted the guts of a month. When she returned to work in the second week of May, she immediately asked for Finbarr Flood's investigation to be hurried.

She met the investigator on May 12th to help him finalise his work. From then on, judgement was in Mr Flood's hands. He completed the job, attached the appendices and handed it to the three-person audit committee on May 19th Ms Lynch and Mr Clarke had to wait another 10 days to find out what he said about them.

First, Ms Lynch was told the details would be passed on to her on May 28th, at a gathering of the company's audit committee. This involved Lady O'Reilly and directors, John Osborne, Jim Beecher and Trevor Stewart. They decided this meeting should take place in a non-threatening environment. It was arranged that it would be held at Lady O'Reilly's mansion which dated from 1717. Her home crowned a Castlemartin Estate made up of 850 acres of Kildare's finest farm land. Ms Lynch asked for permission to bring her mother. Mr McStay said no. He said he was concerned because the details of the report were highly sensitive, and he did not know how much Ms Lynch's mother knew about the episode. The company secretary also felt that he should first ask Lady O'Reilly's permission before inviting somebody who was not connected to the company into her house.

Ms Lynch's mother eventually turned up at Castlemartin's security gates with her daughter and Lady O'Reilly did not make an issue of it. Whether there was delicate information in Finbarr Flood's report, or not, turned out to be irrelevant. The stallion nominations manager expected to get a full copy of Mr Flood's findings that day. Instead, what she got was the briefest possible summary.

"I found the meeting extremely distressing. I was handed a printed page containing only one paragraph of Mr Flood's report in quotation marks," she said. So she demanded the complete report.

She testified before Ms Justice Mary Laffoy that Mr Beecher said at the meeting: "The Flood report is history and today we are moving on from it."

When she insisted on getting a copy, she said Mr Beecher replied: "We will give you a copy of the report when and if we feel like it and keep this up and you won't ever see it."

Mr McStay said the Board never intended to give Ms Lynch the report, because it was still in the hands of the audit committee. Ms Lynch left Castlemartin upset, angry and without the findings of the inquiry carried out into her complaints. She had also been told the Board wanted to bring in a facilitator, to help the two senior members of the management team work together.

That evening she went to the races at Leopardstown. There, she bumped into the Stud's chief executive. He had also been a principal subject of the Flood Report.

"I attempted to be cordial in an effort to demonstrate that I was willing to seek, together with a facilitator, to find a means of working together. It was clear Mr Clarke was not so willing in any way," she said. Ms Lynch met Mr Beecher at the same race meet. But she did not raise what went on earlier in the day. She did e-mail him 24 hours later to thank him for being patient with her, even though she had gotten "more and more distressed".

The morning after the races Ms Lynch looked for a private meeting with Lady O'Reilly to explain her position. She made the journey back to Castlemartin.

"I informed her in detail of the bullying and victimisation that I had been subjected to. I indicated the effect it was having and that it had led to my attempted suicide.

"[Lady O'Reilly] expressed concern Mr Clarke would lose his pension and have nothing to live on should he be dismissed.

"It was clear to me from that meeting that the chairman's main concern lay with protecting Mr Clarke and ensuring that the Board did not become aware of Mr Flood's findings in respect of his conduct," she said. Mr McStay said the comment about the chief executive's pension was not meant as a major point of principle.

"[Lady O'Reilly] did indicate that Mr Clarke would have a modest pension were he to leave the employment of the company but that comment was incidental to the thrust of the entire discussion.

"At the meeting Lady O'Reilly became concerned as [Ms Lynch] had with her a bag of drugs and she explained what each drug was for.

"She provided considerable detail of the suicide attempt to such an extent that Lady O'Reilly was very concerned for her welfare," he told the High Court.

By the end of the meeting the chairman had suggested that the stallion nominations manager take time off work. But Ms Lynch was still determined to at least catch sight of what Mr Flood had recommended. She made a number of phone calls that day. She received a number of refusals.

Eventually, the full Flood Report was e-mailed to both her and Mr Clarke. In it was a damning vindication of her claims that her chief executive bullied her.

Mr Flood was as experienced as anybody in the realm of labour relations. His assessment was that the ending of the affair had a dramatic effect on the two people involved. He reckoned this was because it had become a big problem within Mr Clarke's home on the grounds of the Stud.

Mr Clarke had lived at Tully House with his wife, Monica, since he joined the company. The five-bedroomed bungalow, extended in the late 1990s, had been renovated in stages in recent times. First built in 1970, the house was smack-bang in the middle of the complex. The side gate was just yards from the visitors' centre. A high, thick hedge gave the manager some privacy. The location of the house gave Mr Clarke the shortest possible clockwise commute to the mare and foals' paddocks, his office block, the stallion boxes behind it, the horse museum, the foaling unit, the Sun Chariot yard for expecting mares and the visitors' centre.

A number of the Stud's staff also lived on-site. Their presence gave an extra layer of protection and it meant that their necessary skills were at the ready for late-night deliveries during foaling season.

Ms Lynch was among the workers who resided on the campus, although her house was in a different area. This meant she was still living close to Mr Clarke and his wife, Monica. The Flood Report said the relationship between the two women had been particularly strained after the affair ended. Ms Lynch had confronted the Clarkes at Dublin airport in December 2008. Still, the Clarkes and Ms Lynch had to travel to the same international sales and racing events for the Stud. This was made worse because the entire debacle was well-known in what was a tightly-knit and gossip-hungry industry.

Finbarr Flood said that, when things changed in Mr Clarke's home, in August 2007, his attitude towards his former lover altered.

"It would appear that as a result of pressure on Mr Clarke, Ms Lynch was treated to repeated inappropriate behaviour, direct and indirect, that would have to be regarded as undermining her.

"While this was due to the personal, rather than work situation, this bullying treatment certainly humiliated, intimidated and belittled her leaving her extremely upset," he said.

Mr Flood did not make any finding on the allegation of sexual harassment, because he did not have enough evidence. However, the former Labour Court chairman did contest the general view that what had gone on only affected those involved. Mr Flood said both of the people he investigated insisted their problems had not contaminated other sections of the operation, and that the business of the company had not been compromised. However, Mr Flood maintained it had spilled over to impact on the work of office manager, Eileen Kavanagh, human resources manager, Orla Hennelly, and the company secretary, Mr McStay.

"A significant amount of time has been taken in dealing with the problem on an ongoing basis.

"There has been a significant involvement of senior management and, in recent times, the chairman and directors of the organisation.

"There is also the damage done to the Irish National Stud by virtue of the fact this problem seems to be fairly well known throughout the business," he said.

Mr Flood said the fallout was much worse than the Stud appreciated. After the first Castlemartin meeting, the directors decided the best course of action was to appoint a facilitator to help everybody to work without conflict. Both Ms Lynch and Mr Clarke expressed the view that this approach could work. So, the Board turned to John Malone.

He was a former secretary general at the Department of Agriculture and, thereby, Mr Beecher's ex-boss. Since his retirement, he had gained valuable hands-on experience of dealing with personnel allegations when they threatened to cripple State-sponsored companies. In 2006, he was asked to report on 50 allegations of bullying and mismanagement made against the then president of University College Cork, Gerry Wrixon.

Mr Malone's report, published in 2007, said only some of the allegations stacked up and those that did were too minor to justify a separate investigation by Education Minister, Mary Hanafin. However, even with Mr Malone's know-how, Mr Flood's report prophetically said that any facilitation strategy at Tully would not work.

"Given the background to this case and the way it has developed over the last few months, I do not believe that it is possible for the two parties involved – Mr Clarke and Ms Lynch – to work together for the Irish National Stud," he said.

Ms Lynch told the High Court that, despite the troubling contents of Mr Flood's report, her chief executive's behaviour did not improve.

"He became progressively more obstructive of my work and undermining of my position.

"In particular he was determined to delegate functions which were mine to the management assistant working under me. He also sought to promote her to clients and customers of the Stud as being the stallion nominations manager," she said. Her perceived treatment by the Board also failed to improve in the immediate aftermath of the Flood Report's circulation.

First of all, she had her tickets for the Epsom Derby cancelled, the day before she was due to travel. This was in early June and Sea the Stars was bidding to complete a once-in-20-years event, by adding the Derby to his 2,000 Guineas success.

The company began to focus on Ms Lynch's health. It asked her to see certain psychiatric doctors in Dublin and Kildare. On June 26th Mr Beecher wrote another letter to Ms Lynch to tell her the company had made an appointment for her to see a psychiatrist. Ms Lynch said she went to two doctors to certify she was fit to work. She said initially the only response from the Board was a letter from Mr Beecher threatening her with disciplinary action if she turned up at the office. She was worried that the longer she was absent from work, the more others in the industry would think she was unable for the job.

The company said the fact she had attempted suicide since the initial assessment, had changed the early medical advice. The company began to demand that, for her to return from sick leave, she would have to produce further medical reports. It suggested when she did come back to the office, there would be a facilitator there to bring clarity to everybody's role. This person would also police the requirement for mutual respect in the office.

A dispute about the appropriateness of the doctors and the advice they provided continued between Ms Lynch and the Board for eight more months. She eventually decided it could not be resolved. So she went to the High Court in an attempt to keep her €60,000-a-year job intact.

The outcome for Mr Clarke was different. Mr McStay said the Stud had intended to discipline him. But this was put off because the chief executive told the Board he was suffering from stress.

Soon the Board felt that such action was no longer necessary. This was because Mr Clarke informed them that he would shortly leave his €129,550-a-year post at Tully. The Board had already been involved in lengthy discussions with the Department, and in turn the Department of Finance, to work out how he could depart. The company told the Department it wanted to secure his retirement and, to do so, it worked out a package with him. But documents released to the *Irish Examiner* showed that officials said this was not acceptable. Instead the Board offered Mr Clarke consultancy work after he left. But he rejected this as inadequate.

Mr McStay told the Department a better arrangement would have to be worked out or they would not encourage the CEO to leave. "His 'proposed' departure is subject to the final agreement on the terms which will be sanctioned by the Department. If we cannot reach an agreement soon, the Board will 'persuade' Mr Clarke to remain on," he said.

The Department was made aware of internal human relations problems involving Mr Clarke but the secretary general advised that this would have "no relevance in the Minister's consideration" of the deal. In the meantime Mr McStay and Department agreed that, on the basis of legal advice, Mr Clarke was effectively due four pay rises which had not been sanctioned because of a technical dispute over his contract. This meant he could claim the backdated amounts and his salary would rise from the 2007 level €104,668 to €129,550. He was also paid compensation from holidays he did not have the chance to take in 2009. It proved acceptable to all parties. Mr Clarke wanted a new challenge and took his early retirement.

He took with him his 27 years of experience, international contacts and a special link to the brightest star in the world of racing.

CHAPTER
12

Promise Emerges from the Past

A cocktail of bankruptcy, bitter business and bad luck brought the Irish National Stud its most spectacular boarder. She stayed until 10 days after her 20th birthday.

Until that day, and since, she helped beam the Stud's brand around the globe and link its name to the sport's most brilliant star. As a filly she crossed continents, grafting a career on the track. Afterwards she was shipped from stud to stud to share her special genes with the best working stallions in the world. Hers was a fairytale and a tragedy, which ended months before her already lofty legend reached its zenith.

It began with a gregarious, middle-aged Frenchman. Just above medium height, with dark wavy hair, he had an eye for promise and a fate that destined him to ill-fortune.

Jean Lesbordes ran a small-scale training yard and stud in Normandy during the late 1980s. He had moved himself into the trade from a family connected to workhorses in the vineyards around Bordeaux. The circumstances which paired him with a horse, later to be named Urban Sea, were typically chaotic.

At the time, Japan's stallion industry was in frenzy. From the land of the rising sun, an art dealer arrived in France with a dream of winning the prestigious Prix de l'Arc de Triomphe. He had 10 million francs and no idea what to spend it on.

Mr Lesbordes was brought on board to scour the markets and sales rings for year-old horses with potential. In a latter-day interview with

Paris' *La Liberation* newspaper, Mr Lesbordes said he happened across a placid, but steely-eyed, filly. A stretched white diamond, a hallmark she had inherited from her mother, Algeretta, sat between her eyes. It broke an otherwise perfect chestnut coat. She had been born in Kentucky a year earlier at Paul de Mossac's Marystead Stud. There was good breeding in her.

Mr Lesbordes took to her immediately. At the top sales event, Deauville, he bid 280,000 francs [€55,000]. It was a third of what he was willing to pay for the filly. On the day, it was enough to bring her home. She would have been oblivious, but it was a helter-skelter time. Many in the industry were struggling to survive. Inevitably, the collapse of Japan's inflated, property-based economy crashed against the Lesbordes training stables in Chantilly. The east-Asian money-man, who had sent Mr Lesbordes searching the sales rings, had gone bust. The stock was transferred to a partnership of Hong Kong businessman, David Tsui, and Lillian Oung.

The prized filly, Urban Sea, had yet to stretch her legs when a friend of Mr Lesbordes' introduced him to Mr Tsui's wife, the shrewd business-woman Ling Tsui.

Over the years, Mrs Tsui and her family have kept a thin veil of secrecy around the family business which is generally, and loosely, described as real estate, manufacturing and international trading. But they had, and have, money.

In 1990 Mrs Tsui, a young and successful mother of two, had been doing business with a satellite company in France, Matra. Its chairman, Jean Luc Lagardere, was a horseracing nut. He invited her to Longchamp where she caught the bug. When the floating bloodstock at the Lesbordes yard became available, Mrs Tsui seized on the opportunity to get involved.

Her husband, David Tsui, went over with a team to check out the stock. They were pleased with the product. The horses were retained and, in 1992, they bought out Mr Tsui's business partner for 3,000,000 French francs at the Goff's Arc Sale.

Mrs Tsui was most passionate about the family's foray into racing. She studied pedigrees and breeding patterns. She soaked up the soundings from the yard and learned all she could from a horse she instinctively believed could win the Prix de l'Arc de Triomphe.

The Tsuis' son, Christopher, was studying in Paris. He was 10 years' old. At weekends, he went to Mr Lesbordes' stable where he first met Urban Sea as she rested in her box. Using the likes of Urban Sea, the French trainer taught Christopher and his sister, Christine, to ride horses. Their father learned the same way. Mr Lesbordes' son, Clément, was Urban Sea's rider for her daily gallops. The tall, thin understudy watched the horse, prepared her and minded her. When she travelled, Clément was known to take a hammock and sleep in Urban Sea's stable.

Over the years, Mrs Tsui displayed a habit of picking and trusting loyal officers in Europe to help manage her growing passion for bloodstock. Even among this mixed bag of lieutenants, Mr Lesbordes had a special place. Urban Sea was their special endeavour.

In 1991, the promising two-year-old won her first race. The next season she ran seven times, winning twice in lower-grade events. In the search for success, she was shipped to Dusseldorf in Germany, where Mick Kinane, who would feature strongly in the family's future, rode her once. Then she went to California and Canada.

In March of the next year she was on the road again, and she won. This was followed by two more mediocre performances in Hong Kong and France. There was a second place in the Prince of Wales stakes at Ascot. In July and August she rediscovered form on French soil. But there were scant signs in her racing career to suggest that the faith Jean Lesbordes and the Tsuis showed in her was justified. Nothing she had achieved could convince anybody that the first weekend of October in 1993 would define her legacy.

Her task was to gallop faster than any other horse around a 1½ mile track to claim the Prix de l'Arc de Triomphe, the biggest prize in European racing.

All day the clouds hung grimly over the Hippodrome de Longchamp. The ground was sodden. A sweet-natured Urban Sea had been paired with the 28-year-old Eric Saint-Martin. It was an uninspiring duo. Punters lost interest. The odds bookies gave for them winning the race drifted out the closer it got to the off. She began at 37/1.

Urban Sea's record was drab. And Mr Saint-Martin was a forgotten, former new hope for French racing who had never lived up to the public's wild expectations. His father was a legend. Four times Yves Saint-Martin had won Europe's top race around the same circuit on the banks of the River Seine. He was his nation's favourite jockey. Eric had raced alongside his father, and lost. Later he had successes, but nothing near enough to satisfy the ambitions for him.

Cash Asmussen, the lauded American rider who won the race two years earlier, had been taken off the Tsuis' entry. So Mr Saint-Martin slipped into the family's canary yellow racing top, adorned with its broad purple stripe. He strapped on the matching purple hat with its big bright yellow star.

Urban Sea was a cool animal and innately able for one of the most intimidating parade rings in racing, the steep rising gallery wedged with an unforgiving Parisian crowd. Others were not as well-equipped.

Award-winning American racing writer, Bill Christine, recalled how Mr Tsui was new to racing and only laid a small wager to avoid bringing bad luck. Mrs Tsui stayed away from the track altogether. It all mattered little once the green gates opened shortly after 4.30pm.

Urban Sea and Saint-Martin started slowly. When they turned right, into Longchamp's sweeping final straight, Mr Saint-Martin was still elbowing for space in the crowd. The hotly-tipped Opera House and lesser-light White Muzzle made their break for the front. Urban Sea was penned in along the rails. But she stayed steady. She kept in touch, just. Then, as others faded, Mr Saint-Martin spotted a gap. He snapped the whip with his right hand. Urban Sea kicked her legs to sneak ahead on the right-hand side of the two leaders. The commentators barely noticed the blazing yellow silks of Mr Saint-Martin when he made his move. With 29 strides to the post, the Kentucky-born mare nudged in front. Fourteen strides from the line, she was a length clear. White Muzzle scrambled to catch up and made progress. Mr Saint-Martin, whip now in the left hand, cracked his mount towards the line. It proved to be enough. Urban Sea, quickly derided as the worst horse to win the great race, had shown the speed and stamina needed to beat the best on show.

Jean Lesbordes broke down in tears. Clément lost his voice. As he crossed the line, Mr Saint-Martin's thoughts turned to his father.

Mr Saint-Martin senior was there to greet him in the winners' enclosure. For the first time in 10 years of racing, Eric did not feel embarrassed by people taking pictures of him.

"I don't know if I am ever going to be a king like him [his father], but I have won the big one. Now I have money to pay some rent," he said.

For the photo, Eric Saint-Martin stood beaming with the trophy. Behind him, Mr Lesbordes, in a long, dark overcoat and brown fedora hat, held his own prize aloft. Visible behind Mr Lesbordes' left shoulder was the slender 12-year-old Christopher Tsui in a red blazer, matching tie and thick-rimmed red spectacles. His fresh-faced father shared in the smiles behind a pair of large, dark shades. Sixteen years later, Christopher said that that afternoon was still emblazoned in his memory.

Neither horse, nor rider, nor trainer, repeated that phenomenal feat. Mr Saint-Martin had a good career, but never matched his father's exploits. He and Urban Sea returned to the track in 1994. They won, in typically bolshie fashion. But the horse only raced twice more. A fetlock injury dashed her hopes of repeating the success at Longchamp.

It was to prove incidental. Mrs Tsui had fallen for Urban Sea and had another career in mind. The filly was retired to Mr Lesbordes' yard to mate. At weekends, Christopher Tsui visited her from school. As a youngster, he considered Urban Sea as much a family pet as a prized asset.

"I grew up with Urban Sea and it was unbelievable to own her. She was very quiet, good tempered, brave and determined to win.

"My mother considered Urban Sea a goddess; as all the Chinese Emperors used to say 'when you get a good horse, you get the country'," he said.

Genetics has always been the essence of bloodstock and Urban Sea had to prove there was more to her Prix de l'Arc win than a good run against a bad field.

In the spring of 1995, she was pregnant for the first time. A year later her first son, Urban Ocean, was born. He raced in the Tsui family colours, sprinting to success and drawing worldwide attention to the genes his mother carried.

The value of future progeny from the Tsui's special mare rose exponentially. In 1998 her filly, Melikah, sold for Stg950,000, a record price at France's Deauville sales for a horse of her age. But the international trends were against the Tsuis' 50 horses living at the Normandy stud and the prospects were no better for the stable's doyenne. Fortunately, by that time Mrs Tsui had let in another key advisor, Brian Grassick.

The Irish bloodstock agent told her she was not making the most of her assets. According to Mrs Tsui, Mr Grassick convinced her to relocate away from France. He said the farm had too many poor-quality mares and she would be better served ditching the make-weights. The idea was to buy younger, and better bred, mares in Ireland where the highest class animals were available. So she did.

The substandard stock was flogged and the best moved to Ireland. Urban Sea was readied for the premier stallions on the planet. For these, there was really only one stud farm the mare could go to – Coolmore.

At the time, the Irish stallion nominations' market was estimated to be worth IR£28m. The monstrous Coolmore stud was responsible for 73 per cent of that. Coolmore and the Tsui stable appeared the perfect union.

Everything the matriarch of the Tsui operation had achieved by investing in her belief in one mare, and the bloodlines of her mother, was preceded by the acumen of Coolmore's patriarch, Vincent O'Brien, and a stallion he had found nearly three decades earlier. At that time, the masterful and controversial Mr O'Brien had travelled to the Windfield stables in Ontario, Canada on behalf of the millionaire minerals' mogul, Charles Englehard. There was a horse there that Mr O'Brien was supposed to look at. But the Tipperary-based Corkman was not impressed. Instead, he urged Mr Englehard to sign over a record $84,000 for an untried yearling.

The horse was called Nijinsky. He grew up to be a peerless animal, blitzing the racing circuit in 1970. But he was only a signpost. Mr O'Brien was just as interested in his heritage and his father, the Kentucky Derby-winning Northern Dancer. In time, he became one of the most influential animals in bloodstock history.

Mr Englehard died and Mr O'Brien went into the stud business himself for the first time. He was joined by a family friend, his son-in-law, John Magnier, who dreamed up the idea of raiding the American sales' rings for the best horses on Northern Dancer's family tree. The two men were partnered with the British money-man, Robert Sangster. Their cavalier actions drove prices up. The trio reaped the rewards.

By the time Northern Dancer turned 20, the syndicate which owned him rejected a takeover bid of $20m. The blitzkrieg on Northern Dancer stock, coupled with the lucrative Irish tax breaks, introduced the year after Nijinsky came to Ireland, helped the Coolmore team to build a global empire. They bred with stallions more often, and cornered the market for the best DNA. The aggressive nature of their acquisitions attracted enmity. As a result of their antics, the posse was daubed "Sangster's Gangsters". It all worked in their favour.

The heated exchanges served to stoke up prices in a market they already dominated. When the Arab investors arrived in earnest in the mid-1980s, they outbid Sangster's Gangsters and paid $10.2m for

Snaafi Dancer. The horse was a scrawny, untried one-year-old but, crucially, he was also among the last of the unrivalled Northern Dancer line.

By the mid-1990s, the limelight around Coolmore had moved to the superb sire, Sadler's Wells. In April 1997, this was the beast Urban Sea was sent to be covered by. History has since proved the stars aligned themselves perfectly for the mating pair. But, at the same time, the lights went out for Mr Jean Lesbordes.

In Normandy, 24-year-old Clément Lesbordes, who shared more with Urban Sea than any other person, was out cycling. A rider at the yard had been injured and a small group cycled to get treatment. En route, the front wheel of Clément's bike clipped the one in front of him. He wobbled, swerved out onto the road and hit an oncoming truck. He died instantly.

The immensely popular Jean Lesbordes watched his world fall apart. It was a heavy loss for all involved in a project guided as much by emotion as by evidence.

Mrs Tsui and her husband were not steeped in horse racing. But Ling Tsui had been a quick and shrewd learner. She had faith in Urban Sea. She wanted to remain a part of the mare's success.

The Tsuis entered a foal-sharing arrangement with Coolmore's front company, Orpendale. Three years later, the marriage had produced the greatest colt among his peers. Galileo, the horse conceived the month Clément died, was a phenomenon. Yet, no sooner had he blossomed than the Tsuis and Coolmore started to drift apart again. Neither side has ever explained why. But, as part of the distancing, the Tsuis pulled their mares from the Tipperary stud.

Galileo was the standout success of the short-lived breeding synergy. At birth he had been registered jointly in the name of the Tsuis and Orpendale. The shared-ownership system did not last long. By the time Galileo debuted as a two-year-old, the Tsuis had moved off his ticket. The colt's owner was listed as Mr O'Brien's daughter and Mr Magnier's wife, Susan Magnier.

The Tsuis had sold their interest in Galileo for a reputed £400,000. Some close to the deal believed this price at least suggested the Hong Kong family underestimated the colt's ability early on. Until that sole excursion in Susan Magnier's name, Galileo was sheltered from public scrutiny.

It was October before he raced. Little was known about him. But his pedigree, the son of Urban Sea and the consistently brilliant Sadler's Wells, made him an automatic favourite. He eased home on a rain-soaked Leopardstown with the length of two articulated trucks to spare.

He returned to race the following April. This time, the owners were listed as Mrs Magnier and Coolmore's business associate, Michael Tabor, the Monte Carlo resident who was cash-rich after selling 114 betting shops across Britain.

Galileo's exploits that summer led to hysteria. Mick Kinane, who had ridden Urban Sea once in 1992, was so desperate to stay on his saddle that he went to the High Court to block a two-day riding ban, which would have stopped him steering Galileo around Ascot. Together, jockey and colt won the Epsom English Derby in June by a margin that made a mockery of the opposition. Galileo was defying the doubters with every outing.

On July 1st a handler picked up a clutch of grass to wipe the sweat off a horse appearing to badly overheat. It was moments before the start of the Irish Derby. Two minutes and 26 seconds later, the horse had become the second fastest winner in the history of the Curragh's most lucrative race. He was only the 14th horse ever to win the English-Irish derby double. The racing world was enthralled.

Mr Tabor gushed that his new acquisition was "something to savour". The three-year-old was hailed as one of the greats even before his racing campaign petered out with a sixth-place finish at Belmont in America. The question asked was whether it had all come as a surprise. The words of Galileo's trainer, Aidan O'Brien, suggested it had not.

On that July afternoon in the Curragh, Mr O'Brien said Galileo's pedigree was never in doubt. He said that, since the son of Sadler's

Wells was a foal, "he had a great presence about him and that has just grown".

"It's just a matter of keeping him in one piece. We always knew he was a serious horse and you just have to hope it happens and goes well on the day."

The Tsuis had missed out on a jaw-dropping return. There would have been a share of Galileo's £1.6m race earnings. Then there were the millions he generated siring 61 individual winners who together took home €2.9m in the five years after his first crop began racing. On top of that there was the lucrative access to him which has since seen Coolmore's mares give birth to another generation of exceptional racehorses.

But, by 2002 when the retired Galileo was training to start his first season at stud, the Tsuis had decided to step back from the foal-sharing partnership with Coolmore. The mechanics of the Galileo arrangement was as much history as it was a mystery.

Mrs Tsui and her son, Christopher, have frequently been quoted bemoaning the difficulties of running their Sunderland Holdings outfit from eight time zones away. They have praised their small band of loyal lieutenants who acted as middlemen until Christopher grew old enough to take more control. Both they, and the industrial-sized Coolmore clique, knew the value of a good prospect. Not long after its outright takeover of Galileo, Coolmore spent $70m on the successful racer, but unproven sire, Fusaichi Pegasus.

The Tsuis and Coolmore were also to learn that the worth of Urban Sea was not fleeting. A year after Galileo wowed the world, her second son from Sadler's Wells, Black Sam Bellamy, was winning as well.

Following Galileo's scintillating season, Urban Sea bred once more with Sadler's Wells. But hopes of replicating the success of Galileo were dashed when she did not produce a foal. By that stage the Tsuis had decided it was time to move away from Tipperary. When Mrs Tsui opted to relocate her beloved Urban Sea, Brian Grassick was again on hand to advise her.

Taking such a horse was difficult for a lot of studs. There would have been security concerns and fears it would upset the mighty Coolmore. The Irish National Stud was suitably neutral and adequately equipped. Mr Grassick sounded out the deal and Urban Sea was soon sheltered at Tully.

The Stud's then chief executive, John Clarke, quickly struck up a close business relationship with Mrs Tsui. He became her spokesman on occasions and, later, would leave his job to advise the family's breeding business.

Mr Clarke has denied any knowledge of the reason for the separation between Coolmore and the Tsuis' Sunderland Holdings. He was not involved at the time, but he pointed to the repeat business Mrs Tsui has given to Coolmore, by sending mares to its stallions, as evidence the split was not as acrimonious as people make out.

"I don't know what that [the split] was about. But I do know Ling Tsui has sent mares to Galileo every year. She remains a client of Coolmore, Darley and the Irish National Stud," he said.

The Sunderland Holdings shift meant that, when it came to the latter part of Urban Sea's career, the Tsuis were in complete control. There was no sharing arrangement involved with her final foal born with a Coolmore sire. That was with the stallion, Giant's Causeway. When this filly foal was put on the market in 2002, at the December Tattersalls' sales, the Tsuis were the sole beneficiaries. It was the Irish National Stud, through Mr Clarke, that organised the deal.

This filly had spent her early months at Tully and had obviously impressed, despite a slightly awkward step on her. Two of the main bidders, in a frantic tit-for-tat conducted by Tattersalls' chairman, Edmond Mahony, were directors of the Stud: Pat O'Kelly and Lady Chryss O'Reilly. They scrapped it out with a corps of cash-is-no-object buyers in the ring.

Lady O'Reilly's stud manager, James Kelly, got in early. Coolmore made a fleeting attempt to compete, when the figure nudged towards £1m. But that was not even entertained because it coincided with another offer. Mr Kelly threw out a whopping bid of £1.8m at one stage. But the American heiress to the Campbell's Soup empire, Charlotte Weber, was more determined. Michael Youngs, the representative of Ms Weber's Florida-based Live Oak Stud, laid down the final pitch of £1.9m. It was a world record.

Mr Youngs said the temptation to trade was not inspired by the filly's father but, rather, her mother, Urban Sea. "I couldn't find a dirt performer in the female family." The Stud was chuffed with the success of its new business partner. "The owner and I are delighted Michael got her. She vetted extraordinarily well and was a collector's item," Mr Clarke said just after the hammer came down. Flush with success, the Tsuis directed Urban Sea at stallions owned by Darley's boss Sheikh Mohammad instead.

Coincidently, the ruler of Dubai had been in an ongoing and bitter feud with Coolmore. At various stages, he refused to bid on Coolmore stock in the sales' rings, so his enormous buying power would not unduly inflate the Tipperary stud's profits. Yet, second to Coolmore, he had the best animals in Ireland for Urban Sea to be covered by.

Twice, she was sent to the Maktoum's anchor-stallion, Green Desert. In 2005, owing to the gut instinct of Mrs Tsui overriding all other counsel, Urban Sea made her most successful journey yet. This was to the until-then maligned son of Green Desert – Cape Cross. The result was a strong, heavy and well-shaped foal. The Tsuis called him Sea the Stars. To help establish Christopher Tsui as the centre of their thoroughbred business, his parents nominated him as the owner of their new racer.

The 27 year-old's first racehorse did not hit the track. He transformed it. Sea the Stars' speed and stamina culminated in a stunning victory in the same famous race that his mother clinched 16 years earlier.

In October 2009, Sea the Stars trotted, as his mother had done, towards the winners' enclosure at Longchamp. Christopher Tsui rushed through the crowd to greet him. All the while, the eager hand of one balding 64-year-old man remained gripped to his right shoulder. It was Jean Lesbordes in a fedora hat dashing after him. The Frenchman said the young Mr Tsui was like a god-son. Although the years since they had last stood with the trophy at Longchamp had treated the two friends very differently.

The polite and delicate-looking Christopher Tsui had chased his dreams. He qualified for the Canadian professional golfers' tour in 2003. He failed to make the cut, or even hole a birdie, in his three tournaments. Yet the ability to emerge from the ranks was still a remarkable feat.

He lived on the same secure Florida housing estate as his most famous competitor, Tiger Woods. He studied for a master's degree in business in London. He returned home to Hong Kong. With college friends he established a night club on the former colony's Causeway Bay. In tandem, he took an increasingly active part in the management of his family's broader business.

Meanwhile, Mr Lesbordes had lost his son, and a lot more. Just after retiring, his main jockey, Didier Mescam, was training a horse when he was killed in a fall. Soon afterwards, Mr Lesbordes' business floundered. He decided to cut his losses. Mrs Tsui was there to help.

"I was burnt out, tired, worn out. Continue? For whom? With the death of my son, I lost an arm. Again, if I am here today in this office, it is thanks to Mrs Tsui.

"She advised me to declare myself bankrupt. She invited me to come to rest at her place in Vancouver," Mr Lesbordes said. He followed her advice and recomposed himself.

He got a job writing for France's horse racing paper, *Paris Turf*.

"It has been a terribly emotional period and an unforgettable experience to be so close to the Tsuis and their great champion," he said.

Mr Lesbordes felt that when Sea the Stars emerged from the crowd to win the Prix de l'Arc his son, Clément, was looking down from heaven. Alongside him was his favourite horse, Urban Sea, to witness her son repeat her achievement.

Urban Sea did not live long enough to enjoy the praise heaped on her. On March 2nd, 2009, she was carrying a foal from the Irish National Stud's great stallion, Invincible Spirit. First, Mr Clarke phoned Hong Kong to tell Mrs Tsui that her new foal had been born healthy. He reassured the anxious businesswoman she could go to sleep. Moments later, the 20-year-old chestnut mare took a turn. She haemorrhaged badly.

Urban Sea rose up to lick her new son clean. She could not stay standing. The vessel for the Tsui's 20-year odyssey lay down lifelessly on the floor of the Tully foaling unit. Her last son was orphaned and nicknamed "Reborn". Her second last foal, Sea the Stars, was still two months away from his first classic race.

He had been born in the same secure section of the Stud. Tully's workers had been there to rear him. They taught him to walk properly and prepared him for training. That was during more carefree seasons. Now the company was bleeding money, losing its strength and struggling to stay upright.

That spring the Stud looked longingly at its son, Sea the Stars, with an awareness of what he could achieve on the track. With this came a belief that he would soon return to Tully to stand as a stallion and anchor a new era of financial security.

Late on that March night, John Clarke had to put the phone down after passing on the news that the darling Urban Sea had not survived. As he did so, all at the Stud shared in the hope that the spirit of the great mare would soon be restored and that the Tsuis would decide to allow her son to come back and live at his first home. Many feared that the prospects for the flagging company recovering from its most distressing period hinged largely on this decision.

13

Chasing the Greatest Ever Racer

A lot of excitement was swirling around Tully in the autumn of 2007. Dominant on the agenda was news that Sheikh Mohammed's Darley had just sealed the extraordinary re-syndication of Invincible Spirit, valuing him at an eye-watering €42m.

This colossal investment dazzled all involved. But the Stud still needed to compose itself and focus on the future. The company's chief executive, John Clarke, picked up the phone to call his good friend, John Oxx.

The famously successful Currabeg trainer had known the boss at Tully for a long time. He was a former director of the Stud, as was his father, John Oxx Snr. In the 1980s Mr Oxx Jnr had a spell as the company's chairman, when Mr Clarke was finding his feet on the job.

The quiet and clerical Currabeg trainer was always among the most honest and trustworthy in the business. When he was chairman of the Stud, his Board had striven to serve small breeders. He was in charge when Coolmore wrested Ahonoora from the yard for £7m.

But this phone-call was not to discuss old times. It was to sort out what was ahead.

Mr Clarke had on his hands a yearling who was born 20 lbs heavier than the average foal. His ungainly birth weight marked the start of a trend. In the 18 months that followed, he developed as if he was from a bigger breed than his peers. His pure, bay-coloured, upper body stood on powerful jet-black legs. Wide shoulders stretched the distance between his head and his torso. His mother, Urban Sea, was a bona fide marvel as a broodmare.

The Stud did not own either the dam or her son although the people who did, the Hong Kong-based Tsui family, were good customers of the company. Mr Clarke routinely advised them on breeding and buying.

At Mr Clarke's request, Mr Oxx made the short journey from his Currabeg yard to the lands around the Black Abbey. Mr Oxx knew something about what to expect. He had already been involved with the Urban Sea line, even if this had not worked out too well.

"I had his year-older half-brother by Green Desert [Seas Legacy], who was a lovely horse but had a few fairly major problems and never raced.

"But I was not particularly aware of this younger brother until John Clarke phoned me and said that Mrs Tsui would like me to go and see this fellow at the National Stud. She was not selling him and wanted him to put him into training.

"So I went down to see him for the first time and he more than fulfilled my expectations," he was quoted as saying in the *Racing Post's* book about Sea the Stars.

The yearling had already picked up the basics before Mr Oxx arrived. He had to go to Currabeg to learn his trade. Once there, he was a dozy enough animal, happy to chill and avoid being flustered. He kept himself quiet and curious, always peeking out of his box to watch the comings and goings around the Oxx yard.

By mid-2008 he was ready for his first shot out of the stalls, at a straight course on the Curragh. The ground was good and he had seven furlongs in front of him. Seventeen other horses lined up alongside Sea the Stars. The incredibly successful jockey, Mick Kinane, sat on his saddle. Mr Kinane could not go all-out that day. It was the juvenile's first outing. He shot out of stall number 10 a little hastily. The horse needed to settle and this left him bunched in the thick of the field. The racers had thinned out before he was given space on the rails. Sea the

Stars lost his opportunity. He flicked back his ears with two furlongs to go and hared after the leaders. To find a clean line in the closing stages, he had to check his run. The best he could offer was a dogged sprint for the line. The débutant finished fourth behind Driving Snow, who was owned and bred by Lady O'Reilly.

It was another month before Sea the Stars returned under the same canary yellow silks and purple cap that his mother, Urban Sea, had carried at the beginning of the 1990s. Since then, the only change in the Tsui family colours was the disappearance of the broad purple diagonal stripe from each shoulder. This had been lost in the transition of ownership from David Tsui to his son, Christopher.

For his second race, the ground was softer. The prize money was an identical €13,000. Mr Kinane knew his charge's capabilities. Sea the Stars' odds were slashed. He started as favourite. The bookies knew what they were doing. The horse won that opening race at Leopardstown by two and a half lengths.

There was still a more prized outing on his horizon for 2008. This was the six-horse, Juddemonte Beresford Stakes at the Curragh on September 28th.

The grey gates snapped open in front of Sea the Stars just after 2.20pm. Twenty-eight miles away, a Sunday afternoon Cabinet meeting was mulling over the wisdom of an imminent and sensational blanket guarantee to rescue the country's banks. Fourteen miles away, Goff's was preparing for the opening of a sales' week which marked the tipping-point into Ireland's equine recession. But one mile in front of Sea the Stars stood the most lucrative finishing-post of his young career.

It had been a dreadfully wet summer. The sun-drenched track provided a rare opportunity to run on his preferred good ground. The win was never in doubt. From fourth place half-way out, he shifted gear, led with a furlong to go and passed the post in 1 minute, 42 seconds. All involved were delighted. Immediately, the Stud was promised the sniff of a larger slice of the action. This was according to the recollections of the matriarch of the family that owned him, Ling Tsui.

"When he won the Beresford Stakes, he got home by only half a length and people did not pay too much attention to him. Some people even said it was not a Group Two race.

"But I already liked him so much that I told John Clarke that if he ever won another race as a two-year-old, he could take him on at the Irish National Stud. He agreed, because Sea the Stars had such a good pedigree and is so handsome," she said.

Crucially, after two wins in three starts, it was decided not to race him again as a two-year-old. The chance of him falling into the Stud's lap was gone. If it wanted him, it would have to take fate into its own hands. An obvious option was to buy a stake in him. The Board met early in October and mulled over a valuation of €8million. A quarter share, at €2million, could have been repaid quickly based on early projections. The industry had suffered virtual collapse in the days previous. The country's banks were not alone in suffering acute cash-flow problems. Opinion was mixed on whether it was the right time for such a big gamble.

Goff's was concerned about it sales' returns. Eyes anxiously moved to the upcoming event at Tattersalls. Breeders were showing resistance to the Stud's proposed stallion fees and administration charges. Mr Clarke was given clearance to offer discounts if necessary. He had even proposed chopping down some of its forest to release money. The omens were blackening for the Stud just as they were brightening for Sea the Stars.

After two wins from three starts, his focus was trained on May the following year. Spring training for Sea the Stars did not go according to plan, however. His mother, Urban Sea, died at the beginning of March while giving birth to an Invincible Spirit foal. Two weeks later, when Sea the Stars was due to ratchet up his speed work, a viral infection ignited his temperature. This laid him low until the beginning of April.

He still struggled to find his groove as the clock ran down towards his debut as a three-year-old. The target was the illustrious 2000

Guineas at Newmarket. The bookies initially gave the younger sibling of Galileo little chance. They had begun to see sense closer to the day. He was still only 8-1 going to the start, with a handful of others deemed to be better bets. Coming up the hill towards the line, Mick Kinane cracked the whip across Sea the Stars' powerful right hind-quarter. The winter's training paid off and he drove passed Delegator with ease. He had clinched his first classic.

There was an unavoidable hype surrounding Sea the Stars after his Newmarket victory. Punters and pundits slowly started to make their minds up about whether he had the physique to emulate his half-brother, Galileo, and win the Epsom Derby. The crux of their concerns was whether his proven speed compromised his ability to last longer distances. The Derby was always the true test of three-year-olds, with rises, dips and a lightening-fast downhill run. Prize money was buoyed by packed grandstands and international interest. It all conspired to provide a timely opportunity for the eternally sociable industry to don the traditional top-hats and waist-coats. It was an event that offered the chance to network with the best in the business.

The Stud's stallion nominations manager, Julie Lynch, had planned to be there. She had her tickets for the Queen's Stand. These passes entitled her to the same access as owners and trainers. She was interviewed by the *Sunday Tribune* a week before, and was asked for her views on an increasingly divisive distance debate surrounding Sea the Stars' capabilities.

"I think he will stay in the Derby. Cape Cross [his father] has already sired a course, and distance, classic winner in Ouija Board. Urban Sea won 'the Arc' over a mile and a half. Galileo is also a course, and distance, winner and another half-brother, Black Sam Bellamy, is a dual Group one winner at the distance," she said.

During that interview, she bit her tongue about everything that was going on at the Stud and her dispute with Mr Clarke. Given the opportunity, she sold the Stud's product and explained the philosophy of the Irish National Stud, contrasting it with the industrial environment at Coolmore.

"We are run as a commercial organisation, first and foremost. But there is still a great feeling of national pride. We still do our best to represent the Irish thoroughbred industry and as vendors we are one of the biggest consigners to the Goffs' sales each year. It is important that Ireland has a national stud and our stallion roster has never been as strong as the current one."

This was printed while the animosity between her and Mr Clarke was at its height. John McStay later told the High Court that, on June 3rd, Ms Lynch sent a message to her human resources manager, Orla Hennelly. It said "I want him fired". The day after this message was sent, Ms Lynch said her flights and tickets to the Epsom Derby were cancelled. She was to miss one of the greatest days of the year.

The festival was in mourning. The master trainer and breeder, Vincent O'Brien, had died five days earlier. He had trained 2 of just 34 horses good enough to win the 2,000 Guineas and the Epsom Derby in the same year since 1813.

Although almost three dozen horses had achieved the double, most of them did so in the very early years. When Sea the Stars arrived at the track as the 2,000 Guineas champion, the feat had not been achieved since Nashwan passed the post on the same June day 20 years earlier.

Leading up to the great three-year-olds' race, Sea the Stars was tussling for the favourite's tag alongside the Aidan O'Brien-trained Fame and Glory. The choice would have been clear-cut. However, there were lingering doubts about Sea the Stars' ability to sustain his speed over a longer distance. His father, Cape Cross, was a horse that excelled at mile-long races. But the length of the Derby did not suit the progeny from his paternal line. Sea the Stars was so quick at Newmarket it was thought unlikely he could also possess the added qualities needed to last.

"It's just that invisible brick wall near the furlong pole that concerns me. To win a Derby you've got to stay and we just don't know for sure he will," Mr Oxx told the *Daily Telegraph*.

Mr Oxx was not the only person fretting about the length of the course. The matrix of family traits and the criss-crossing of DNA made it an impossible conundrum. Urban Sea had given birth to two foals from Sea the Stars' grandfather, Green Desert. These were nowhere near the calibre of those she had with Sadler's Wells. The best of her Sadler's Wells family was the Derby winner, Galileo.

Before he covered Urban Sea, Green Desert's meeting with Park Appeal was more successful. This resulted in Cape Cross. Cape Cross went on to sire Ouija Board and Sea the Stars.

Ouija Board won the 2004 Epsom Oaks in admirable style. She beat All too Beautiful into second place. It just so happened that All too Beautiful was an older half-sister of Sea the Stars. She was Urban Sea's last filly from Galileo's father, Sadler's Wells.

Ironically, Ouija Board was the reason Sea the Stars existed at all. Her win sparked Mrs Tsui's interest in her family tree. So, despite questions from her advisors about the wisdom of sending her aging mare to Cape Cross, Mrs Tsui put her foot down. The subsequent mating completed a tapestry which allowed Sea the Stars to calmly trot out for the Epsom Derby. It was up to him to prove he could take the best talents of his wonderful mother and overcome the nagging suspicion surrounding his father's sprinting genes.

Seconds before 3.53pm on June 6th 2009, Sea the Stars was the third last horse into the stalls. The bugles blared. And Christopher Tsui's horse kicked off from stall number four. His team watched on. Mr Oxx said he was more nervous than when he won his only other Derby with Sindaar at the beginning of the decade. Sindaar was not expected to win. Sea the Stars was.

Mick Kinane settled him into a steady stride within two furlongs. Mr Oxx relaxed a bit. After that, it became an easy race to enjoy. It was so straightforward.

Sea the Stars climbed the 110-foot hill, in the first seven furlongs, neatly tucked into fourth place. He had an unobstructed view of what was ahead. Mr Kinane kept him near the rail as they approached the heaving crowds on both sides of the track. The galleries' screaming tended to unsettle the young colts. The quick downhill stretch could also be a shock to many horses as they faced into the final five furlongs. Sea the Stars used it as a slingshot. He moved into third place and released himself on the two pace-setters out in front. He overhauled Golden Sword with just a furlong to go. This was where many thought the Currabeg-trained horse would tire. The pack chased. But no horse's stamina looked better suited to shouldering the strain than Sea the Stars'.

The win primed him for a run at the Irish Derby. A victory here would have seen him become the first horse since the legendary Nijinsky to complete the treble – the two Derbies and the 2,000 Guineas.

The significance of such a bid is that it showcased an expansive spectrum of skills in a horse. The sprinter's burst of speed revealed in his first run at Newmarket was topped by the extra bit of stamina needed at Epsom. The Curragh could have shown he had the ability to turn it all around in three weeks and triumph over his fellow three-year-olds once again.

As June developed, the stubbornly rainy Irish summer brought uncertainty to his bid to replicate Nijinsky. The Curragh had watered the track and it was vulnerable to more rain. Sure enough, the clouds came.

At Tully, Ms Lynch had been put on a period of sick leave, which she disputed, and she was anxious to attend the Derby.

"I was concerned that by not being at the Derby it would be clear to people that I could not cope with my job and that my employer was justified in suspending me on medical grounds," she said.

For two days she sent and responded to e-mails. Ms Lynch was looking to clarify the terms under which she could go to the festival without the Stud disciplining her. The conditions set down meant that she felt unable to talk to clients or congratulate them on their successes.

At the Curragh it was hoped that Sea the Stars would be among those earning plaudits. But on Friday, the eve of the race, torrential rain soaked the track. The ground was wet, far too wet for Sea the Stars. He was pulled from the Dubai-sponsored Irish Derby and denied the chance to win its €855,000 prize.

The depressing weather, and the disappointment of the champion not running was not the only source of gloom in Kildare during the festival. The attendance at the Curragh was 15 per cent down on 2008. The €1.6m bets made at the course produced a tally €500,000 below the previous year. Racing was in trouble. Sea the Stars was not. The deluge in Ireland left an opening on the calendar and the attention switched to Sandown and the Coral Eclipse Stakes on July 4th.

Missing the Irish Derby and moving to the Eclipse pitted him against five older horses. He had only faced three-year-olds up until then. This time, the oldest in the field was the five-year-old Land Shining. The oldest jockey was ten times that. It was Sea the Stars' rider, Mr Kinane. He had celebrated his 50th birthday two weeks earlier.

The Eclipse field included two sons of Sea the Stars' sibling, Galileo. One of those was Rip van Winkle, whom he beat into fourth at both Epsom and Newmarket.

Untypically, Sea the Stars broke out early. It upset his rhythm and he was challenged with two furlongs to go. Whether through habit, intelligence, lethargy or modesty, Sea the Stars never looked to win a race by more than a length. Mr Oxx had suggested to Mr Kinane before the off that if the horse was winning, he should stretch him out. This would show him off to the crowds. But the pitch-black legs of Sea the Stars did not want to work more than they had to. Besides, one length was more than enough. Rip van Winkle's challenge trailed away. Sea the Stars became only the fifth horse in 110 years to win the Guineas-Derby-Eclipse treble.

Each race had laid out its own unique challenge. Each win had proved just how much Sea the Stars was able for them. The more obstacles he overcame, the more talents his genes offered future quests to breed the perfect racehorse. He was a speed merchant and a stayer. Sea the Stars was increasingly becoming the ideal stallion.

"He didn't win the Guineas by being out of bridle, and out last, and just running on and getting up like a Derby horse in the last stride. He won it all the way.

"After the race we thought, my god, now isn't this great? He's a half brother to Galileo and he's won the Guineas. The world and his wife will want this fellow at stud," said Mr Oxx.

But the Board at Tully did not care about the world or its wife when it knew it could steal a march on the market. The company felt there was a chance of winning the competition to craft the colt's stud career. The Irish National Stud was keenly aware that bringing him back home, with the multi-million euro industry he was soon to become, would provide security to its already struggling stables.

14

A Star Shines but Hopes Die

Enticing the genetic godsend, Sea the Stars, to Tully was not an idle dream. Bringing him back home became an obsession for the Irish National Stud.

Ever since the Tsui family had followed Brian Grassick's advice, and sent their champion mare, Urban Sea, to Tully, a trusting relationship had developed. Over time, the Stud's chief executive, John Clarke, was taken in as one of Ling Tsui's lieutenants. He helped advise her and lay out the options for her brilliant broodmare band.

The year that Sea the Stars was born, Mr Clarke offered to put the foal in the December sales. It was a bumper year. He had a perfect pedigree. The young horse would have got a fantastic price. On this occasion, Mrs Tsui opted to keep hold of her horse. She wanted her family to send him out as a colt.

As Sea the Stars grew up and strengthened, it was Mr Clarke and his stallion nominations manager, Julie Lynch, who kept the savvy Mrs Tsui sweet on the Stud.

The breeder's importance to the farm was not taken for granted. Staff worked hard to make sure she got value for her money. The Stud consigned yearlings to the sales' rings on the family's behalf. Mr Clarke monitored the markets for prospects. In 2008, the company and its customer combined their best assets: Urban Sea became pregnant for the final time with the Stud's strongest sire, Invincible Spirit.

The Irish National Stud believed its relationship with the Tsuis' Sunderland Holdings' operation could be tied up with an even more elaborate knot. There was a chance the Tsuis' impeccably-formed racer, Sea the Stars, could return to live at Tully as its anchor income-earner for a new decade. The directors knew its trump card in a bid to secure Sea the Stars was John Clarke.

Ling Tsui tended to watch Sea the Stars' races on her laptop at home. After the runs, the chief executive discussed each outing with her. Following the juvenile horse's second win in 2008, the Hong Kong businesswoman promised Mr Clarke that if the novice racer claimed one more title as a two-year-old, she would move him to stand at Tully. The Board never got to call in this commitment because Sea the Stars did not run again until his third year. This did not mean the Tsui's relationship with Tully had deteriorated in any way.

At Newmarket, in May 2009, Mr Clarke was the man selected to represent the family and accept the 2,000 Guineas trophy. Meanwhile, back in Kildare, all involved in his upbringing joined in the feverish excitement building around his career.

Seven months earlier, the Stud had gone to great lengths to secure a €2m, long-term stake in the soon-to-be stallion. At this time, its economic position was precarious. The Goffs' and Tattersalls' sales had come and gone with brutally poor returns for yearlings. Banks and builders, whose custom had helped sustain the Stud, were in trouble. The outlook for breeders was grim. The market was heavily overstocked.

The Stud had come to realise that capturing an interest in such a good prospect would greatly improve its chance of riding out the turbulence in the thoroughbred industry. The Board asked Mr Clarke to see if he could seal the deal.

His successor, John Osborne, was one of the directors at this time. Mr Osborne said everybody at the Stud had been watching Sea the Stars since he was delivered in its foaling unit at a weighty 142 lbs.

Sea the Stars had not been trumped-up or fully tested at the age of two. This gave the company the edge over its competitors. It knew of Sea the Stars' abnormally strong hind-quarter and the long bulging muscles along the top of his back legs. These drove his hooves from under his body with every stride. They provided a natural gearbox for a horse with speed coursing through his family. Another winter's growth would allow his body to strengthen and his instinct to improve.

"Due to the fact that Sea the Stars was foaled and raised at the Irish National Stud before being transferred into the care of a former chairman of the Stud, Mr John Oxx, we have always monitored his progress closely. He is a most beautiful horse.

"Even as a two-year-old he was obviously a contender but he was not yet the Real McCoy. We entertained great hopes that one day he might return to us," Mr Osborne said.

In October Mr Clarke flew to Hong Kong with Air France, on a business-class flight that cost €5,000, to see what could be done. Crude early estimates put the juvenile's value at €8 million. On this basis, the Stud would have been happy to relax its purchasing policy and settle for a minority stake.

Mr Clarke had a strong bond with the matriarch of the Tsui family, Ling Tsui. Even though her son, Christopher, was Sea the Stars' registered owner, she would make the final decision on the horse's impending stud career. Mr Clarke had been an advisor to her since she parted with Coolmore in 2001. The chief executive and his client mostly communicated via e-mail or by telephone. She split her time between Vancouver, in western Canada, and Hong Kong.

The Stud had taken various opportunities to show its gratitude for the Tsui's continued custom. In 2003 Mr Clarke had signed for a framed oil painting of Urban Sea by Newbridge artist, Carolyn Alexander. It was a €2,300 gift, on behalf of the Stud, to the mare's owner. Mr Clarke kept her up to date on the family's stock in Kildare. Christopher Tsui said the chief executive's regular communication was a valuable part of the Stud's product. It helped minimise the hazards of running a breeding operation from the other side of the world. This geographical disconnect helped build a bond. However, it also meant that the Stud had to extend itself in the effort to convince the Tsuis to sell a stake in Sea the Stars.

"The owner of Sea the Stars lives in various places across the globe and the Board took the decision to investigate whether there might be a possibility of purchasing an interest in him when he was a two-year-old.

"This would have been a huge punt on the part of the Stud. However, the Board decided to at least investigate whether the owner was prepared to do business," Mr Osborne said.

Mrs Tsui was not. In May the following year, a doubling of the valuation was met with the same response. Later, in the summer of 2009, it was Mr Clarke who emphatically ruled out such a strategy and killed off the courtship of every other prospective buyer.

"The horse is not for sale. I speak to Ling Tsui a lot and everyone is enjoying the fun of an unbelievably good racehorse and I just feel privileged to be part of what is a great adventure for the Tsui family," Mr Clarke told the *Racing Post*.

The treble titles – the 2,000 Guineas, the Derby and the Eclipse Stakes – had raised the possible price tag for Sea the Stars' stud career to €60m. Another run of wins before he signed off on his racing career would send his stock even higher.

For July, Sea the Stars went back to Currabeg, where he enjoyed the bones of three weeks' trotting, relaxing and recovering. Then, he had to get primed again. This time, it was for a four-horse field at the £340,620 International Stakes at York. Sea the Stars was up against three challengers from Aidan O'Brien's stable. All three horses were owned by the people who once shared Galileo with the Tsuis: the Magniers and Michael Tabor.

John Oxx's independent entry was last for almost the entire race. At three furlongs to go, the two weakest competitors, Set Sail and GeorgeBernardShaw, parted. This allowed their stable companion and sprint specialist, Mastercraftsman, to slip between them. Sea the Stars did not have time to go wide. With two furlongs to go, Mick Kinane had to guide him through the same two-horse gate. On sentry duty were the two struggling Ballydoyle colts. It was tight. But track was running out.

When Sea the Stars made it past Set Sail and GeorgeBernardShaw, he still had to haul down Johnny Murtagh on Mastercraftsman. For a second, Sea the Stars slipped off the pace. His kick appeared absent, as his rival powered for the line. Mastercraftsman went a length and a half clear. Mr Murtagh cracked the whip a bit too often for the stewards' liking. A serious slight on Sea the Stars otherwise incredible record was two hundred metres away.

Then the champion bolted. Within 22 strides left he was eye-to-eye with the challenger. He did not linger. After 11 more he was a length clear and claiming his fourth Group One win.

His team was not in the mood to stop there. His fans wanted more and his owners were happy for him to deliver. On September 5th, Sea the Stars came to Leopardstown for what would be the only home run by Ireland's greatest ever three-year-old. The event was the country's highest profile flat race, the Irish Champion Stakes. That afternoon, the crowds came out to celebrate him. What they saw was even better than anybody expected.

He let it all stretch out in front of him. There were five contenders from the Ballydoyle stable, each anxious to smudge the champion's record with a defeat in Dublin. They put up a ferocious fight. A dozen lengths lay between the Derby winner and the leader when the field turned for home. Johnny Murtagh, this time on Fame and Glory, was allowed make a clean sprint for the line. It was an opportunity this horse had been denied in all his battles against Sea the Stars. The Aidan O'Brien-trained Fame and Glory had won the Irish Derby, but only after the rain forced the Tsuis' horse to pull out. He did not figure when Sea the Stars was in the mix.

With a furlong and a half to go in the Champion Stakes, Sea the Stars needed to show another set of talents simply to get back in contention. He had four Group One wins behind him, but a lot of ground to make up in front of him. Yet again, Mr Kinane put the clutch down, found the right gear and, by the time they reached the post, Sea the Stars had blitzed his rival with a couple of lengths to spare.

Every win increased the anticipation about who would get to stand the horse once he retired. The international media was equally curious as to how, and by whom, he would be managed. At least one part of this puzzle became clearer after his Leopardstown victory.

On September 14th, Mr Clarke announced he was going to retire. No mention was made of the stress the chief executive told the Board he was under, or the disciplinary process the company had threatened once he was well enough to take it.

"For some time now I have been considering going out on my own as a bloodstock consultant and I feel the time is now right as the Stud had had so many successes in the last few years.

"Twenty-seven years in the same position is a long time and despite the current difficulties of the industry the long term future of the Stud is bright. I look forward to seeing the Irish National Stud continuing its role in the Irish bloodstock industry," he said

Similarly, there was no sign of ill feeling in Lady O'Reilly's statement on the same day. This was despite the horseracing press already speculating about tensions between senior management colleagues.

"I have enjoyed working with John. He has made an enormous contribution to the success of the Irish National Stud over almost three decades.

"This is a new beginning for him and he leaves with the best wishes of the Board for his new venture. I know that if he brings the same determination which characterised his time at the Irish National Stud that he will achieve much success," she said.

John Clarke opted for early retirement. But the Tsuis were determined that Sea the Stars would go all the way before signing off on his career. The prize they craved most of all was the Prix de l'Arc de Triomphe, the title that defined his mother's legacy in 1993. For this race, Sea the Stars was back to a longer run of a mile and four furlongs.

He was facing the same route around the aubergine-shaped track on the banks of the Seine. This was the idyllic vista his mother, Urban Sea, had faced 16 years before.

He was caught in the bunch for the first section of the race, as the pack passed the browning leaves of the towering trees to their left and the golden grass in the pasture to their right. With 600 metres to go, the horses started to meet the 55,000-strong crowd. Sea the Stars was still well back and without room to move. It was an almost identical predicament to that which his mother had met when she turned the final bend of her glory year.

At the 400-metre mark, Urban Sea had come off the railings, changed gear and burst into a gap caused by the field fanning out for the final sprint.

At the 400-metre mark, Sea the Stars came off the railing, changed gear and burst into a gap caused by the field fanning out for the final sprint.

With 250 metres to go, Urban Sea had emerged from the crowd to figure in a frantic, three-way dash for the line.

With 250 metres to go, Sea the Stars emerged from the crowd to figure in a frantic, three-way dash for the line.

When she hit the final strip of advertising hoardings, Urban Sea had pulled a length clear. At the same point, her son had gone a length better. Urban Sea passed the post, fending off a late challenge from White Muzzle. A fight was also on behind Sea the Stars, but he was too far in front for it to matter. Following the finish, it was all about family.

Urban Sea, owned by David Tsui, had posthumously shared her finest moment with her penultimate foal. While David and Ling Tsui's own son, Christopher, was the owner of their latest Prix de l'Arc champion.

Jean Lesbordes, the trainer of Urban Sea, was at Christopher's side. But Mr Lesbordes' son, Clément, was not. His father said Clément was in heaven. He added that watching down, alongside him, was the horse he loved to ride – Urban Sea.

The win was also about the Tully family and, more specifically, the three men responsible for so much of its legacy: John Oxx, its former chairman and Sea the Stars' trainer; John Clarke, its outgoing chief executive and the Tsui family's advisor; and John McStay, the long-time company secretary of the Irish National Stud. Mr McStay's son, Barry, wrote a post on his blog afterwards that heaped praise on Sea the Stars and on his father's friends, who were so involved in the victory.

"John [Oxx], his wife, Caitríona, and children, Aoife, Deirdre and Kevin, have been wonderful friends to us.

"[The] Tsuis' advisor in all these matters, John Clarke, is my brother's godfather and his son, Jonathan is Killian's [McStay] best friend.

"The three families, Oxx, Clarke and McStay, with their three Johns, have been inseparable since I've been on this earth. Today was a small celebration of that, as much as a massive celebration of the magical Sea the Stars," he said.

Immediately after the celebrations, attention turned to where Sea the Stars would stand as a stallion. The *Guardian* newspaper spoke to Mr Clarke and he was adamant Tully would be able to handle the hottest property in bloodstock, but it would be Mrs Tsui's call as to where he went.

"Mrs Tsui will make a decision once his racing career is over on what she wants to do with the horse long-term.

"But it would be no problem at all to stand a horse of the calibre of Sea the Stars at the Irish National Stud. We used to stand Indian Ridge for €80,000, so we have the infrastructure and it would hold no fears for our staff to be dealing with a horse of that quality," he said.

Mr Clarke also pointed to the fact that a life at the Irish National Stud would make Sea the Stars accessible to the thousands of fans who made the trip to Longchamp to see him, and the millions more who cheered him on from home.

"People wouldn't be able to get too close to him, of course. But they would be able to see him in his paddock and so on. He has a huge following, particularly here in Ireland.

"Everybody wants him, obviously, and I don't think there's ever been a prospect quite like him, to be honest.

"It's unfair to compare others with him because there's never been a horse with so much potential. He's possibly the greatest racehorse of all time, and he has the perfect pedigree, the perfect physique and the perfect temperament. When you add all those together, what you have is perfection in the thoroughbred," he said.

After Paris, there was one other possible run for Sea the Stars – the Breeders' Cup Classic in Santa Anita, California. He did not need the win, against horses of all ages, to prove his power. Yet, there were potential sire earnings to consider. A victory in America, where Galileo had failed in his final race, would have put him in the shop window for the big-money breeders across the Atlantic.

In the end, the team behind the horse decided on discretion and declined to ship a horse who had been training since the spring, off to the Pacific Coast for a seventh top-class outing of the season. The owners also knew that, with every race, comes a reputational risk. Just as each win proved something different about his talents, so a defeat would have raised questions about prospective weaknesses. Many horses had seen great early season runs compromised by uncharacteristic defeats later in the year.

Sea the Stars straight six-from-six season left no such doubts. Emotion would have flown him to Santa Anita, but caution kept his feet grounded in Ireland. At this stage the wise thinking in the industry was that the Irish National Stud would soon be revealing a new money-spinning lodger.

As is often the case, newspaper report followed newspaper report. Pretty soon it was assumed that Sea the Stars' return to his birthplace was imminent. Just like when his dam, Urban Sea, arrived at Tully, the blissfully neutral status of the National Stud was considered crucial for the champion. Coolmore's name was thrown around, but the separation between the Tsuis and the Fethard franchise made this highly unlikely.

Sheikh Mohammed, who was busily fighting to rearrange the debts of his Dubai principality crippled by the property crash, was also mooted to be interested in a €70m bid.

There was a possibility the Tsuis would take a more permanent European position under Christopher's guidance. This would have involved opening their own farm in Europe.

Mr Clarke was asked repeatedly about where the stallion was headed. He gave nothing away. He said the three- year-old "ticked all the boxes" and any stud farm in the world would be happy to have him. But there was another player who did not feature in the initial speculation.

The Aga Khan had visited the John Oxx yard at Currabeg during the summer. While there, he had asked to see the colt. The billionaire had the facilities, the desire and the cash required to support such a stallion prospect.

"If I were the Aga Khan and possessed his wealth and if the possibility of having a stallion such as Sea the Stars arose, [people] can only imagine the lengths I would have gone to secure the services of the said stallion for my Stud," said Mr Clarke's successor as chief executive, John Osborne.

"We were not able to compete with the Aga Khan."

The Stud was struggling financially and it was about to lose its best asset in the quest to secure Sea the Stars – John Clarke.

By October 27th, the guessing game was over. The Aga Khan had made his pitch and Mrs Tsui said she was happy to strike up a relationship with another of Ireland's largest breeding operations. Critically, the Tsuis did not have to surrender a stake in him.

"His Highness was kind enough to let us stand Sea the Stars at Gilltown while keeping ownership of him, and we are most grateful.

"The staff and facilities are top-class and Sea the Stars will enjoy his stay there," she said.

The Aga Khan had a long and proud involvement in the Irish industry, dating back to when the founder of the National Stud, Lord

Wavertree, tempted the spiritual leader's family to take up an interest in equine affairs. Even after such a long and proud tradition, His Highness said this stallion was as good a product as the Gilltown Stud had seen.

"Mrs Tsui and Christopher's decision to entrust the future career at stud of Sea the Stars to Gilltown Stud farm brings to everyone at the Aga Khan studs, as well as to me personally, the greatest happiness. Mrs Tsui and Christopher's decision is certainly one of the most important developments for my operation since I inherited it in 1960.

"This horse could also help develop relations to bring Chinese investment into the European bloodstock market," he said.

There were a lot of factors in the decision. Upfront costs, especially insuring the greatest racehorse in the world, were prohibitive. The first weeks of John Clarke's Tully career had been dominated by the kidnapping of Shergar from the Aga Khan's yard. The legacy of this scandal meant that all studs had to pay a premium for standing superstar stallions. The semi-State company's accounts were in such a sorry position it would have struggled to cover itself against such a loss.

Ironically, such insurance fees played into the hands of those who could afford them, most notably Shergar's former owner, the Aga Khan.

The synergy between the Tsui's Sunderland Holdings and the Aga Khan's Gilltown had an immediate effect on the Irish National Stud. Not only did it lose out on the chance to bring home the champion of champions, he took all those who shared his colours with him. On November 6th, Mrs Tsui's broodmares were shipped out of Tully after an eight-year stay.

By this time, the closeness of the relationship between the Tsuis and John Clarke became clearer. At the Tattersalls' December mare sale Mr Clarke was buying in his capacity as advisor to the Tsuis. He was still an employee of the State, but he was already looking to next season. He bought a mare called Bitooh for the Tsuis, with a view to sending her to Sea the Stars.

However, the most illustrious mare set for a visit to Sea the Stars was already living at the Aga Khan's Gilltown farm. Zarkava had won the Prix de l'Arc de Triomphe the year before Sea the Stars. In doing so, she became the first female in 15 years to win Europe's greatest race. The last one to manage it was an older mare, Urban Sea.

This great broodmare's legacy was to become further entrenched at Gilltown at the Irish National Stud's expense. On January 5th, the Tsui family moved their next great racing hope from Tully's paddocks. The yearling, who was born minutes before his mother died, had been nicknamed Reborn. He was the result of the much-anticipated match-up between Invincible Spirit and Urban Sea. But, for his final 10 months of frolicking before he began training, he was moved to join Sea the Stars, whose father was a paternal half-brother to Invincible Spirit.

"Mrs Tsui has decided to have all her stock in one place so everything has been moved to Gilltown Stud.

"The Invincible Spirit is a lovely yearling. There is a long way to go until he goes into training in the autumn but he's very strong and probably nicer than Sea the Stars at the same stage," Mr Clarke said. Six days later, Mr Clarke had followed the yearling out of the Stud to assume a more prominent role under the Tsui family's umbrella. His finish date had been agreed much earlier with the Board and was chosen, it said, for "practical business reasons".

The Board agreed to pay him €64,775.36 instead of requiring him to work the final six months of his contract. Trading under his own name, he immediately set himself up as a bloodstock advisor, with the Tsuis as his number one client.

The Stud was left with just memories of the fleeting chance it had to bring home its most famous son, Sea the Stars.

"It was nearly a great investment for the Stud. But it did not happen," admitted John Osborne, the man who took over from John Clarke.

15

The Heavens Cave In

The Board of the Stud got itself bogged down in mucky mayhem when it committed to restoring and protecting Owens' Cottage. The quaint, thatched residence had got its name from the man who used to live there, John Owens. He and his wife, Katie, made it their home while Mr Owens worked at the Stud for many years. It had been among Michael Osborne's favourite features when he lived at Tully House.

But, in the three decades since Mr Osborne left, the cottage and its small thatched porch had lost its lustre. Neighbours accused the company of wilful neglect as they looked upon a cottage wrapped in plastic protection. The polythene had been stretched across it as a replacement for a proper roof.

The Stud had intended to replace the reeds. But, when experts looked behind the façade, they found the beams supporting the building were rotting and could not hold up the roof. Then, as the company searched for a solution, a depressing deluge descended. Rain drenched the summer of 2009. The water weighed the old thatching down and the whole roof caved in.

The Stud's office manager, Eileen Kavanagh, told the *Kildare Nationalist* that the company was trying to sort out the problem, but it was mired in financial turmoil.

"We are working very hard on this but we aren't helped by the fact that the bloodstock industry is experiencing a very difficult time at the moment.

"However, the directors are keen to get the cottage back to its former condition and we are doing everything possible to achieve that. We love that cottage and it is disheartening to think that people are under the impression that we left the cottage to purposely fall into disrepair," she said. It was estimated that rebuilding Owens' Cottage, and plugging the leaks which buckled it, would cost €70,000.

Restoring the Stud, and stopping a drip-feed of controversies bringing it to the brink of collapse, proved a far more exhausting and expensive undertaking. The *Kildare Nationalist* printed its article about Owens' Cottage on September 3rd, 2009. This call from the local paper was not the only media query Ms Kavanagh had to field.

At the end of August, Fiona Gartland of the *Irish Times* asked for details on the expenses approved for the retiring chief executive, John Clarke. She sent in a request for a breakdown to be released under the Freedom of Information Act. The Stud was about to be sucked into a much wider seam of controversy.

In the latter years of the boom, the State training agency, FÁS, had basked in a bounty of European social funding. But, throughout 2009, the receipts from expensive trips by senior staff and board members embarrassed the entire organisation and forced a humbling clear-out.

Politicians too had apparently been spirited along by the Celtic Tiger's property-driven tax revenues. A seemingly endless supply of money covered hefty expense bills for entertainment and international travel. But when people began to reflect on this largesse, the political clique started experiencing a nasty hangover.

Over the summer of 2009, a journalist with the *Sunday Tribune*, Ken Foxe, had doggedly tracked down the Ceann Comhairle, John O'Donoghue's, expense reports. Mr Foxe foraged around the accounts documenting Mr O'Donoghue's time in Cabinet and his tenure as Ceann Comhairle. Among other revelations, Mr Foxe uncovered €550,000 worth of travel costs incurred by Mr O'Donoghue and his wife, Mary, during the five years he spent as Sports and Tourism Minister.

Initially, the political consensus was that the investigation would go away. The public did not agree. Readers remained interested and appalled. On Monday, September 14th, after another *Sunday Tribune* news story, Mr O'Donoghue wrote to his peers in the Dáil and, for the first time, defended his expense claims.

"On a personal level, I wish to acknowledge that some of the costs incurred appear high. I sincerely regret, in so far as I am concerned, that some of these high costs occurred although a minister or an office-holder would not be apprised of such expenditure at this level of detail either on an ongoing basis or at all in fact.

"It has to be borne in mind also that, while some costs of the arrangements appear high and have caused disquiet, they were legitimate and in accordance with the Department of Finance guidelines," he said.

By sheer coincidence, this was the day the Irish National Stud announced that Mr Clarke was to leave his position after 27 years. In August he had informed company secretary, John McStay, and the Board of his intention to step down. But the chief executive was asked to wait for a few weeks before making the news public. In a statement, Stud chairman, Lady O'Reilly, said she had enjoyed working with the outgoing boss.

"This is a new beginning for him and he leaves with the best wishes of the Board for his new venture," she said.

Four days later, Ms Gartland was supplied with Mr Clarke's expenses information, without having to go through the Freedom of Information process. Her article appeared large in that Friday's *Irish Times*.

"Departing chief of Irish National Stud defends expenses," ran the headline.

Ms Gartland had information to account for almost €85,000 worth of expenses relating to travel by Mr Clarke and his wife, Monica, between 2002 and 2004.

"The 59-year-old, who was chief executive at the Stud for 27 years, defended the expenses and said he did not use first-class flights. Some flights may have been expensive, but this could be accounted for by last-minute bookings, he said.

"He occasionally took his wife on trips with him with the approval of the Board when the trips were long or where an invitation had been extended to both him and his wife.

"Mr Clarke, who has a company car, had used the chauffeur service mostly to travel to Dublin airport to catch early flights; the cost was cheaper than a taxi from Kildare, he said and he did not like to leave his car at the airport," Ms Gartland's article stated.

On reading the newspaper, Agriculture Minister, Brendan Smith, immediately wrote to the Board looking for an explanation "as a matter of urgency". Two months earlier, he had been in Tully and had warned the Stud about expenses – Mr O'Donoghue's record had just come into the public arena and FÁS had dominated the agenda for six months.

"I would draw your attention to certain control issues that have received a good deal of publicity in some State bodies over the last year.

"I remind the Board to ensure the appropriate controls are in place within the company to ensure that all monies are very carefully spent and that a frugal approach becomes the order of the day," he told the assembled directors in July.

When he requested the expenses' report on September 18th, it was the second time in a week that his office was in contact with the Stud. On the day of Mr Clarke's resignation, Lady O'Reilly wrote to Mr Smith updating him on the first half of the year and explaining the internal financial controls which had been adopted to comply with the Government's Code of Practice.

On the issue of Mr Clarke's claims, the Stud maintained then, and since, that the sums were justified: foreign travel was part of the job and all payments were in line with Department of Finance guidelines.

It had already investigated the issue. Ten months earlier, it had drafted in Kealy Mehigan accountants to audit the travel and motor expenses of its workforce. The independent audit team had arrived at Tully on December 19th, 2008 and pulled up all claims made by staff members for the first 11 months of that year. They prepared a detailed breakdown of Mr Clarke's tally and that of stallion nominations manager, Julie Lynch. The auditors also looked at the pairs' credit card statements and the receipts they provided. There was a special section looking at the cost of meals.

Eventually this audit report was released to the *Irish Examiner* under the Freedom of Information Act. It showed that between January and November 2008, Mr Clarke was responsible for 60 per cent of the company's total staff expenses' bill. For every day covered by the audit, Mr Clarke had been approved for an average of €276 worth of claims. This included €46,927 on meals and hotels and €21,713 on flights, travel and parking. There were also charges associated with hiring a new company car after his own 2001 Volvo S80 was crashed in March. His total claim, up until the end of December, was €92,461.

Kealy Mehigan's analysis also calculated that Ms Lynch was responsible for 15 per cent of the company's claims. The remaining six dozen full-time and part-time staff accounted for the rest of the bill.

The audit laid out how, in 2008, Mr Clarke was initialling and approving Ms Lynch's expenses. This was after an affair between them had ended and a more fractious period had begun. Mr Clarke's own claims were being signed off by Lady O'Reilly. The auditors said these were not always backed up by a proper proof of purchase.

"We vouched all statements to supporting receipts but these were not always present. Twenty-three percent of expenses did not have supporting receipts and of the 77 per cent which had receipts, 32 per cent did not have a detailed breakdown as the credit card slip was the receipt," the report said. These credit card slips had been initialled by Lady O'Reilly, although one month's statement was not signed. Later, it is understood the Revenue Commissioners conducted its own investigation into the sanctioning of expenses after the reports appeared in the *Irish Examiner*. However, the Stud refused to make a statement on the issue.

Separately, the Kealy Mehigan report raised concerns that some items claimed for by Mr Clarke were not travel-related. His bills included €1,404 spent on assorted shrubs and trees for the patio at his company-provided home, Tully House. These were bought at Johnstown Garden Centre, but no receipt was supplied. Entirely independent household expenses showed that, earlier in the year, the company had paid €22,258 to build the sheltered sandstone patio outside the chief executive's house.

The Kealy Mehigan audit described how the company had been underpaying its staff their mileage allowance. This was relative to the approved civil service rates. The anomaly was rectified, but the workers' entitlements were not backdated.

If the company, or Ceann Comhairle, John O'Donoghue, thought that September would carry the last cry of controversy arising from historic expenses claims, they were wrong.

Ms Gartland had submitted a further Freedom of Information request for Mr Clarke's more recent tallies. In another theatre, eleven weeks after the *Sunday Tribune* first published Mr O'Donoghue's expense details, the Kerry South TD was forced to resign from his office.

He had released a full record of receipts, covering his time as Ceann Comhairle, on the day the country was voting on the second Lisbon Referendum. When it emerged that some of the dates he travelled with parliamentary delegations coincided with world-renowned horseracing meets at Longchamp and Melbourne, the scandal became too much. His resignation speech to the Dáil was a bitter volley against the media and those colleagues who had called for his head.

"Transient political benefit will never be a compensation for long-term political damage. The institutions of this State and the dictates of constitutional fairness are bigger than any individual, their political ambitions and their careers.

"In my case I regret to say that I was not afforded the basic principles of a fair hearing. Instead, the sound bite took the place of fairness. The headline achieved was more enticing and politically compelling than the fairness of the process that ought to have been followed," he said.

Mr Clarke was offered no such soliloquy as he edged towards retirement. But, within a few months, he too was asserting a right to defend his reputation.

While the details of Mr O'Donoghue's expenses, and to a much lesser extent those of Mr Clarke, filtered out, the Stud was already looking at deeper problems that were drilling a hole in its finances. Despite its initial outlook, when the market began to hobble, customers did not spend their money on the higher priced stallions.

In 2009, its sires had covered 920 mares, but the sustained interest was at the lower end of the market. Cheaper horses were getting customers more readily.

As it looked to 2010, the Stud was consumed by wrangling about the price to be set for its seven stallions, and the scope for offering the usual discounts to bulk customers.

Five sires had their fee fixed at 2009 levels. In the case of Invincible Spirit, his syndicate committee settled on a €45,000 charge for 2010. This was €30,000 below the figure he had commanded in 2007. Many breeders wanted his owners to go lower. Yet, by Christmas, his diary was full.

Verglas was in more trouble. Despite some brilliant results on the track, particularly in France, owners were not convinced. Almost two-thirds of his foals put up for sale in 2009 did not recover the €15,000 that breeders had paid to have mares visit him a year earlier. Similarly, his yearlings did not get close to turning a profit for their owners, who had forked out for the initial nomination fee.

In a game of brinkmanship with breeders, based on a battle between perception and performance, Verglas's price for 2010 remained static at a firm €10,000.

There was trouble too finding the right pitch when selling access to a more recent arrival, Amadeus Wolf. Disputes about his fee festered among shareholders. His syndicate, whose management committee was led by John McStay's son, Mark, had never seemed to settle on the right market.

In 2009 he covered just 103 mares at an advertised fee of €8,000, although, with discounts, his services were selling at much less. His fee remained at €8,000 for 2010. In an even more depressed economy, customers were not biting.

Despite reluctant uptake from breeders, John McStay told the High Court the Board was concerned that Ms Lynch's efforts to negotiate prices were going too low. He claimed the stallion nominations manager had disobeyed the orders of the Board.

In response, Ms Lynch said that the directors were only concerned about her sales' technique because they were trying to destabilise her. She said there was a sinister agenda behind the Board's orders for her to charge more than the discount prices she shook on with clients.

"Mr McStay and other members of the Board had already sought to undermine me on numerous occasions.

"For example it ordered that the contract for nominations I had sold to a good client for a particular price be cancelled. That was motivated to embarrass and undermine me with that client and within the industry," she told the High Court.

Throughout November and December, Mr McStay said e-mails on the issue flew back and forth between him and Ms Lynch. He tried to put comments made about Ms Lynch in context.

"I say any criticism of [Ms Lynch] in this regard was to protect [the Stud's] commercial interest and because of repeated refusals by [Ms Lynch] to follow the Board's continuing direction. I deny they were motivated to undermine [her]," he said.

While Mr McStay and Ms Lynch clashed via e-mail, Mr Clarke was enjoying a prolonged sunset at the Stud. He was also preparing for the next phase in his career. His days as chief executive were coming to an end but he was still active in the market. He was able to begin bidding in the name of the owner of Sea the Stars, Ling Tsui.

At the Tattersalls' mares' sales, in early December, he was with Sea the Stars' trainer, John Oxx, to check out potential partners for the 2009 Horse of the Year. Mr Clarke paid €283,500 to get a four-year-old mare called Bitooh for Mrs Tsui.

The Hong Kong businesswoman had already announced the Prix de l'Arc de Triomphe winner would not be returning to Tully. Mr Clarke had indicated he was to begin work as her bloodstock advisor. With just days to go in his 27-year tenure, he enjoyed the Christmas holiday and a chance to put the events of the past three years behind him.

But as the clock wound down on a terrible 2009, Ms Lynch was about to upset his plans. She typed out a desperate plea for help and sent it to the Minister for Agriculture, Brendan Smith. The entire affair was just weeks away from exploding into the public domain.

CHAPTER

16

Investigations and Recriminations

The Stud had known 2010 would begin on a dour note. At the beginning of January, Sea the Stars' half-brother, the son of Invincible Spirit and Urban Sea, was moved from the yard. Ling Tsui's decision to stand her wonder stallion at the Aga Khan's Gilltown farm, and not Tully, had already seen her mares move in the same direction. Now, Sea the Stars' younger brother, first nicknamed Reborn, was leaving as well.

It was a bitterly cold spell. Ice and snow brought the country to a screeching halt. Temperatures plummeted to their lowest levels for 40 years; the departure of Invincible Spirit's yearling was a dark and gloomy reminder of how the glow of a glorious summer had died.

The company could have forecasted some early-year shivers. Its chief executive, John Clarke, was days from his departure. The financial year, which began on January 1st, started with a €3m overdraft and €5.7m in accumulated debts. However, nobody would have predicted the sharpness of the snap brought on by events that occurred in the final hours of 2009.

First, director Pat O'Kelly announced she was to retire after 18 years on the Board. She said her resignation was motivated by the disappointment at not securing Sea the Stars and by the company's decision to curtail the number of students allowed on the highly regarded, but loss-making, breeders' course. Ms O'Kelly said people who thought that Tully could not have handled Sea the Stars were wrong.

During her time as a director she had journeyed extensively with Mr Clarke to investigate potential purchases. Ms O'Kelly considered him a "very good chief executive".

In latter years, stallion nominations manager, Julie Lynch, had joined the travelling party. Now Mr Clarke was leaving and Ms Lynch was on the brink of a decision from which she could not turn back.

On December 30th, 2009 she typed a deeply personal e-mail and sent it to Minister Brendan Smith. This laid bare her treatment at the hands of John Clarke. Her e-mail informed Mr Smith of various corporate governance issues at the Stud. She requested the Minister to intervene.

Mr Smith, a small, stout Cavan man, was considered sincere and approachable. He was the gentle public persona of the Fianna Fáil front bench, but he had failed to inspire confidence since his promotion to Cabinet.

The Minister read Ms Lynch's plea. On January 8th, he e-mailed the Stud chairman, Lady O'Reilly, to draw her attention to it. He followed this up on January 13th with a letter asking her to investigate. This included a copy of Ms Lynch's e-mail and her subsequent correspondence, which had a more comprehensive account of what had gone on. The next day, Mr Smith's private secretary, Dymphna Keogh, sent a letter to Julie Lynch.

This letter said that Mr Smith would wait for a report from the Board on the corporate governance complaints before deciding what to do. It also explained that the Minister would not entertain her request to examine Mr Clarke's behaviour.

"The Minister will carefully consider the report of the Board into the allegations you have made, once he has received it. In light of the serious allegations/complaints you made, the Minister expects you to cooperate fully with the Board in relation to whatever process it institutes.

"In response to the second issue [the bullying]... while the Minister is obviously concerned by what you have written, it is not correct for the Minister to intervene in the ongoing human resources issues of the Irish National Stud," he said.

He said if Ms Lynch was not happy with that, she should seek her own legal advice. She did just that. Four days later, Lady O'Reilly sat down, took out a pen and hand-wrote her response to the Minister's request for an inquiry. On lined and personalised headed paper, she penned 225 block-lettered words, with one scribbled-out mistake, and said that her report would be ready within two weeks. The single-page faxed message was addressed to Ms Keogh and said the Board would also make every effort to look into all the allegations made by Ms Lynch.

"Kindly assure the Minister, and be assured yourself, that the Board of the Irish National Stud is fully focused on the Stud's business and successful running, and takes its responsibilities with the utmost seriousness, and never more so than during these challenging economic times.

"The Board is aware of the seriousness and urgency of the matters raised and will furnish its report as soon as possible as a matter of the highest priority. With kind regards, yours sincerely, Chryss O'Reilly."

The Board was already aware of the substance of the allegations Ms Lynch made to the Minister. It was furious that its internal affairs had arrived on the desk of its political patron. But, at that stage, it had to concede the matter could not be kept within Tully's 1,000-acre compound. It also knew that its attempt to shield the affair from public scrutiny had failed.

The *Irish Times* article on Mr Clarke's expenses had been well aired. In addition, the relationship between him and Ms Lynch was widely rumoured within sections of the bloodstock industry. Ms O'Kelly's departure and her comments to the *Racing Post* had attracted more interest.

On New Year's Eve, the *Irish Examiner* was aware of the general issues and the imminent departure of the chief executive. The newspaper sent simultaneous questions to the Stud, the Department of

Agriculture and the Department of Finance on the outgoing CEO's parachute payment and his pension entitlements.

Finance said it had no role to play. Agriculture said it was a matter for the Irish National Stud. The Stud said company secretary, John McStay, would see how much information could be released under the Freedom of Information Act.

The Department of Agriculture subsequently confirmed Mr Clarke would be paid €64,775 when he left. This was in line with the terms of his contract and was in lieu of him working the final six months of his term. RTÉ, the *Irish Field*, the *Irish Times*, the *Mail on Sunday* and the *Irish Examiner* were all aware that there was more to the story. Journalists were probing various quarters.

The Stud had known for quite a while that time was running out. In October, Ms Lynch had referred her case to the Rights' Commissioner, under the safety at work legislation. On January 4th, the Stud was told it would have to answer this case on February 18th. The hearing was five weeks away. The noose was tightening.

On Monday, January 11th, the *Irish Examiner* contacted the Stud. It said it was in a position to report that the Minister had ordered an investigation into serious allegations regarding the Stud's governance. On Wednesday the first evidence of the debacle was printed for the public to peruse. Later that day, Mr Smith's private secretary wrote a letter to Lady O'Reilly reiterating his request for a detailed explanation.

More questions from the press arrived. These included a Freedom of Information request to have Finbarr Flood's report released in full. There was also an application to have the details of deals between the company and its directors published, along with their expenses. A separate query called for the company to outline how much had been spent defending legal actions taken by its employees. This made specific reference to the case of Pat Mullarkey. There was panic in the Stud.

Initially, the press pursuit honed in on the Flood Report. By Friday, January 15th, the *Irish Examiner* could publish the results of the investigation in full. As the Board had learned seven months earlier, this report exposed the victimisation that Mr Flood had identified. It also recounted the details of the love affair which had started it. The Stud had originally been loath to distribute the report to even the smallest circle because of the damage its contents could do. Now, Mr Flood's assessment was freely available on news-stands across the country. Independently, the relationship between the Stud and Ms Lynch was on the verge of complete collapse.

Mr McStay said he was concerned by the tone of e-mails the stallion nominations manager had sent to her assistant, Sinead Hyland. Ms Lynch had also contacted the company's solicitors in a way Mr McStay felt was inappropriate. On January 14th, Ms Lynch sent Mr McStay an e-mail.

"Quite frankly, fuck you. I dare you to fire me you horrible fucker, just try it," she said. The company secretary said he replied to this briefly and politely. The same day Ms Lynch sent a text message to Lady O'Reilly.

"I am going public with everything today," she said.

The company continued to demand that Ms Lynch attend doctors before it would allow her back to work. Mr McStay said a medical report it received deemed her to still be a "serious suicide risk".

Meanwhile, the Board appointed John Malone, the former director general of the Department of Agriculture, to help run the company in Mr Clarke's absence.

In 2009 he had been brought in to facilitate the chief executive and the stallion nominations manager in their efforts to work together. This was in the wake of the Flood Report's findings. The tactic did not succeed. By the time Mr Malone was in place, Ms Lynch felt she had been frozen out completely.

On January 19th, Ms Lynch's laptop crashed. It was sent to the IT department. Here, she said, it was confiscated. The next day, she looked for it back. Failing that, she wanted access to vital information that she had stored on her hard drive. Ms Lynch said the IT section refused to

217

give it to her. This was on the grounds that Mr McStay had told them she was suspended, Ms Lynch claimed.

That morning, Mr McStay and HR manager, Orla Hennelly, hand-delivered a letter to Ms Lynch at her home. This asked her about her recent visits to doctors.

Mr McStay's letter told Ms Lynch that she was being relieved of all her duties, her phone was to be diverted, her e-mails redirected and she would have to live away from the Stud. Ms Lynch interpreted the message as a move by the company secretary to kick her out of Tully.

"Without any hearing and/or without being provided with a copy of any medical report or evidence that was being relied upon to ground the decision, I was informed by Mr John McStay that I was to leave the office and that I was being required to vacate my house.

"I was given no forewarning that this decision was imminent. I was not afforded any opportunity to challenge the decision. I had to leave the premises immediately," she said.

Mr McStay said his actions were taken because one of the doctors had suggested it might be beneficial for her to take a break and live some place else. Ms Lynch did not want to leave her home. The company said it would give her €750 a month towards a new house.

The former director, John Osborne, had just been confirmed as the new chief executive. On February 3rd, he and Ms Hennelly called to Ms Lynch's house. They again asked her to vacate the property. Once more she refused.

At this stage, the media's focus had switched to the multi-million Invincible Spirit windfall. On February 1st, the *Irish Examiner* sent a series of questions to the Stud asking it to explain aspects of the syndication. It asked for: the total amount involved and a breakdown of benefits for each director and Mr McStay; the number of shares they held when the deal went through; on what basis Lady O'Reilly was selected to sit on the management committee; and how much Mr McStay paid for his extra shares in 2006. These were forwarded by the company to Mr McStay for him to prepare a response.

The next day a statement, attributed to a spokesperson for the company, gave an extended account of how the Invincible Spirit offer came about. It spelled out how the company had rearranged its own shareholding. However, the statement said the positions of individual shareholders, even those who sat around Tully's boardroom, were not something the company would comment on. The Freedom of Information Act gives State agencies some room to manoeuvre and discourage requests. The Stud was a small operation dealing with an increasingly large volume of these applications.

On February 15th, it responded to two applications from the *Irish Examiner*. The first had looked for information on the Invincible Spirit syndication deal. The Stud said that to get paperwork together would take 40 hours. At €20.95 per hour and €0.04 per photocopy, it proposed a €918.15 charge to consider the file.

On the same day, it dealt with another *Irish Examiner* request. This had looked for records of transactions between directors and the company. The Stud said this would be released subject to a payment of €1,268. Mr McStay, who was the subject of both requests, signed the letters on behalf of the company.

The Stud did not respond to a number of other FOI applications that were before it. Nor did it supply any explanation for the company's decision not to address these. Eventually headline data from the second query, and others, were released free of charge. The Invincible Spirit data was withheld because it was commercially sensitive.

Requests under the Freedom of Information Act can be legitimately thwarted, minimised or delayed. Demands from the Minister or the High Court cannot.

Four days after the Stud replied to the two Freedom of Information letters, a High Court summons arrived. Julie Lynch had taken her case. She was demanding the company's decision to put her on administrative leave be declared void. She wanted the Court to set aside the Stud's insistence that she move out of her house. Ms Lynch asked the Court to grant an injunction to stop the company from suspending her, taking her name off the website or cancelling her mobile phone account. In addition, she looked for her laptop to be given back without any information deleted.

Some of those involved in the Stud had a personal affection for Ms Lynch and wanted the case handled sensitively. Others wanted to crush her. But now the company had more than its stallion nominations manager, a High Court judge or the national media to answer to.

On January 29th, Lady O'Reilly delivered the report Minister Smith had requested. This was triggered by Ms Lynch's e-mailed allegations. On February 24th, Lady O'Reilly, Mr McStay and Mr Clarke's replacement, John Osborne, appeared in front of the Minister and his key advisors to account for this document.

Minutes of the meeting show that Mr Smith was far from satisfied with the Stud's handling of the controversy. He asked why the Stud had not implemented procedures that would make it clear how employees could make confidential disclosures and still feel protected. These were supposed to come into effect in May 2009 under the terms of a revised Code of Practice.

"Mr McStay admitted that he had not brought the provisions of the revised Code to the attention of the Board but undertook to ensure full compliance," the minutes said.

The Minister also made it clear that, while the company's dispute with Ms Lynch was an internal human relations one, it should not have been kept a secret from him.

"[Mr Smith] made the point that when it became clear that the matter was affecting or could potentially affect the reputation or administration or financial stability of the Irish National Stud this should have been brought to his attention by the Board.

"He also pointed out that [Lady O'Reilly's report to him] would appear to suggest there was not full clarity of roles and authority of all senior staff in the Irish National Stud and, while not wishing to interfere in operational matters, said this is an issue that the new CEO should address," the minutes said.

Mr Osborne agreed. The Minister reiterated his dissatisfaction in a letter sent exactly one month later. By the time that document left his offices on Kildare Street, the situation had become far more complicated. Moreover, the public got to pore over revelations, flagged in the Flood Report, in even more explicit detail. The February 18th date with the Rights Commissioner had been cancelled. A far more troublesome, and costly, hearing in the High Court was looming.

On March 3rd, John McStay went into a glass-fronted office block on Sir John Rogerson's Quay to sit down with Emmet Quish of McCann Fitzgerald solicitors. There, he swore an affidavit claiming the company had no choice but to keep Ms Lynch from her work, because her presence was damaging the business. He said she had e-mailed one customer in an unacceptable tone. Another customer wrote directly to Mr McStay to raise concerns. And, according to a log taken by John Clarke, she reported a further client to the Gardaí. This included allegations of threats made against her.

"How can [the Stud] even start to quantify the damage which it may suffer should this Court order that [Ms Lynch] be returned to work before she receives the treatment she requires.

"That would expose [the Stud] to further inappropriate behaviour or worse," Mr McStay said.

In her affidavit Ms Lynch said she was being shut out of the industry and the Stud was spinning a different story to various sources in order to justify her absence.

"I have been completely isolated. My colleagues are too intimidated by the Board to even contact me, they have said as much.

"The Irish National Stud has sought to prevent all contact between [me] and any party within the industry. The damage which this action is causing to my reputation and standing within the industry is immeasurable and ongoing," she said.

Ms Lynch said the tactics of the company had left her exposed, vulnerable and without her right to privacy.

"Perhaps my gravest concern is the fact the Irish National Stud appear to feel that they have the right to access my personal medical records in order to conduct an effective audit on the opinions of my doctors and their views that I am fit to work," she said.

On Friday, March 20th, a determined Ms Lynch went into the High Court. Accompanied by her mother, she wore a black dress, her short blonde hair brushed tightly back off her face. Ms Lynch's legal team read out her extensive affidavit. The Stud's barrister went through the account of company secretary, John McStay.

John Osborne watched from the back of the room as Ms Justice Mary Laffoy became increasingly frustrated by the minutiae of personal detail being raised through the legal arguments. The next day the affair was not confined to one publication or media outlet. It was broadcast and printed across the country. The Stud had been shamed. This served it with notice about what could come out if a full civil trial went ahead.

After a weekend's reflection, the company settled the immediate dispute – the injunction sought by Ms Lynch. The case was put on hold until a full hearing could take place. Continued wrangling between the sides has meant the case has yet to go ahead. It is not scheduled to go ahead until May 24, 2011.

Four weeks after initial court appearance, Lady O'Reilly wrote to the Minister to express her regret about what was going on in the Four Courts. She also assured him the company had complied with the Code of Governance and its failure to have confidential whistle-blowing procedures in place would be addressed at its next Board meeting.

"As chairman I agree on the importance of bringing any matters that could affect the reputation and financial stability of the company to the attention of the Minister.

"We are now reliant on our legal advisors to resolve the present case in the best interests of all involved.

"From the very beginning of this matter, the Board acted according to the Code of Practice and in the best interests of the employees of the Irish National Stud and in the best interests of the Irish National Stud, taking professional advice at all times.

"It is most regrettable that it is now the subject of litigation, as every position was taken to do the right thing for all concerned at all times," Lady O'Reilly told the Minister. But, within days, the company's legal problems doubled.

John Clarke was also unhappy. He followed his former lover and went into the High Court to present a case before the same judge, Ms Justice Mary Laffoy.

The former chief executive wanted the findings of the Flood Report quashed. The Stud decided it would fight this case as well. It was now fighting two battles before the same judge arising from the same affair. If the semi-State company was to lose both, it would have to budget for costs in the region of €1.5m.

Mr Clarke filed his case on April 26th. The next day it was announced he had landed a job working for the rising Italian auction house, SGA. He was taken on as a bloodstock consultant as it worked to build up its profile in the industry.

Meanwhile, with a whopping legal bill to contemplate, the Stud was now preparing to be hauled before its political masters to account for how it all went wrong.

17

Explanations and Humiliation

Three days after John Clarke began his High Court tussle with his employer of 27 years, his successor was in the dock. John Osborne and the company's new financial controller, Anne Lawlor, attended a meeting on the seventh floor of Agriculture House.

The main item on the agenda was money and the Stud's lack of it. Four officials from the Department of Finance attended, with two from the Department of Agriculture. There were a number of problems to address. The company estimated it would soon be posting a €3.9m loss – the final figure turned out to be €4.2m. It had appointed a solicitor to chase down its bad debts. This had become an increasing problem as a result of its international ambitions. Those who owed it money, and their assets, were now dispersed around the world. The company was doing the best it could. Where its debtors had saleable animals, the Stud was using its contacts to help get those to the market quickly. This income contributed towards repayments.

The Stud's pension scheme was also a concern. There was now a widening deficit in the plan. The 2007 windfalls had not been used to fill the hole. But, in 2008 and 2009, the company had put in a combined €300,000 to try and stem the liability.

Mr Osborne spelled out to the senior civil servants how the Stud intended to alter the scheme and make the debt more manageable. The Department of Finance said the Stud was a commercial semi-State so it could choose its own course of action. But its officials warned the company it must protect the rights of individuals already in the scheme and any change would have to be approved by both departments.

On the subject of its stock, Mr Osborne said the Stud needed to add some stallions to its roster to maintain its earning power. He said it would have to borrow more money to do this. The Stud boss had already met with its bank to discuss its loans and how these could be paid off.

The Department of Finance team said any extra debt would have to be based on a strong business case. Officials would have to be sure the Stud had the ability to fund the repayments. Unlike in times gone by, there was no prospect of a bailout from taxpayers. No additional shares would be purchased. Ten months earlier, Minister Brendan Smith had told the directors in brutally simple terms "the Stud cannot look to the stakeholder, i.e. the State, to make funds available from the exchequer. Accordingly, the company will have to rely on its own resources into the future".

At the April 2010 meeting the new chief executive also warned the civil servants that the bad news that had been emerging since January was about to get worse.

It was the second time in two months that Mr Osborne had to attend Agriculture House to account for problems in the company he was now in charge of. But this was not the last time he would have to go to Kildare Street to explain what had gone on at the State's stud farm.

Mr Osborne had joined the company as a director almost 12 years earlier. Long before that, he had spent part of his childhood at Tully. His father was Michael Osborne, John Clarke's immediate predecessor, who was credited with transforming so much about the Stud and the Irish bloodstock industry.

Like his father, the 45-year-old Mr Osborne was a qualified vet. He was an investor in thoroughbreds. He worked as a pinhooker, spotting good prospects as foals and selling them on for a profit before they reached racing age. When he got the chief executive's job, he said it "was just like going home".

Michael Osborne had lived to the age of 71. He died just before Christmas, 2005. After implanting his vision into the heart of the Irish National Stud, he projected his enthusiasm onto the biggest vistas the world would allow. He was the architect for the Dubai World Cup, an effort to recreate motorsport's Formula One championship for the planet's top racehorses.

"It was Michael who established the Dubai World Cup as a great international race," said its sponsor and Michael Osborne's long-time employer Sheikh Mohammed. Closer to Kildare, he was treasured even more. At Mr Osborne's funeral Mass, Fr Joe McDermott praised a man he described as a selfless, appreciative and grateful person.

"Michael was an amazing and immensely popular person whose influence extended to many far-flung parts of the world, but he never lost the common touch," he said. John Osborne also spoke at that Mass, four years before he succeeded his father as the boss of the Stud.

"We listened to him and on occasion managed to burst some of his bubbles.

"We argued with him and sometimes thought he was mad, but he took us on an incredible journey," he said.

Mr Osborne left an estate worth €650,891 and an indelible legacy on the thoroughbred landscape and on the institution of the Irish National Stud. His son was appointed to his old post at the end of January 2010, after speculation had linked him to the position for weeks.

The Board had decided to advertise for applicants in November. Director Jim Beecher told the Department of Agriculture that adverts were to be placed in the *Irish Field* and the *Racing Post*. The Department of Finance was not happy. It said the two specialist papers would not be enough.

Agriculture officials e-mailed company secretary, John McStay, and told the Stud it should flag the opening in at least one national newspaper,. This was done. The interview process was followed. Mr Osborne, married with four children, was offered the job.

The Naas-man had seen difficult times at Tully, both as a youngster living on the farm and as a director in the boardroom. But his first six months in charge were worse than anything previously witnessed. Three weeks after he and Ms Lawlor briefed the Departments on the state of the company, Fiona Gartland of the *Irish Times* was finally given the paperwork she had sought under the Freedom of Information Act. An almost identical request was pending from the *Irish Examiner*.

Ms Gartland then published an aggregated travel bill for John Clarke and his wife, Monica. This averaged €100,000 annually for eight years. The report also revealed the amount the Stud had paid to heat and light Tully House while the Clarkes lived there. Combined with the cost of renovating the property, buying furniture and providing household goods, the bill for the chief executive's house had amounted to €134,000 since 2000.

On a broader and more troubling note, the articles revealed how the Stud had spent €700,000 defending itself against employees who took cases against it. This included fighting the challenges of Pat Mullarkey and Andrew Lacey, who each claimed they had been bullied. In the month before Finbarr Flood was drafted in to help Julie Lynch and Mr Clarke work together, the settlements had spurred the Board to begin preparing a new staff handbook. It also considered re-issuing the bullying policy to all staff. It was too late to avoid its largest bill yet.

The company barely had time to gather itself. The following morning, after the articles in the *Irish Times*, the *Irish Examiner* published information gleaned from a separate Freedom of Information request. This showed how business deals worth €718,000 were not put out to competitive tender and were, instead, awarded to entities linked to key personnel at the Stud. This included the work carried out by McStay Luby, the accountancy firm of company secretary, John McStay; €93,000 of Waterford Crystal products bought by the company's gift shop from a business then controlled by Lady O'Reilly's family; €157,945 in training fees the Stud paid to Dermot Weld; and a Renault horse box, worth €73,188, that was purchased from director, Mick Leavy's, Burke Brothers' garage. The Stud subsequently said Mr Leavy's garage only put a 3 per cent margin on the deal, so its profit was €2,000. The company got the invoice from the French manufacturer to prove it.

Aside from the enthusiastic interest of former Agriculture Minister, Joe Walsh, the Government had generally kept the Stud at arm's length. It did not meddle in the affairs of commercial semi-State companies. However, the Department of Agriculture was put on notice that it would be difficult to abdicate all responsibility for the scandals at the Stud.

In late 2009, Fine Gael's Agriculture Spokesman, Michael Creed, had asked the Department about its role in overseeing the conduct of the National Stud. In February, Sean Sherlock of the Labour Party had put down a parliamentary question to seek Minister Smith's views on the Flood Report. Still, nothing prepared the Department's secretary general, Tom Moran, for the morning of Thursday, May 20th.

He and his officials were attending a cyclical meeting of the Dáil's powerful spending watchdog, the Public Accounts Committee. After working through his Department's spending habits, and the cost of the contamination of Irish pork 18 months earlier, attention switched to the Irish National Stud. Immediately he was ducking from a barrage of questions on how the Department had allowed the semi-State company to deteriorate.

"As secretary general and accounting officer, does Mr Moran believe there is a need for the Department to carry out an investigation into a litany of reports in newspapers in recent times on foreign travel, expenses incurred by individuals, the procurement practices being followed, or otherwise, and a link between individuals who are Board members and companies which offer services to the Stud?" Committee chairman Bernard Allen asked.

Mr Moran repeated again and again that the company was a stand-alone entity. It managed its own affairs. The Minister had discretion to intervene but this was only if he felt the Stud's reputation was at risk. Mr Allen asked if the Department felt the Stud had adhered to the Code of Practice for corporate governance. Mr Moran said it did, and the Minister was given assurances by Lady O'Reilly to this effect. She had done so since the initial media reports, he said. The secretary general maintained he had no responsibility for how a semi-State body spent its money. The Committee was not impressed.

"I am amazed nobody [in the Department] is asking the hard questions," Mr Allen said. The Committee chairman was joined in his criticism by members of his own Fine Gael party and Fianna Fáil, who likened the regime to the ridiculed structures at FÁS. These comments were then aired across most sections of the media.

The Stud's effort to keep its reputation intact was floundering.

Within 24 hours, it had issued a response. In its most extensive statement yet, the company said its non-executive directors were people with specialist knowledge and expertise. It claimed all dealings between the company and the directors were spelled out in each annual report. The statement itemised the transactions involving directors.

Mr Weld, it said, was one of the most celebrated trainers in the world and the horses he trained for the Stud earned €80,000 more in winnings than it cost to train them. He stepped out of any Board discussions about those animals, it said. Regarding Mr McStay, the company said he had made himself available for many unbilled hours and provided a range of voluntary advice to the company. Furthermore, competitive rates were paid to McStay Luby to cover the costs of a staff member who carried out work for the Stud.

"The management and Board of the Irish National Stud will continue to act in the best interest of the good name and reputation of the Stud and Ireland internationally," it said.

Two days before the meeting, an even more detailed fax was sent from Lady O'Reilly to the Minister to defend the company she chaired.

She said the coverage in the press had been "sensationalist" and she was "most distressed" about the problems it created for Minister Smith.

Lady O'Reilly said the travel and entertainment bill for Mr Clarke, which averaged €100,000 a year was not unduly large, given the nature and scale of the business. His wife had been paid for but she had voluntarily acted as the chief executive's unpaid assistant.

"It is vital for an INS CEO to assess the horses firsthand and to maintain direct contact with the owners so that they may consider the INS as a favoured place to stand their future stallion or send their mares to.

"Many owners consider their racing activities as social outings to be enjoyed with their spouses and families. It is therefore natural that much of the necessary contact with owners of future stallions and indeed broodmares who pay to patronise INS stallions takes place in a social context," she said.

Lady O'Reilly asked the Minister not to be distracted by the distorted coverage in the newspapers.

"It is easy for journalists to create sensationalist headlines and regrettably they do so with no understanding of the nature of the INS's business, which has been conducted in a transparent and honourable way and compliant with governance guidelines.

"The INS received no credit for employment it creates, its major contribution to the tourism sector, the educational opportunities it supplies and the successful stallions it stands," her handwritten fax to Mr Smith said.

This did not spare the Minister his uncomfortable moment under the spotlight. His department had fielded a number of increasingly detailed parliamentary questions throughout the month of May. On May 26th, because of the ministerial rota, it was his turn to stand in the Dáil to answer routine questions about his brief.

Fine Gael's Mr Creed asked for the Minister's impression of the expenses, tendering issues and connected contracts at the Stud. Mr Smith said he had got a report from Lady O'Reilly, about the expenses' issue, and was happy they were in line with Department of Finance guidelines. The Minister did not address the contracts awarded or the procurement practices.

"It is important to distinguish between the role of the Board in meeting the requirements of the Code [of practice] and those of the Department in monitoring compliance with the terms of the Code.

"It is not the responsibility of the Department to have in place a parallel system of management to that of the Board," he said. After listening to the Minister's response, Mr Creed said it was not enough.

"Notwithstanding the recent appointments of two fine and able people, does the Minister not accept that the cloud hanging over the remainder of the Board of the INS requires that the Board now tender its resignation?

"In order to safeguard the interests of this valuable industry, which has a global reach and is one of the few areas in which we distinguish ourselves internationally, and to protect all the associated employment, a new Board is required. We need to move on from this," he said.

The Minister had made changes. Mr Osborne had left the Board, to become chief executive, and Ms O'Kelly had resigned. On the eve of the Public Accounts Committee meeting, Mr Smith appointed his fellow Cavan man, Sean Brady, and national hunt trainer, Jessica Harrington, to the Board. Mr Brady was living in Kildare and would not have been regarded as a Fianna Fáil stalwart. But he had a reputation for meticulous and thorough performances as a Board member. Ms Harrington was one of the foremost national hunt trainers in the country. And, while the Stud had traditionally focused on flat horses, it had recognised the growing appeal and earning power of jump racing.

These were not to be the last new faces announced during that Dáil exchange. Minister Smith revealed that more changes were planned. He said these were to be made known by the end of June.

"I will be making four new appointments which will include those with expertise in the bloodstock industry and persons with expertise in finance and law," he said. The Minister did not carry out the wholesale changes he had promised by the end of June. He did appoint one new director. He left the fate of three others hanging.

By the time that last appointment was made, Mr Osborne had been back to Dublin city centre, again flanked by the company's financial controller Anne Lawlor. After months of allegations and recriminations, the Oireachtas Agriculture Committee invited him to account for the increasingly unsavoury situation at the Stud. It was Wednesday, June 11th and he was asked to open up about the affairs of the Stud over the past decade and the mire it had found itself in.

The Agriculture Committee had become one of the least aggressive in the Oireachtas. Deputies and senators with farms and farming constituencies tended to negotiate seats on it. This gave all concerned a chance to speak on issues affecting their rural voters. It also meant that this team was less likely to criticise their countryside base in a Dublin city political chamber.

Different audiences provoked different positions. Fianna Fáil deputy Ned O'Keeffe had been at the Public Accounts Committee two weeks earlier. At it, he had called for the Stud to be hauled before the Committee to answer for its FÁS-like expense habits. In the Agricultural Committee, he argued the opposite. Mr O'Keeffe said semi-State employees sent to sell Ireland overseas could not travel on "the back of a bus or on a donkey and cart".

"We left all that behind us in the age of leprechauns. All sorts of people argue that we overspend. If we do sell Ireland the country must have a good image.

"Irrespective of who travels, if they do not stay in a good hotel, travel on a good airline or arrive at an exhibition or trade fair in a good car, it is a minus for Ireland," he said. However, while Mr Osborne would have endured a more difficult morning had he been before the Public Accounts Committee, he was not spared a grilling.

Fine Gael's Mr Creed, who had already quizzed the Minister on the matter, asked for an account of directors' dealings, Mr McStay's role in the Invincible Spirit deal and Mr Clarke's conduct as chief executive. His colleague, Senator Paul Bradford, went in pursuit of how the company lost the opportunity to stand Sea the Stars. Mr Osborne was frank. He said the prospect of a rapid decline of what had been a hero industry was very real. This was a threat nobody could shrug off as inconsequential, he said. The Stud had lost €4.2m in 2009. The environment was not good to spur a recovery. The number of new broodmares registered was down 30 per cent for the second year running. Stallions were getting older. He accepted the Stud had a disproportionate amount of staff problems for a small company. Plus, it would have to look at how it spent money.

"A lot of things were different in the last decade and things are going to have to be different from now on if any of us are going to survive in business and meet the challenges we face," he said.

The new chief executive told the Committee the commercial viability of the Tully enterprise was precarious. The Stud was ticking over because of the continued heartbeat of Invincible Spirit. He assured taxpayers the Stud had not wasted their money. Windfalls were ploughed back into improving facilities. It had built a museum, office, recreation areas for staff, student accommodation and a warren of stables around the sprawling yard. He had plans to turn the ship around. There was a flash of his father's innovation.

"The Stud has never been an annual drain on the exchequer. While it is a shame to be in a loss-making position because it constrains what we could do, we will soon be better fixed and I have all sorts of ideas about what we could do in such circumstances," he said.

At stages, Mr Osborne looked exasperated. He sighed, his face dropped, and his eyes screamed with an assertion that the Stud's sorry situation was not as simplistic as had been presented.

Sinn Fein's Martin Ferris queried Mr Clarke's expense account. Mr Osborne pleaded for a chance to put it in context. Mr Clarke was chasing big money deals for the company and the bills were comparatively small. No first-class tickets were bought.

"It is slightly coy to say that we adhered to the guidelines. The guidelines specifically state that there is no first class travel. There was never first class travel, although there was business class travel," he said.

But Mr Osborne was prepared to debate the merits and necessity of luxury travel. It cost a lot more but, on landing, highly paid professionals were more productive, he said. The Stud had stuck to the letter of the law, even if they flirted with the spirit of it.

Mr Osborne was brought back to the issue of directors' dealings. But, he claimed, there was no conflict of interest. Instead, he said, taxpayers were better off because wealthy Board members had used their money to buy the Stud's bloodstock products.

"Which is better for all of us?" he asked.

Mr Osborne said it would be ridiculous to force this handful of connected individuals to do business with the company's competitors.

"There would only be a conflict if one of them had a stallion prospect for which they wanted to find a home or sell to the market.

"That would be a huge conflict, but it would be flagged and that situation has not arisen," he said.

He accepted the company had to beef up its performance in the area of corporate governance. But, he said, Mr McStay, in particular, had performed countless hours of unpaid work and had been a valuable asset to the company. Mr Osborne said, regardless of what had gone on before the Invincible Spirit re-syndication, no outside party, such as the Queen, had been "excluded from the party".

He said that when director Jim Beecher had investigated the grumblings about directors' dealings, he found that being a Board member was a hindrance, not a help.

"There was an obvious potential for an accusation of favouritism, so it was worth investigating how we measured up.

"The measure was that if one took the average fee to the general and the average fee afforded to the directors, then one was worse off if one was a director," he said. The Stud has not been able to find a copy of this report to make public.

"The majority of people on the Board acted from a genuine, old-fashioned spirit of public service," the chief executive said.

But Mr Osborne evaded questions regarding the conduct of his predecessor, John Clarke. Mr Creed and Mr Bradford wanted to know to what extent the former chief executive was conflicted in his duties because he was also working for the owner of Sea the Stars.

Mr Osborne said he could not comment because of the legal papers filed by Mr Clarke against the company. However, the 45-year-old attempted to convince TDs and senators that the regime had changed for the better. Three people in the Stud were now meeting twice a week to ensure the company complied with corporate governance rules. A dedicated human relations officer had been appointed to deal with personnel issues and the management structure had been reformed and strengthened. While he was reluctant to deal with past problems, he said, his was to be a new era.

"There has been a significant change of style with the new CEO and we are having weekly management meetings.

"There is a good atmosphere in the workplace and everybody is working well together... I would find it very disappointing if we ran into any of these difficulties in future," Mr Osborne said.

A Case for Survival

In January 2007 Mick Leavy wrote to Agriculture Minister Mary Coughlan to thank her for the honour of appointing him as a director of the Irish National Stud.

"I have a life-long interest in the bloodstock industry. And both as a native Kildare man and thoroughbred owner I have a particular interest in the future success of the National Stud.

"I am happy to say I am fully committed to the development of the Stud, in all aspects, as a major resource and showcase for the area, county and country," he said.

In June 2010 he resigned from the Board before the company's annual general meeting. For health reasons and other commitments, the Stud was something he would have to let go. Mr Leavy had always been a credit to his county. As a key member of the Kildare Supporters' Club, he pulled hard to entice the legendary Mick O'Dwyer to manage the Lilywhites' football team. The storied partnership between a downtrodden Kildare side and Ireland's most successful manager owed much to the determined teamwork of Mr Leavy and the former manager of the Irish National Stud, Michael Osborne.

Ten years later, when the Government felt its Stud would benefit from a representative of the town with which it was so intrinsically linked, it turned to the owner of the local Burke Brothers' Garage, Mick Leavy. Down through the years and, like most people living in Kildare town, the peaceful walks around the Black Abbey had been as much a neighbourhood recreation area as a national asset.

In 2008, when he was a director at Tully, Mr Leavy's garage, Burke Brothers, sold a Renault Master Platform horse box to the Stud for €73,188. The deal was not tendered for. It was arranged with his son, not himself. The Stud said it needed a company nearby which could service the vehicle at short notice. Reportedly, the margin the garage charged was minimal. It only made an initial €2,000 profit on the deal. Then the cab kept breaking down. The warrantee did not meet the costs. So Mr Leavy's service yard ended up fixing it for free.

The untendered purchase came to light in May 2010 along with €718,000 worth of business deals involving directors. The trade became the most public issue to emerge from his relatively short time as a director. Mr Leavy had been planning to resign long before the transactions between the company and the boardroom became known. Without fuss, he stepped down the following month. Agriculture Minister Brendan Smith appointed PJ Fitzpatrick in his place.

Mr Fitzpatrick was a former chief executive of the Irish Courts Service and was part of a Dublin-based company that trained business people to become better executives.

Lady O'Reilly was told about her new Board member on June 23rd, 2010. Mr Leavy was the third change to the Board thrust upon Mr Smith. Pat O'Kelly had resigned in December 2009 after 17 years at Tully. John Osborne was appointed chief executive a month later, so he could no longer be a director.

When Mr Smith was under attack in the Dáil he had promised more dramatic changes. He said he would introduce legal and business expertise to the beleaguered Board before the beginning of July. When he left office almost a year later this had still not happened. The spine of the Class of 1992 and 1993 – Lady Chryss O'Reilly, Jim Beecher, Dermot Weld and John McStay – were still in place in one guise or another. However in his final days in office he quietly beefed up the Board by adding the name of Galway business leader Paul Shelly to its list of directors.

Politically, the summer of 2010 was the first quiet period in three years. Mr Smith briefly had the opportunity to pause and reflect. The Stud did not. On June 24th the partially refreshed Board gathered at Tully to sign off on the annual accounts for 2009. These showed a situation worse than the one suggested by Mr Osborne a fortnight earlier, at the Oireachtas Agriculture Committee.

The company had sold €5.6m worth of services in 2009. But it cost the Stud €9.8m to get these to the market. The loss after tax was €4.2m. Lumped on top of 2008, the total shortfall hit €6.6m for 24 months. The Stud was owed €4.3m. It was indebted to the banks to the tune of €5.7m. There was a €894,000 hole in its pension plan. It needed a break. The company had plans and ambitions. Moreover, it was anxious to prove it was capable of righting itself.

There were already signs of a transformation in transparency. The 2009 accounts were very different to those produced throughout its 65-year history. They gave a more thorough insight into the directors' dealings with the company. Information was provided on stallion syndicates involving the Stud and parties connected to its key personnel. These arrangements earned a combined €2m in 12 months. This was shared among the company, its Board and its Company Secretary. The profit was reportedly a drop of €1.8 on the same income stream in 2008. At all times the Stud took the bulk of the money.

"No individual director or secretary had interests in such syndicates greater than 15 per cent," it revealed.

This section of the accounts also took the opportunity to register the 2008 purchase of the horsebox off Mr Leavy, which had not been mentioned when the deal was done the year before.

However, the new format did not deal with the make-up of the sire syndicate committees, the identity of the shared stallions or the people involved. Nor did it reveal if there were purchases of the Stud's yearlings and foals by directors or connected entities. For the first time, the documents accounted for all meetings attended by directors and listed how much each Board member was paid for their services.

Lady O'Reilly received €12,950, retired civil servant Jim Beecher was paid €6,750 and the rest were given €8,325. It showed the attendance of each director at meetings. Dermot Weld arrived for three out of five, Trevor Stewart was present for four and the rest of the Board had a 100 per cent record. There were eight meetings of the Audit Committee. Furthermore the Board had underpinned this group with independent expertise. John Malone, who was originally drafted in to facilitate Julie Lynch and John Clarke working together, was installed on a full-time basis.

Changing the structure of the accounts was not enough. The prevailing climate in the industry was darkening. The Stud was not just sheltering from a passing shower. Tully was facing a nuclear winter. From Dubai's Persian Gulf, to the bluegrasses of Kentucky and the pasturelands in Tipperary, the lush era was over. An arid landscape was ahead.

At the end of 2009 the Irish Thoroughbred Breeders Association produced a report on the future of the indigenous bloodstock industry. It was researched under the direction of former Agriculture Minister, and new chairman of Anglo Irish Bank, Alan Dukes. He and his team said the volume of bloodstock sales in the country had dropped by 65 per cent in two years. Employment in the industry would fall by at least 20 per cent. Economically the value of the equine trade jumped 64 per cent between 2002 and 2007. It suffered an abrupt collapse immediately afterwards.

By then there were almost three times as many broodmares in the country as there were in the boom of 1984. These 20,000 mares, along with more than 30,000 foals, yearlings and stallions, were owned by 10,106 breeders. The cost of keeping these animals was €225m a year. An estimated €188m was generated in stallion fees and €216m worth of thoroughbreds were exported in 2008. In previous times these had mostly gone to Britain. Now that market was not interested in buying.

The Irish industry was being attacked on two fronts. Money had evaporated. Other countries had become more attractive. The vulnerabilities were brutally evident at the Irish National Stud. By mid-2010 it had not managed to buy a stallion in two years. Instead it boosted its stature on the back of the success of one of its lodgers, Elusive City. He covered 160 mares in 2009.

The 10-year-old Elusive City had arrived with the scrappage of the doomed Huma Park Stud in Meath. But 75 per cent of the syndicate who owned him was French. Tully had no stake. His managers wanted him home. Duly, he left. Elusive City was a small part of a sizeable shift in power to mainland Europe. The cash available to Irish customers collapsed. Bonuses were available elsewhere. The stallions followed the money.

In two years Ireland's competitive edge had been blunted. The stallion tax exemption was withdrawn on August 1st, 2008. At home it left bloodstock fighting with every other sector to attract the interest of the few remaining investors. In contrast, foals born in France benefited from a premium prize at international races held in the country. For these events the French authorities laid on an exclusive pot for locally-born horses that finished in the top five. This was two thirds of the overall prize fund for three-year-olds. It meant owners were handsomely rewarded for keeping their broodmares at home.

After four decades of Irish incentives, suddenly it made more sense for a foal to be born in France and carry the signature FR branding. The erstwhile appeal of the IRE tag ebbed. Normandy was gaining. Kildare, Cork, Tipperary and Meath were losing. Rapidly, the flood of bloodstock investors drained away. The bountiful flow of 12,000 newborn thoroughbred foals per season began to dry up.

Meanwhile, another sparkling source of nourishment, which had made Tully such an ideal breeding ground for thoroughbreds, was weakening to a trickle. Despite disputes with Kildare County Council, the construction of the motorway through the Grey Abbey section of the Stud had gone ahead. With it came a remarkably rich seam of money for the Stud to exploit. The route had affected all six major stable complexes and disrupted the balance of the yard. But there was a payback.

First came the €1.2m for the tract under the road. Then the value of the annexed section multiplied and the company was given permission to sell up and keep the revenue. It earned almost €1m an acre from the first auction. There was always a fear the work would impact on the delicate environmental balance of the Curragh. It did. After 2006 most of the springs from the calcium-rich channels feeding the Japanese Gardens dried up. Two pumps had to be rented to replenish the lost water. In winter the waterfalls cascading down the showpiece monastic island of St Fiachra's Gardens had to be shut off, because the flow was so poor. Water pressure was a problem in one quarter. Elsewhere the drip feed of controversies was an even more pressing, and costly, concern.

The financial drain brought on by staff disputes in previous years was about to be dwarfed by the legal actions arising from its most complicated and public bust-up. The High Court became the theatre. The Stud was the reluctant actor. This role was one its flagging accounts and its battered reputation could ill afford. Two separate cases were taken against the Stud. These were totally independent in purpose, yet inextricably linked in their origins. They involved a couple of workers whose private affair unwittingly exposed the company to extraordinary public scrutiny.

Julie Lynch, the stallion nominations manager, was fighting to keep the job she worked so hard at. In July her legal team told the Court both sides were still trying to secure key documents from each other. A hearing was to be fixed for later in 2010, if a settlement was not reached beforehand. This was postponed on two more occasions as the sides fought for copies of documents. Following another interim settlement a trial was scheduled to begin on May 24, 2011. This was to be decision day. The company had the Spring to decide if it wanted to scrap for scant spoils in public or settle and save face in private.

In April 2010, John Clarke began his bid to restore his standing and reclaim the investigation report into allegations made against him. No date for a final hearing had been set down. In the meantime he had taken the job as a consultant to the Italian auction house, SGA. His business, John Clarke Bloodstock, was based in a single room apartment in a luxury Dalkey complex. A cautious calculation of the final exposure for the company exceeded €1m. The closer prospective public hearings got, the more they threatened the Stud. If public trials went ahead all the fights and failings of the semi-State organisation would be broadcast to the widest possible audience.

Back at Tully, the Stud was still using whatever implements it could to plug leaks. It opted not to cooperate with the publication of his book. The Board decided against explaining the issues about its performance, or the events which submerged it. It appealed to the Information Commissioner, Emily O'Reilly, to block a decision by the Department of Agriculture to release a catalogue of correspondence. This file related to corporate governance issues at Tully and was requested under the Freedom of Information Act.

Subsequently, the Board sought to snatch from the public domain the documents which had humiliated it. In a letter, it cited four different legal arguments and laws to stop the publication of key elements of the saga.

Firstly it wanted the report of Finbarr Flood to be buried.

"The publication of the investigation report prepared for the Irish National Stud by Mr Flood would be a breach of confidence in that the report was confidential between the parties and remains as such," the Stud said.

It also asked that the outcome of the settlement reached with former farm and tourism manager, Pat Mullarkey, be kept under wraps. These had already been revealed by Justine McCarthy in the Sunday Times and discussed in the Oireachtas.

"Any details in relation to the agreement reached with Mr Mullarkey are also confidential between the parties. The disclosure of such matters may also be a breach of privacy," it said.

The Board claimed its concern was not just to protect itself but other people who were involved.

"Any such breach of confidentiality/ privacy is actionable by the Irish National Stud and/or any affected third party.

"The use and disclosure of personal data and sensitive data may also constitute a breach of data protection acts."

Without citing any evidence, the letter suggested paperwork had been provided from within the ranks of its own staff roster and this should not be printed in public.

"Any information provided to you by employees of the Irish National Stud would be in breach of their confidentiality obligations to the Irish National Stud and any involvement by you and/or the Irish Examiner in such breaches could constitute inducement to breach of contract," it said.

The semi-State company asked for all the material it fought to keep from public scrutiny to be shredded.

"The Irish National Stud would therefore request that copies of any such confidential information which has been provided to you in breach of confidentiality obligations owed to the Irish National Stud and others are returned to the Irish National Stud or destroyed."

The Stud also warned that any of the people connected to it, or the goings on at Tully over the past 20 years, would sue if they felt their reputation had been harmed because of this book.

"Any defamatory statements may also be actionable by the affected parties.

"The Irish National Stud reserves the right to take legal action to it if any such information is used, including published, by you or any other third party," it said.

The letter was signed by chief executive, John Osborne. Three days earlier an interview he gave to the Racing Post was published. In it he told Richard Griffiths that he had assured staff his tenure would be different. He was adamant the company's finances would improve.

The Stud was still trading and Mr Osborne was confident the Department of Agriculture would approve extra borrowing if Tully spotted a stallion it wanted. The new chief executive said he had studied market trends since the Stud was first conceived by Col Hill Walker. While this latest collapse had been prolonged, historically the market always rebounded quickly. This research formed the basis of a five-year plan Mr Osborne drew up for the Board, as it argued for its own recovery.

"The Stud and the industry needed to show resolve," he said.

"There have always been periods when greed takes over for a while and then fear kicks in for a while; we are probably in a fearful period right now.

"We ought to be more prudent in good times and we ought to be more brave in the bad times. But it goes against human nature to do it that way," he said.

As he spoke the 2010 season was coming to a finish with a chink of light emerging from an old flame. Invincible Spirit, who had stunned the world after his first season at the Stud, was reaping the rewards of that standout success. The high worth breeders attracted to him after 2007, those willing to pay his inflated €35,000 covering fee that year, had set him on course for a world record. By the end of 2010 he had 42 winners among his two-year-old crop. However, this dispersed family told its own tale about the rot in Irish racing and the increasingly international direction taken by the State's stud farm. Of those winners 23 were registered in the UK, Italy and Ireland had 7 apiece, France had 4 and Denmark had 1.

The shareholding the Stud had fought to retain in Invincible Spirit, coupled with his success at supporting a €60,000 price tag for 2011, lifted an otherwise depressing situation. The company's stallion roster had been augmented by two low grade additions, Big Bad Bob and Lord Shanakill, their fees were set at €6,000 and €7,500 respectively. Lord Shanakill was left trailing by Sea the Stars in his three-year-old season in 2009. Of the eight horses standing at Tully for the 2011 season, Invincible Spirit was alone in his ability to justify a fee in excess of €10,000. But Invincible Spirit was special for many reasons. Already anticipation was building on the prospect of his only son with Urban Sea, Born to Sea, emulating his mother's other offspring. At the end of 2010 the Tsui family entered Born to Sea in the Epsom Derby for 2012. He was the last half brother of Sea the Stars and was born minutes before his mother died. Yet he was still to begin racing under John Oxx's direction. His juvenile debut was scheduled for the end of the summer in 2011. Further success from this line would cement the belief in eternal promise but, at the same time, remind the company of its lost opportunity with the hero of 2009 - Sea the Stars.

Meanwhile, in the office building in Tully, Mr Osborne had to finalise his recovery plan for the Board. However, by the end of the summer of 2010 he was also charged with compiling an argument for its very survival. Because, in the midst of a chaotic year at Tully, Finance Minister Brian Lenihan decided the country was creaking under its own debt. If there were assets that could be sold off they should be.

Mr Lenihan brought in University College Dublin economist, Colm McCarthy. A year earlier he was the author of the seminal shopping list of €5.3 billion in budget cuts contained in the report of An Bord Snip Nua. In the second half of 2010, Mr McCarthy's new Review Group on State Assets began to strip bare 27 commercial semi-State companies and assess if it was prudent to put them on the market.

There were giant utility firms and minnow port companies to be picked apart. The prospects for all of them were expected to be spelled out in an initial report. This was delayed as the Fianna Fail-Green Party government fell asunder, the International Monetary Fund was called on to rescue Ireland and voters were given the chance to elect a new Dail in February 2011. The often controversial and always dour Mr McCarthy was typically blunt. He laid out the figures and said that during the previous eight years the Stud had reported an annual loss in every set of accounts bar one. That exception was down to a once-off sale of land, he noted.

The UCD professor said while the company was solvent, because it had strong assets, its savings were depleted and there was a limit to how long this could continue before another bailout from taxpayers would become necessary. Damningly he said the idea that Ireland still needed a national stud to boost breeding prospects was dead.

"The National Stud no longer plays a critical role in providing access for Irish breeders to the best stallion lines and accordingly the need for retaining such a facility in state ownership should be reviewed.

"The Review Group recommends that the National Stud be disposed of," the report said.

The 47th recommendation in his report went largely unnoticed in the fuss surrounding higher-profile companies. But it roared loudly through a Tully compound in the height of breeding season. However, this season it was at times unusually quiet and uniquely frenzied. The Stud had to shut its doors to tourists for short period in order to prepare for one of the most special visitors in its storied history. Queen Elizabeth II had made a decision to come to Ireland for a four day visit designed to help put centuries of ghosts to bed. She tentatively stepped down onto the tarmac at Baldonnell unsure about how welcome she and her husband, Prince Philip, were.

Her visit was anchored on opportunities to remember and reflect on the men and women who fought for, and against, her forces. However, the first State visit to the country by the British monarch since Independence, also provided a stage on which to celebrate and savour the interests shared across the Irish Sea. The Queen looked puzzled during a trip to Croke Park and intrigued by a stroll through Trinity College. But she was at home when the great and good of Irish breeding turned up to welcome her to the Irish National Stud.

In 2007 it was the underlying desire to entice the Queen to invest in Invincible Spirit that heightened interest in the sale of loose shares by syndicate members. This attempt to secure the stallion in Ireland, with traffic from the Queen's stables, did not come off. At the time existing members, including company secretary John McStay, used their rights of first refusal to buy additional stakes instead. This was all in advance of the mammoth multi-million dollar re-syndication of the star stallion. But the breakdown in the Royal plan for Invincible Spirit did not sour the burgeoning relationship. Through her racing manager, John Warren, the Queen agreed to send mares to Invincible Spirit. Just before the Royal couple's visit General Synod, her three-year-old son of the record breaking stallion, had his second run of the year. That horse, like his father had fared better in shorter sprints. But unlike his father General Synod had so far failed to turn his pace into wins. On the Saturday before her she departed for Ireland the colt took to the track for the fourth time but turned out his worst performance.

May had not been a good month Her Majesty's mounts. She had spent the year hoping in vain that her runner, Carlton House, would fulfil his promise and win the Epsom Derby. The last reigning monarch to enter a winning horse in the Derby was King Edward. This was Minoru, a colt bred by Col Hill Walker at the National Stud in Kildare and donated to the King to help boost the morale of the monarchy. Contrastingly his great granddaughter had to watch Carlton House come up short while the glory went to a French raider in a further sign of its increasingly dominant thoroughbred industry.

As with much of the Queen's visit, her visit to the Stud was a procession of protocol and pomp. But the time in Tully also allowed chief executive John Osborne and chairman Lady O'Reilly to show off one their wares in a stallion parade dominated by Invincible Spirit. It was a bitter-sweet moment for the company chairman. For the first time the trail of chestnut and bay coloured sires was not broken by a flash of almost brilliant white. On the day the Queen landed at Casement Aerodrome Verglas died following a freak accident in his stable. According to the Stud he never enjoyed having his mane shortened and reared up when he was being groomed. Verglas lost his footing and fell awkwardly against the stable wall. He fractured the bottom part of his spine and died of internal haemorrhaging with a vet alongside him. There was cleaning, hosing and frenetic activity outside the boxes as workers prepared for the Queen's visit. But the Stud said an investigation showed there was no connection between the commotion outside and the accident inside. He had covered 66 mares in 2011 at a price of €10,000.

The 17-year-old sire had been a winner for Lady O'Reilly before embarking on a stud career in France that faltered until he was brought to Ireland in 2005. Standing for €10,000 Verglas was one of the only stallions on the Stud's books with a pedigree worth celebrating. His progeny had 28 stakes' wins amongst them. Before turning in triumph to welcome the Queen chief executive Mr Osborne reflected on a sickening prelude to a treasured occasion.

"Staff are distraught at the news, which followed a tragic accident during the normal course of business.

"Along with Invincible Spirit, Amadeus Wolf and Jeremy, he was among our top stallions and has left behind him an incredible legacy of wins," he said.

If the parade provided a sad reminder of what the Stud had lost so too did the Queen's itinerary. After leaving Tully her motorcade drove away from the throngs of cameras and 1,000 visiting journalists. It headed to the Aga Khan's stud where the Queen spent an hour in the company of the wonder horse, Sea the Stars. She followed this up the next day with another personal visit to the world-renowned Coolmore operation in Tipperary.

As the Queen departed Tully to inspect the farm's prodigal son those left behind had to turn to the mess he walked away from in January 2010. Four days after the Queen's trip to Tully the Stud was back in Court. This time the Board was prepared to draw a line under its bitter and undignified battle with its stallion nominations manager, Julie Lynch. The seemingly intractable dispute between employer and employee was expected to take at least four-weeks to resolve in Court. Had the Stud lost the cost of almost a month in the High Court would have towered over a legacy of legal bills, already grossly disproportionate for a firm of its size. Worse still, the hearings would have involved detailed discussions on both the business and the personal failings inside the semi-state company.

On Tuesday May 24, 2010 Ms Lynch's barrister, Frank Callanan, stood up before Mr Justice Michael Peart. He read a statement agreed between both sides and announced that the two-year standoff had ended with an "amicable arrangement in full". The terms were confidential but the explanation was public. The Stud said it regretted "any injuries caused to Ms Lynch" and praised her contribution to the company. She was recognised for having helped bring in a record number of mares to be covered at a time when an unprecedented amount of money was created. The joint statement said Ms Lynch had decided to "pursue interests of her own".

Dressed in black coat, Ms Lynch walked out of the High Court and away from dark and troubling time in her life. She left her job, her home and the stallions she helped to bring to the attention of the world. She also left a company which had hired her with high hopes but parted acknowledging the injuries which brought her to the brink. The Stud had been spared becoming the centre of a summer of sensation and sex scandal. The financial cost of this privacy will be hefty. Its standing in its sector had suffered. But while it was left to pay the bill and rebuild its reputation it also had to convince a new and cash-strapped Government that it should be allowed to retain its status as the Irish National Stud.

Previous Publications by Hillgate Publishing Ltd.

SONNY – For the Good Times
Sonny Knowles in conversation with Frank Corr
Author: Frank Corr
ISBN 0-978-0-9541819-2-5

Martin Molony – A Legend in his Lifetime
Author: Guy St. John Williams
ISBN 0-95418190-0-5

T. P. Burns – A Racing Life
Author: Guy St. John Williams
ISBN 0-9541819-1-3

The Cheltenham Gold Cup Immortals
Author: Guy St. John Williams
(Limited Edition)

Cecilia Come Back
Gee Gee Al Fan Lie
Author: Sr. Mary Cecilia Delany
Limited edition

T. P. Burns – A Racing Life

Author: Guy St. John Williams
ISBN 0-9541819-1-3

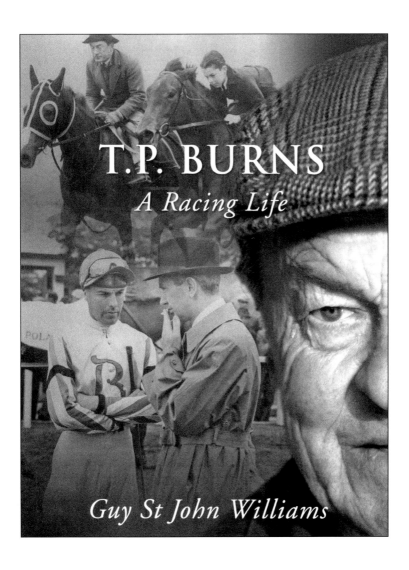

Martin Molony – A Legend in his Lifetime

Author: Guy St. John Williams
ISBN 0-95418190-0-5

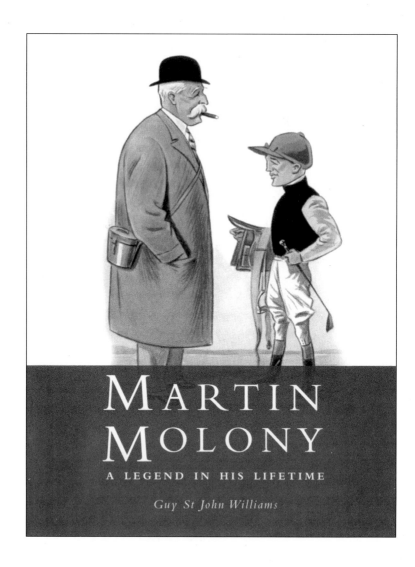

MARTIN
MOLONY

A LEGEND IN HIS LIFETIME

Guy St John Williams